ETHNICITY AND THE DEMENTIAS

ETHNICITY AND THE DEMENTIAS

edited by
Gwen Yeo
Stanford Geriatric Education Center
Stanford University
Stanford, California

and

Dolores Gallagher-Thompson
Veterans Affairs Palo Alto Health Care System and
Stanford University School of Medicine
Stanford, California

Taylor & Francis
Publishers since 1798

USA	Publishing Office:	Taylor & Francis
		1101 Vermont Avenue, N.W., Suite 200
		Washington, DC 20005-3521
		Tel: (202) 289-2174
		Fax: (202) 289-3665
	Distribution Center:	Taylor & Francis
		1900 Frost Road, Suite 101
		Bristol, PA 19007-1598
		Tel: (215) 785-5800
		Fax: (215) 785-5515
UK		Taylor & Francis Ltd.
		1 Gunpowder Square
		London EC4A 3DE
		Tel: 0171 583 0490
		Fax: 0171 583 0581

ETHNICITY AND THE DEMENTIAS

This work was partially supported by a grant from the Bureau of Health Professions for Geriatric Education Centers (Gwen Yeo, PhD, Director) and by grant 90AM0829 from the Administration on Aging (Dolores Gallagher-Thompson, PhD, Principal Investigator).

1 2 3 4 5 6 7 8 9 0   BRBR   9 8 7 6

This book was set in Times Roman by Harlowe Typography, Inc. The editors were Kathleen Baker and Catherine Simon. Cover design by Michelle Fleitz. Printing and binding by Braun-Brumfield, Inc.

A CIP catalog record for this book is available from the British Library.

⊗ The paper in this publication meets the requirements of the ANSI Standard Z39.48-1984 (Permanence of Paper)

Library of Congress Cataloging-in-Publication Data
Ethnicity and the dementias/edited by Gwen Yeo and Dolores Gallagher-Thompson.
    p. cm.
    Includes bibliographical references.

    1. Dementia—United States—Cross-cultural studies.
2. Minorities—Mental health—United States.   3. Psychiatry,
Transcultural.   I. Yeo, Gwen.   II. Gallagher-Thompson, Dolores.
RC521.E86   1996
616.8′3—dc20   95-52587
                                                                    CIP
ISBN 1-56032-436-8 (case)
ISBN 1-56032-437-6 (paper)

This book is dedicated to our husbands, Dick and Larry, whose support and understanding have helped make this book possible, and to the staff of the Stanford Geriatric Education Center and Older Adult and Family Center at the VA Health Care System, who have assisted us in all aspects of this work.

Contents

PART 2: ASSESSMENT OF COGNITIVE STATUS WITH DIFFERENT ETHNIC POPULATIONS

               American Elders   59
               F. M. Baker

               Overview of Recent Research in Dementia   60
               Psychosocial Considerations for Studies of Dementia in
                   African Americans   62
               Epidemiologic Studies of Dementia in African
                   Americans   64
               Screening African American Elders for the Presence of
                   Cognitive Impairment   66
               Conclusion   68
               References   71

CHAPTER 7   Cross-Cultural Testing and the Cognitive Abilities
               Screening Instrument   77
               Evelyn Lee Teng

               General Considerations in Cross-Cultural Testing   77
               The Cognitive Abilities Screening Instrument   80
               Adaptations from CASI E-1.0 to CASI C-2.0 for Use
                   with a Predominantly Illiterate Chinese Population 82
               Conclusion   83
               References   84

PART 3: WORKING WITH FAMILIES OF DEMENTIA PATIENTS FROM DIFFERENT ETHNIC POPULATIONS

Asian/Pacific Island Americans

               Dementia   89
               *Kathryn Sabrena Elliott, Mariann Di Minno,
               Darrick Lam, and Alicia Mei Tu*

               Conceptual Models   90
               Barriers to Care   92
               Strategies for Practitioners Working with Chinese:
                   Learning to Identify Where Your Patient Is on the
                   Continuum   98
               References   107

PART 4: SPECIAL ISSUES AND SPECIAL POPULATIONS

PART 5: IMPLICATIONS FOR THE FUTURE

Contributors

MARIE S. CHAVIS AUSBERRY
Family Caregiver Alliance
425 Bush Street
Suite 500
San Francisco, CA 94108

F. M. BAKER, M.D., M.P.H., F.A.P.A.
Professor, Department of Psychiatry
University of Maryland
School of Medicine
645 West Redwood Street
University Center
Baltimore, MD 21201-1549

SUSAN G. COOLEY, Ph.D.
Chief, Research and Evaluation
Office of Geriatrics and Extended
    Care (114B)
U.S. Department of Veterans Affairs
810 Vermont Avenue, NW
Washington, DC 20420

AL CROSS, M.S.W.
716 North Third Street
San Jose, CA 95112

MARIANN Di MINNO, R.N., M.A.
Program for Alzheimer's Disease Care
    and Education
University of California (PACE)
1350 7th Avenue
CSBS-228
San Francisco, CA 94143

KATHRYN SABRENA ELLIOTT, Ph.D.
Medical Anthropologist and
    Sociocultural Gerontologist
University of California, San Francisco
Memory Clinic and Alzheimer's Center
1350 7th Avenue
CSBS-228
San Francisco, CA 94143-0848

SUZANNE HANSER, Ed.D.
126 Clark Street
Newton Center, MA 02159

J. NEIL HENDERSON, Ph.D.
Department of Community and Family
    Health and Suncoast Gerontology
    Center
University of South Florida Health
    Sciences Center
Box MDC56
13201 Bruce B. Downs Boulevard
Tampa, FL 33612-3805

CATHERINE HAGAN HENNESSY,
    Dr.P.H., M.A.
Aging Studies Branch
Centers for Disease Control
    and Prevention
Mailstop K-51
Atlanta, GA 30333

DOROTHY HOWE
Senior Program Specialist
Health Advocacy Services
American Association of Retired Persons
601 E Street, NW
Washington, DC 20049

YUKIMICHI IMAI, M.D.
Department of Psychiatry
St. Marianna University School
  of Medicine
2-16-1 Sugao, Miyamae-Ku
Kawasaki 216, Japan

ROBERT JOHN, Ph.D.
Director
Minority Aging Research Institute
P.O. Box 13438
University of North Texas
Denton, TX 76203-6438

DESSERIE JONES
Division of Nephrology and Hypertension
Drew University of Medicine and Science
King/Drew Medical Center
Los Angeles, CA 90059

KATHLEEN KELLY, M.P.A.
Executive Director
Family Caregiver Alliance
425 Bush Street
Suite 500
San Francisco, CA 94108

SHIRLEY KIRCHEN, R.N.C., M.S.
Associate Chief Nurse, Extended Care
Department of Veterans Affairs
VA Medical Center
4150 Clement Street
San Francisco, CA 94121

B. JOSEA KRAMER, Ph.D.
Associate Director for
  Education/Evaluation
Geriatric Research Education
  Clinical Center
Sepulveda VA Medical Center
Associate Researcher, Anthropology
University of California at Los Angeles
School of Medicine
16111 Plummer Street
Sepulveda, CA 91343

DARRICK LAM, M.S.W.
Self-Help for the Elderly
Director of Client Services
407 Sansome Street
Suite 400
San Francisco, CA 94111

ERIC B. LARSON, M.D., M.P.H.
Professor of Medicine
Medical Director
University of Washington Medical
  Center
University of Washington School
  of Medicine
Seattle, WA 98195

IRENE DANIELS LEWIS, D.N.S.C.,
  F.A.A.N.
San Jose State University
School of Nursing
HB 420
One Washington Square
San Jose, CA 95192-0057

MORTON LIEBERMAN, Ph.D.
Professor and Director
Alzheimer Center
University of California, San Francisco
1350 7th Avenue
San Francisco, CA 94143

MELEN R. McBRIDE, R.N., Ph.D.
Stanford Geriatric Education Center
703 Welch Road
Suite H-1
Palo Alto, CA 94304-1708

DONALD E. MORISKY, Sc.D.,
  M.S.P.H.
Professor and Vice-Chair
Department of Community Health
  Sciences
UCLA School of Public Health
Room 26-070 CHS
10833 LeConte Avenue
Los Angeles, CA 90095-1772

DAN MUNGAS, Ph.D.
University of California, Davis
UC Davis Alzheimer's Disease
   Center
1771 Stockton Boulevard
Suite 2005
Sacramento, CA 95816

HEIDE PARRENO, M.S.
Clinical Team Manager
Community Home Health Care
2023 Vale Road
Suite 203
San Pablo, CA 94806

MARCEL PONTÓN, Ph.D.
Department of Psychiatry
University of California, Los Angeles
Los Angeles, CA 90024

ROSA RAMIREZ, M.S.W., M.P.A.
El Portal: Latino Alzheimer's Clinic
Alzheimer's Association
Los Angeles Chapter
5900 Wilshire Boulevard
Suite 1710
Los Angeles, CA 90036

LONNIE C. ROY, M.A.
Research Scientist
Minority Aging Research Institute
University of North Texas
Denton, TX 76208

ANN SAITO, O.T.R.
1578 Willowgate Drive
San Jose, CA 95118

MARGOT L. SALVINI, M.S.W.
Research Scientist
University of North Texas
Minority Aging Research Institute
Center for Studies in Aging
Chilton Hall 273
P.O. Box 13438
Denton, TX 76203-6484

MELISSA TALAMANTES, M.S.
Instructor
Department of Family Practice
University of Texas Health Science
   Center
7703 Floyd Curl Drive
San Antonio, TX 78284-1175

I. MARIBEL TAUSSIG, Ph.D.
4251 Gulf Shore Boulevard North
Suite 11-C
Naples, FL 33940

PHYLLIS M. TEMPO, L.C.S.W.,
   M.P.H.
Department of Veterans Affairs
San Jose Mental Health Clinic
1888 Senter Road
San Jose, CA 95112

EVELYN LEE TENG, Ph.D.
Professor
Department of Neurobiology
University of Southern California School
   of Medicine
1474 Rose Villa Street
Pasadena, CA 91106-3523

ALICIA MEI TU
Family Caregiver Alliance
425 Bush Street
Suite 500
San Francisco, CA 94108

IRENE VALVERDE
Program Coordinator
Alzheimer's Association of
   Monterey County
2700 Garden Road
Monterey, CA 93940

HARRY WARD, M.D.
Professor of Medicine
Drew University of Medicine and Science
Associate Professor of Medicine
UCLA School of Medicine
Chief, Division of Nephrology
   & Hypertension
King/Drew Medical Center
Los Angeles, CA 90059

Preface

The purpose of this book is to share current knowledge about the impact of ethnicity and culture on dementing disorders. At first glance, the reader may wonder why this is the topic of an entire book; after all, aren't the dementias (such as Alzheimer's disease) first and foremost diseases and disorders of the brain that should not be strongly influenced by such environmental factors as cultural background, ethnic identification, and race? On the one hand, it is true that dementing disorders are found in all racial, ethnic, and cultural groups that have been specifically studied; on the other hand, it is also true that their prevalence rates vary by ethnicity and race (just as they do by gender). What also varies considerably is the nature of the response of the individual and his or her family to the disease process. Although not a great deal of research has been conducted on these topics to date, studies that have been done have indicated that considerable variability is present (both within and between various racial and ethnic groups) and is related to the participants' ethnic and cultural identification and values. Investigation of this complex and very interesting set of phenomena is a major goal of this book.

In this book, the authors present information on several important dimensions that relate to these areas of inquiry, including chapters on epidemiological studies, methods of assessment of cognitive function in different ethnic groups, and the role of the family (and other social institutions) in providing support to the impaired relative. Several special issues are also covered (such as the increasing ethnic diversity among aging veterans in the United States), and, finally, there is a closing chapter on policy issues at the federal, state, and local levels. Most chapters not only present information but also raise issues and suggest questions to be addressed in future research.

The majority of chapters in this book are based on presentations given at a conference titled "Ethnicity and the Dementias" that was held in September 1994 at Stanford University. The conference was cosponsored by many local, state, and national groups, including the following: the Department of Veterans

Affairs (including the Bay Area Consortium for Geriatric Education; the Veterans Affairs [VA] Palo Alto Health Care System; the Palo Alto Geriatric Research, Education, and Clinical Center; The Long Beach Regional Medical Education Center; and the Office of Geriatrics and Extended Care at the VA National Headquarters and Central Office in Washington, DC), Stanford University (including the Stanford Geriatric Education Center, the Aging Clinical Research Center, and the Alzheimer's Disease Diagnostic and Treatment Center), the American Association of Retired Persons, the Greater San Francisco Bay Area and Monterey County chapters of the Alzheimer's Association, the California Geriatric Education Center, and the Family Caregiver Alliance Program in San Francisco. Note that some additional topics are included in this volume that were not represented at the conference, in order to improve the scope of the volume and increase its breadth of coverage.

This book is intended for researchers and clinicians who find themselves interested in these topics and who possess a genuine interest in learning about the many ways in which culture and ethnic identification interact with the biological changes that typify the dementing disorders. The authors of this volume hope that it will be useful to a wide variety of researchers, health care providers, and students in training by providing insights based on currently available data and highlighting the gaps that need to be filled by future reflection and research.

Dolores Gallagher-Thompson and Gwen Yeo

Acknowledgments

This work was partially supported by a grant from the Bureau of Health Professions for Geriatric Education Centers (Gwen Yeo, PhD, Director) and by grant 90AM0829 from the Administration on Aging (Dolores Gallagher-Thompson, PhD, Principal Investigator).

Part 1

Overview of Issues

The increasing ethnic diversity of the older population in the United States is rapidly putting a rainbow in the graying of America. To ignore the implications of dementia, arguably the most devastating and widespread set of geriatric conditions, for the growing population that does not fit into the typical European American mold is to deny the importance of the unique needs for the soon-to-be one fifth of older Americans.

The unique dementia-related issues for elders and their families from ethnic minority backgrounds include lack of research with specific ethnic groups, indications of differences in risk (and conflicting data for some populations) for certain types of dementia, need for culturally and linguistically appropriate assessment techniques, variations in cultural meanings attached to changes in cognitive function, and lack of education in cultural competence to enable providers to work appropriately with elders and their families from different ethnic backgrounds.

Chapter 1
Background

Gwen Yeo

After the dramatic increase in the past decade in knowledge about Alzheimer's disease and other dementias, the time has come to explore the relevance of that knowledge to the rapidly increasing population of elders of color in the United States. Although the literature on the epidemiology, assessment, and family support of people with dementia among the ethnic minority populations is still relatively thin, this book represents an effort to present the current level of understanding and to increase the resources available to clinicians and researchers.

DEMOGRAPHICS

The populations that fall into the four federally designated ethnic minority categories in the United States are the focus in this collection. These designations are American Indian/Alaska Native, Asian/Pacific Islander, Black, and Hispanic.[1] These ethnic minority populations of older Americans are growing even faster than the exploding population of older adults as a whole. By 2020, elders (those ages 65 and over) in these categories are projected to make up more than 22% of all older Americans (U.S. Bureau of the Census & National Institute on Aging, 1993). In California, these elders of color already constitute more than

---

[1]The following designations are also used for three of the categories: American Indian/Eskimo/ Aleut, African American, and Latino.

3

Table 1   Older U.S. Populations in Ethnic Minority Categories: 1990 Census

	65 and older		85 and older	
Race or ethnicity	n	%	n	%
Total	31,241,831		3,080,165	
American Indian or Alaska Native	114,453	0.4	9,205	0.3
Asian or Pacific Islander	454,458	1.5	29,738	1.0
Black	2,508,551	8.0	230,183	7.5
Hispanic origin[a]	1,161,283	3.7	94,564	3.1

Note. Table compiled from data from the U.S. Bureau of the Census (1992).
[a]Hispanics may be of any race.

20% of the older population; this percentage is projected to reach 41% by 2020 (California Department of Finance, 1988; U.S. Census of Population & Housing, 1990). Although far from perfect, the best estimate of the current size of the ethnic minority population comes from the decennial U.S. Census, based on respondents' self-reported identification. Because the risk of dementia increases with age, Table 1 presents the numbers and percentages of elders 65 and over and 85 and over in the ethnic minority categories in 1990. Slightly more than 27 million people age 65 and over classified themselves as non-Hispanic White, and almost 313,000 classified themselves as "other race."

HETEROGENEITY

It is important to recognize that within these categories immense variability is found, much of which affects the perception and response to dementia. The most important source of diversity within the four ethnic minority categories is national origin and culture (tribal in the case of American Indian populations). As an example, Table 2 indicates the major groups identified in the 1990 Census within the Asian/Pacific Islander category of elders. Among the elders lumped together in this, the most rapidly growing of the four categories, 70% were born outside the United States, ranging from 28% for Native Hawaiian and 17% for Japanese American to 98% for Vietnamese and Cambodian, with the large Chinese and Filipino groups reported to be 84% and 95%, respectively (Young & Gu, 1995).

Even within these subcategories of discrete national origin (e.g., Filipino), there is a wide range of levels of acculturation and ethnic identity, education, income, length of residence in the United States, rural or urban background, religious affiliation and participation, and family support; any one of these may influence the interaction between provider and patient with suspected cognitive impairment or that between the provider and family members. For example, in the metropolitan areas of many states on both coasts, at least three different language groups are found among elders labeled Chinese, including elders who were born in mainland China, Taiwan, Hong Kong, or Vietnam; whose income

Table 2 Ethnicity of Asian and Pacific Islander Elders 65 and Older: 1990

Ethnic group	N	%
Total Asian	439,723	96.8
Chinese	133,977	29.5
Japanese	105,932	23.3
Filipino	104,206	22.9
Korean	35,247	7.8
Asian Indian	23,004	5.1
Vietnamese	18,084	4.0
Cambodian	3,724	0.8
Laotian	3,697	0.8
Hmong	2,535	0.6
Thai	1,416	0.3
Other Asian	7,901	1.7
Total Pacific Islander	14,735	3.2
Hawaiian	10,233	2.3
Samoan	2,047	0.5
Guamanian	1,523	0.3
Other Pacific Islander	930	0.2

Note. Table compiled from data from the U.S. Bureau of the Census (1992).

varies from well below poverty level to extremely wealthy; and whose educational backgrounds vary from no years of schooling to graduate degrees.

Almost every interaction with an older patient and every decision a provider must make about care are affected by the cultural backgrounds of both patient and provider, from assessment of function to prescription of medications to working with family caregivers to executing advance directives about life-sustaining care. Some of the most difficult issues for physicians and other members of the geriatric team involved with management of dementia patients include those discussed briefly below.

1 *Taking an adequate history and obtaining appropriate assessments of cognitive function with elders who speak little or no English.* Use of interpreters makes adequate assessment problematic, especially if family members are doing the translating. Because there are no language equivalents for many concepts, because some assessment instruments developed in the United States contain questions that are not appropriate for other cultures or other languages, and because family members may not understand the importance of exact translations or may feel protective of an older relative, the diagnostic process can become extremely difficult. There are few cognitive assessment batteries that have been developed and validated for non-English-speaking elders in the United States; most of those that do exist are featured or referenced in this volume.

2 *The variation in the meaning of cognitive impairment and behavior change in old age in different cultures.* In many cultures, confusion, disorientation, and memory loss are seen as normal parts of aging; in others, they may be associated with a stigma of "craziness." There may be many reasons that family members who experience the gradual deterioration of intellectual function that accompanies dementia would not feel that it is appropriate or desirable to seek assistance from American health care providers. In some societies, there may be a non-Western health care belief that could explain the changes observed, so that family members would be more likely to consult healers from traditions other than Western biomedicine. It is extremely important for providers faced with elders not acculturated to U.S. society to learn to elicit explanatory models of illness used by older patients and their families in order to understand and negotiate appropriate and acceptable management techniques.

3 *Working with family systems and other sources of support.* Western-based models of caregiver education and caregiver support are frequently not seen as relevant in cultural traditions that emphasize the responsibility of the family for the care of the elder or filial piety. Culturally prescribed gender roles may be important in understanding the expectation that an older son or his wife assume a major caregiving burden when a daughter might be available, or that only sons make decisions and daughters provide the day-to-day care. In some traditions, a major source of support for elders, their caregivers, or both is the church or other religious communities.

4 *Differing perceptions of institutionalization and decision making related to health care.* In some cultural groups, nursing home care is considered abandonment and is completely unthinkable, even in cases of extreme stress and burden to family caregivers. In some cases, family members have requested providers to inform the elder that the hospital requested that she or he be moved to a nursing home because they are not able to tell the elder directly. Decisions about health care are sometimes traditionally made or heavily influenced by an individual with authority from outside the family, such as a clan leader.

5 *Variations in response to ethical decision making.* The reaction of family members to issues requiring decisions about life support are frequently influenced by numerous factors that may not be well understood by health care providers. Lack of trust in the provider's judgment or recommendation is frequently colored by the knowledge of widespread historical discrimination and exploitation in health care that has been inflicted on the ethnic or racial group to which the family belongs, an experience that is common among a number of the populations of elders of color. Individual autonomy in health care decision making, a cornerstone of Western biomedical ethics, is not consonant with many traditions, especially some Asian cultures in which it is assumed that family members will protect and provide for an elder, especially if she or he is ill. Surgery, taking blood, and autopsies are also abhorrent in some traditions in which it is believed that blood is associated with the life force and does not replenish itself or that the body should be returned to one's ancestors or to God without being "mutilated."

These and a number of other issues have been identified in the work of the Stanford Geriatric Education Center during the 8 years it has been developing resources for multidisciplinary education of health care providers in ethnogeriatrics. Most of these issues are discussed in some detail in the remainder of this book in the hope that the insights they provide for clinicians and researchers will be helpful.

REFERENCES

California Department of Finance. (1988). Projected total population for California by race/ethnicity. Sacramento: Population Research Unit.

State of California State Census Data Center. (1990). Summary of California Tape File 1: Complete Tables; U.S. Census of Population and Housing. Sacramento: Author.

U.S. Bureau of the Census. (1992). 1990 Census of population: General population characteristics (United States, 1990 CP-1-1). Washington, DC: Author.

U.S. Bureau of the Census & National Institute on Aging. (1993, November). Racial and ethnic diversity of America's elderly population. *Profiles of America's Elderly, 3*, 1.

Young, J. J., & Gu, N. (1995). *Demographic and socioeconomic characteristics of elderly Asian and Pacific Island Americans*. Seattle, WA: National Asian Pacific Center on Aging.

Chapter 2

An Overview of Dementia and Ethnicity with Special Emphasis on the Epidemiology of Dementia

Eric B. Larson
Yukimichi Imai

Dementia has been recognized worldwide through the millennia. It is found in all cultures. Previously, dementia was primarily a problem for individuals and their families. As greater numbers of persons have reached old age, however, dementia has become a societywide problem. This chapter reviews the general topic of dementia, its clinical definition, and its epidemiology and concludes with a discussion of the interaction between ethnicity and dementia as well as describes ongoing efforts to unravel the interaction between ethnicity and dementia.

OVERVIEW OF DEMENTIA

Dementia is a syndrome characterized by global loss of cognitive function, especially of memory. The loss of function must be sufficient to impair social or occupational function (American Psychiatric Association, 1987, 1994). As a syndrome, dementia may be caused by a number of diverse diseases (Christensen et al., 1994).

The most striking feature of dementia is its association with age. More so than almost any other disease or syndrome, dementia increases dramatically with age (Jorm, Korten, & Henderson, 1987). Dementia is extremely rare in persons under the age of 60, but starting at age 65 the incidence of dementia doubles approximately every 5 years (Hofman et al., 1991). On the basis of recent

9

published reports, for persons over the age of 85 the prevalence of dementia varies from more than 30% to approximately 50% (Evans et al., 1989; Folstein, Anthony, Parhad, Duffy, & Gruenberg, 1985; Hofman et al., 1991; Rocca et al., 1990).

With the aging of most societies, there is increased awareness of dementia. Dementia causes considerable dysfunction and distress to individuals and families. From a societal perspective, dementia increases the need for services, especially long-term care services, dramatically. Thus, as societies have aged, there is increasing public and private awareness of dementia (Schneider & Guralnik, 1990).

In countries like the United States, ethnic, racially diverse elderly populations are growing twice as fast as the general population. Less is known about dementia in these populations, but information about them will be extremely important in the future.

Among the multiple causes of dementia, most studies have emphasized four as being particularly common. The most common cause is Alzheimer's disease, an illness typically of gradual, insidious onset that is invariably progressive (Larson, Kukull & Katzman, 1992). The pathologic features are those of neurofibrillary tangles and senile plaques found predominantly in the hippocampus but diffusely present through the brain (Terry & Katzman, 1983; Terry, Masliah, & Hansen, 1994). The second most common cause is so-called vascular dementia, often called multi-infarct dementia. This form of dementia is usually caused by multiple cerebrovascular accidents throughout the brain. It is strongly associated with hypertension and risk factors for stroke (Johansson, 1994; Tatemichi et al., 1994). Less common are the dementias associated with alcohol-induced brain damage—so-called alcoholic dementias (Tatemichi et al., 1994). Most studies have also reported a fairly high frequency of Parkinson's disease (Korczyn, 1986; Still, Jackson, Brandes, Abramson, & Macera, 1990). Complicating factors of dementia include coexistent depression in persons with dementia. On the basis of 30 studies of Alzheimer's disease to determine the prevalence and phenomenology of affective and psychotic symptoms in patients with Alzheimer's disease, depressive and psychotic symptoms occur in 30–40% of persons with Alzheimer's disease (Wragg & Jeste, 1989). Drug side effects and acute illnesses also make persons with dementia worse (Bowen & Larson, 1993; Haines & Katona, 1992; Taft & Barkin, 1990).

There are more than 30 other causes of dementia. These illnesses may present singly or in combinations. These illnesses are very important for the individuals who experience them, but are less important from a public health perspective (Clarke, 1993; Larson et al., 1992).

One of the problems of dealing with dementia is the difficulty of detecting it. Because dementia is typically insidious, it may be mistakenly identified as normal aging (Feher, Larrabee, Sudilovsky, & Crook, 1994). Furthermore, dementia is almost invariably associated with social isolation and, in some cultures, a sense of shame. Thus, most studies have indicated that at least 50% of cases are not known and usually not recognized until a person is quite severely impaired (Ineichen, 1987; Winblad, Aguero, Ericsson, Fratiglioni, & Nordberg, 1993). This is a particular problem in studies of racial minorities who may also be less well integrated into the majority public health and medical care systems.

INTERACTION OF ETHNICITY WITH DEMENTIA

One question that is frequently asked about chronic diseases is whether there is variation by ethnic or racial groups. There is strong evidence that genetics play a role in determining the risk of Alzheimer's disease (St. George-Hyslop, 1994). There are persons with autosomal dominant patterns in which approximately 50% of persons in an affected family will have Alzheimer's disease (Bird, 1994; Hirst, Yee, & Sadovnick, 1994). There is also evidence of so-called polygenic factors that cause Alzheimer's disease to cluster in certain families. However, twin studies have demonstrated that there must be environmental factors that play a role in dementia as well (Breitner & Murphy, 1992).

The key questions with regard to ethnicity and dementia are these: First, is there a difference in overall rates of dementia in certain populations? Second, is the distribution of causes of dementia different in those populations?

Overall, in North America and Western Europe, reported rates are quite variable. However, some representative rates are shown in Table 1. Pfeffer, Afifi, and Chance (1987) showed that the rates in a U.S. retirement community were 6.2% of those over age 65 and 15.8% of those over age 80. Evans et al. (1989) reported much higher rates in a population of persons of predominantly Italian descent in East Boston, Massachusetts, in which 10.3% of those over 65 and 47% of those over 85 had a dementing illness. Skoog, Nilsson, Palmertz, Andreasson, and Svanborg (1993), in a study from Sweden, reported that approximately 30% of persons age 85 were demented. Overall, the European average is 4.8% of those persons over age 65. By contrast, Zhang et al.'s (1990) studies of Chinese in Shanghai demonstrated that 4.6% of those over age 65 were demented and 24.3% of those over 85 were demented. In Japan, the average of several studies is 4.8% of those over age 65, with a range of 4%–7% (Hasegawa, 1990; Homma & Hasegawa, 1989).

The distribution of causes of dementia in the United States and Canada suggests that approximately 50% (Folstein et al., 1985) to more than 90% (Evans et al., 1989) of persons with dementia will have Alzheimer's disease. Persons with vascular dementia will account for 10% (Kase et al., 1989; Takemichi, Sacktor, & Mayeus, 1994) to 50% (Folstein et al., 1985; Hasegawa & Imai, 1989). In Caucasian, middle-class populations, Alzheimer's disease may account for 90% or more of cases (Evans et al., 1989). By contrast, in African American populations with relatively high levels of untreated hypertension and diabetes, vascular dementia could be the cause of dementia in 50% or more persons with impairment (Folstein et al., 1985; Wallace, 1993). In Caucasian populations in the United States and Europe, vascular disease is considerably less common than

Table 1 Selected Recent Epidemiological Studies for Aged Persons with Dementia in Asia and Western Countries

Study	Country	Year	Age range of elderly	N	Prevalence rate (%)	Etiological classification (%)			
						AD	VD	Other & UD	VD/AD
Karasawa et al. (1982)	Japan	1982	65+	4,502	4.6	1.0	2.5	0.6	2.5
Hasegawa et al. (1985)	Japan	1982	65+	1,507	4.8	1.2	2.0	1.6	1.7
Hasegawa & Imai (1989)	Japan	1985	65+	1,607	4.7	1.5	2.2	1.0	1.5
Imai et al. (1994)	Japan	1992	65+	4,259	3.8	1.8	1.5	0.5	0.8
Zhang et al. (1990)	China	1990	65+	5,055	4.6	3.0	1.2	0.4	0.4
Park et al. (1994)	Korea	1994	65+	5,770	10.7	6.4	1.3	3.0	0.2
Molsa et al. (1982)	Finland	1982	65+	19,482	2.0	1.0	0.8	0.2	0.8
Sulkava et al. (1985)	Finland	1985	65+	8,000	6.7	3.6	2.7	0.4	0.8
Rocca et al. (1990)	Italy	1990	59+	778	6.2	2.6	2.2	1.4	0.9
Fratiglioni et al. (1991)	Sweden	1991	75+	1,810	11.9	6.4	2.9	2.8	0.5
Copeland et al. (1992)	United Kingdom	1993	65+	1,070	4.3	3.3	0.7	0.3	0.2
CSHA Working Group (1994)	Canada	1994	65+	9,008	8.0	5.1	1.5	1.4	0.3
Folstein et al. (1985)	United States	1985	65+	3,481	4.5	2.0	2.0	0.5	1.0
Evans et al. (1989)	United States	1989	65+	2,623	—	10.3	—	0.5	—
Bachman et al. (1992)	United States	1992	65+	2,180	4.1	2.3	0.4	1.3	0.2

AD = Alzheimer's disease or Alzheimer-type dementia; VD = vascular dementia; Other & UD: Other-type dementia and unclassified dementia; 65+ = over 65 years old; 59+ = over 59 years old; 75+ = over 75 years old; and CSHA = Canadian Study of Health and Aging.

Alzheimer's disease (Hofman et al., 1991; Jorm, 1991). By contrast, in Japan vascular dementia is more common (Hasegawa, Homma, & Imai, 1985; Hasegawa & Imai, 1989; Ueda, Kawano, Hasuo, & Fujishima, 1992).

Even with these generalizations, there are considerable differences and heterogeneity of results. For example, in East Boston more than 95% of persons with dementia had Alzheimer's disease (Evans et al., 1989). By contrast, the Swedish study showed that the ratio of Alzheimer's disease to vascular disease was about 50:50 in 85-year-olds (Skoog et al., 1993). Folstein et al. (1985) reported a 50:50 ratio of Alzheimer's disease to vascular disease in a primarily African American population in Baltimore. In Japanese studies, the range of persons reported to have Alzheimer's disease is 12%–40% of all those with dementia, whereas the range of those with vascular dementia is 50%–70% of all those with dementia (Hasegawa & Imai, 1989; Hasegawa et al., 1985; Homma & Hasegawa, 1989; Ueda et al., 1992). In Chinese studies (Zhang et al., 1990), Alzheimer's disease accounted for 60% of those with dementia, whereas vascular dementia accounted for 28%.

What can be concluded from the studies of rates of dementia? First, it is obvious that reported rates differ considerably. These differences may be accounted for by methodologic differences. Definition of dementia and detection may be quite variable, and this could account for some of the differences (Graves, Larson, White, Teng, & Homma, 1994; Wolfe et al., 1992). However, equally plausible is that there may be underlying genetic factors (Heston, 1987; Heston, Mastri, Anderson, & White, 1981) and environmental forces (Karlinsky et al., 1992) that affect the differences in overall rates of dementia.

The distribution of causes of dementia is also quite variable (Takemichi et al., 1994). Again, methodologic differences could explain some of the results. However, there is a growing suspicion that the distribution may, in fact, be quite different in various populations. This suggests that the underlying rate of Alzheimer's disease may be quite different. Given the strong importance of Alzheimer's disease in progressively older populations, this difference may be relevant for public health.

There are at least two key issues that these variable rates raise for public health. First, are there environmental effects that can be discovered through cross-cultural or migration studies? If there are, some of these environmental effects could be amenable to modification and thereby prevention of dementia. Second, are there cultural factors that could lead to more effective adaptation to dementia that can be discovered through cross-cultural and migration factors? The answer to this question could allow researchers to discover the most effective way to deal with dementia for individuals and for society as a whole. Thus, it will be important to understand some of the factors that could explain these rate differences.

There are at least four factors that could explain the rate differences. First, social factors may play a role (Valle, 1994). In some cultures, Alzheimer's disease or dementia of any sort may not be an acceptable diagnosis. This could lead families to hide persons with cognitive impairment or could make physicians reluctant to diagnose a person as having Alzheimer's disease. In addition, in some cultures so-called "senility" may be viewed and accepted as just normal aging. Indeed, this was the case in North America and Western Europe before it was widely recognized that the pathology of so-called senility was usually the same as so-called presenile dementia or Alzheimer's disease (Forbes & Hirdes, 1993).

A second factor that could explain a rate difference relates to measurement. That is, current measures of cognitive function may be less accurate for ethnic minorities. For example, cognitive impairment has been reported to be twice as common in African Americans and Hispanic Americans using the Mini-Mental State Examination (MMSE) in epidemiologic catchment studies (Escobar et al., 1986). This raises the question of whether this measure is an accurate reflection of functional impairment and brain pathology or if the MMSE has a cultural bias that results in lower scores for certain subgroups in spite of similar levels of cognitive function and underlying brain pathology.

A third explanation for rate differences would relate to intrinsic biologic susceptibility to dementia (Dresse, Marechal, Scuvee-Moreau, & Seutin, 1994). For example, one group could be more genetically predisposed to develop dementing illness and thus have higher rates (Tsai et al., 1994; van Duijn et al., 1994). Apolipoprotein E is a protein involved in lipid transfer. The e4 allele has recently been shown to be strongly associated with Alzheimer's disease. In the North Manhattan community study of dementia, apolipoprotein E-e4 allele is a strong risk factor for Alzheimer's disease in Caucasians, an intermediate risk factor in Hispanic Americans, and not a risk factor in African Americans (Mayeux et al., 1993). This may suggest biologic differences in susceptibility.

Finally, environmental factors may differ and thus explain the rate differences. For example, stroke risk factors are much higher in African American populations than in Caucasian populations (Alter, 1994). The rate of multi-infarct dementia is generally believed to be higher in African Americans, presumably as a result of higher levels of hypertension, diabetes, smoking, and other stroke risk factors (Gorelick et al., 1994). Another example relevant to ongoing research is that the prevalence of Alzheimer's disease appears to be increasing in Japan (Imai et al., 1994). Does this suggest a change in survival of the population or a change in exposure to risk factors for Alzheimer's disease and vascular dementia?

ETHNICITY AND DEMENTIAS: RESEARCH ISSUES

Little is known about the cause of many dementias and, in particular, of Alzheimer's disease. In addition, persons with dementia present caregivers and society with unique service needs (Brodaty & Hadzi-Pavlovic, 1990). The increased rate of dementia in an aging society is also a stress on limited health care resources. Society has an ongoing interest in whether there are factors that might promote more successful aging and prolong functional independence (Ganguli, Seaberg, Belle, Fischer, & Kuller, 1993). The importance of these issues suggests that research in ethnicity and dementia may be particularly timely and represent a unique opportunity (Pittman et al., 1992).

Migration of an ethnic population allows one to understand the relationship between genetic and environmental factors—the so-called "nature versus nurture" question. That is, when a minority population migrates across several cultures, they typically maintain the same distribution of genetic factors but are exposed to a dramatic change in environmental forces and the cultural aspects of the majority culture (Farrer et al., 1990; Gatz, Lowe, Berg, Mortimer, & Pedersen, 1994). Studies of Japanese migration from Japan to Honolulu to San Francisco (the Ni-Hon-San Study) helped unravel the relationship between genetic and environmental factors (nature and nurture) in the development of coronary artery disease, cerebrovascular disease, and breast, colon, and gastric cancers (Graves et al., 1994). In the case of stroke and heart disease, this ultimately led to the development of preventive strategies designed to reduce harmful risk factors and promote positive risk factors. Currently, a unique opportunity exists, analogous to the Ni-Hon-San studies, to study aging in Japanese in Japan, Hawaii, and Seattle (Graves et al., 1994). Such studies are designed to determine whether there are environmental risk factors that are important in the pathogenesis of Alzheimer's disease and other dementias (Cohen, 1993). They will also likely define whether the genetic substrate and genetic risk are different in Japanese populations versus a Caucasian, albeit heterogeneous majority population.

The diversity of minority and ethnic groups frequently includes unique service needs. According to a recent report from the U.S. Office of Technology Assessment Advisory Panel on Alzheimer's Disease (U.S. Department of Health & Human Services Advisory Panel on Alzheimer's Disease, 1992), it will be extremely important to describe the unique service needs of minority and ethnic groups in the United States and—given the global nature of health care—in minority and ethnic groups in other parts of the world. Presumably, awareness of unique service needs will result in more so-called "culturally appropriate" services that are more valued by persons in need of service.

It is also likely that the diversity of cultural patterns provides a unique opportunity to view adaptation in a way that improves the understanding of how people adapt to illness, in particular dementing illness, which affects so many aspects of a person's life. Some patterns may be particularly important for the cultural group and thus should be preserved. It is also likely that certain cultural patterns of adaptation to an illness like dementia may be more or less effective. Whether effective patterns can be transmitted and generalized to other groups is an interesting and important question. Thus, an important research agenda would be to describe the cultural patterns of care adaptation in diverse groups.

Finally, it is highly likely that there is an interaction between environment and genetics in the phenomenon of so-called successful aging. In the process of studying dementia across cultures, it may be possible to discover environmental (so-called nurture) factors that promote successful aging (Karasawa, Kawashima, & Kasahara, 1982). Again, the range of environmental change is much broader during migration and is presumably occurring on a base of a genetically more homogeneous population. In general, the phenomenon of ethnic and thereby genetic similarity in the context of dramatic environmental and cultural changes is a characteristic feature of migration and presents a unique "experiment of nature" that is well worth exploiting to improve understanding of many important phenomena.

REFERENCES

Alter, M. (1994). Black-white differences in stroke frequency: Challenges for research. *Neuroepidemiology, 13*, 301–307.

American Psychiatric Association. (1987). *Diagnostic and statistical manual of mental disorders*. Washington, DC: Author.

American Psychiatric Association. (1994). *Diagnostic and statistical manual of mental disorders*. Washington, DC: Author.

Bachman, D. L., Wolf, P. A., Linn, R., Knoefel, J. E., Cobb, J., Bellanger, A., D'Agostino, R. B., & White, L. R. (1992). Prevalence of dementia and probable senile dementia of the Alzheimer type in the Framingham Study. *Neurology, 42*, 115–119.

Bird, T. D. (1994). Clinical genetic of familial Alzheimer disease. In R. D. Terry, R. Katzman, & K. L. Bick (Eds.), *Alzheimer disease* (pp. 65–74). New York: Raven Press.

Bowen, J. D., & Larson, E. B. (1993). Drug-induced cognitive impairment. Defining the problem and finding solutions. *Drugs and Aging, 3*, 349–357.

Breitner, J. C., & Murphy, E. A. (1992). Twin studies of Alzheimer disease: II. Some predictions under a genetic model. *American Journal of Medical Genetics, 44*, 628–634.

Brodaty, H., & Hadzi-Pavlovic, D. (1990). Psychosocial effects on careers of living with persons with dementia. *Australian and New Zealand Journal of Psychiatry, 24*, 351–361.

Canadian Study of Health and Aging Working Group. (1994). Canadian study of health and aging: Study methods and prevalence of dementia. *Canadian Medical Association Journal, 150*, 899–913.

Christensen, H., Jorm, A. F., Henderson, A. S., Mackinnon, A. J., Korten, A. E., & Scott, L. R. (1994). The relationship between health and cognitive functioning in a sample of elderly people in the community. *Age and Ageing, 23*, 204–212.

Clarke, A. (1993). Problems of clinical research in dementia. In G. K. Wilcock (Ed.), *The management of Alzheimer's disease* (pp. 161–173). Kent, United Kingdom: Wrighson Biomedical.

Cohen, G. D. (1993). African American issues in geriatric psychiatry: A perspective on research opportunities. *Journal of Geriatric Psychiatry and Neurology, 6*, 195–199.

Copeland, J. R., Davidson, I. A., Dewey, M. E., Gilmore, C., Larkin, B. A., McWilliam, C., Saunders, P. A., Scott, A., Sharma, V., & Sullivan, C. (1992).

Alzheimer's disease, other dementias, depression and pseudopdementia: Prevalence, incidence and three-year outcome in Liverpool. *British Journal of Psychiatry, 161*, 230–239.

Dresse, A., Marechal, D., Scuvee-Moreau, J., & Seutin, V. (1994). Towards a pharmacological approach of Alzheimer's disease based on the molecular biology of the amyloid precursor protein (APP). *Life Sciences, 55*, 2179–2187.

Escobar, J. I., Burnam, A., Karno, M., Forsythe, A., Landsverk, J., & Golding, J. M. (1986). Use of the Mini-Mental State Examination (MMSE) in a community population of mixed ethnicity: Cultural and linguistic artifacts. *Journal of Nervous and Mental Disease, 174*, 607–614.

Evans, D. A., Funkenstein, H. H., Albert, M. S., Scherr, P. A., Cook, N. R., Chown, M. J., Hebert, L. E., Hennekens, C. H., & Taylor, J. O. (1989). Prevalence of Alzheimer's disease in a community population of older persons. *Journal of the American Medical Association, 262*, 2551–2556.

Farrer, L. A., Myers, R. H., Cupples, L. A., St. George-Hyslop, P. H., Bird, T. D., Rossor, M. N., Mullan, M. J., Polinsky, R., Nee, L., & Heston, L. (1990). Transmission and age-at-onset patterns in familial Alzheimer's disease: Evidence for heterogeneity. *Neurology, 40*, 395–403.

Feher, E. P., Larrabee, G. J., Sudilovsky, A., & Crook, T. H., III. (1994). Memory self-report in Alzheimer's disease and in age-associated memory impairment. *Journal of Geriatric Psychiatry and Neurology, 7*, 58–65.

Folstein, M., Anthony, J. C., Parhad, I., Duffy, B., & Gruenberg, E. M. (1985). The meaning of cognitive impairment in the elderly. *Journal of the American Geriatric Society, 33*, 228–235.

Forbes, W. F., & Hirdes, J. P. (1993). The relationship between aging and disease: Geriatric ideology and myths of senility. *Journal of the American Geriatric Society, 41*, 1267–1271.

Fratiglioni, L., Grut, M., Forsell, Y., Viitanen, M., Grafstrom, M., Holm'en, K., Ericsson, K., Backman, L., Ahlbom, A., & Winblad, B. (1991). Prevalence of Alzheimer's disease and other dementias in an elderly urban population: Relationship with age, sex, and education. *Neurology, 41*, 1886–1892.

Ganguli, M., Seaberg, E., Belle, S., Fischer, L., & Kuller, L. H. (1993). Cognitive impairment and the use of health services in an elderly rural population: The MoVIES project: Monongahela Valley Independent Elders Survey. *Journal of the American Geriatric Society, 41*, 1065–1070.

Gatz, M., Lowe, B., Berg, S., Mortimer, J., & Pedersen, N. (1994). Dementia: Not just a search for the gene. *Gerontologist, 34*, 251–255.

Gorelick, P. B., Freels, S., Harris, Y., Dollear, T., Billingsley, M., & Brown, N. (1994). Epidemiology of vascular and Alzheimer's dementia among African Americans in Chicago, IL: Baseline frequently and comparison of risk factors. *Neurology, 44*, 1391–1396.

Graves, A. B., Larson, E. B., White, L. R., Teng, E. L., & Homma, A. (1994). Opportunities and challenges in international collaborative epidemiologic research of dementia and its subtypes: Studies between Japan and the U.S. *International Psychogeriatrics, 6*, 209–223.

Haines, A., & Katona, C. (1992). Dementia in old age. *Occasional Paper/Royal College of General Practitioners, 58*, 62–66.

Hasegawa, K. (1990). The clinical issues of age-related dementia. *Tohoku Journal of Experimental Medicine, 161*(Suppl.), 29–38.

Hasegawa, K., Homma, A., & Imai, Y. (1985). An epidemiological study of age-related dementia in the community. *International Journal of Geriatric Psychiatry, 1*, 45–55.

Hasegawa, K., & Imai, Y. (1989). Epidemiological study on age-associated dementia in Japan. In M. Mergener & B. Reisberg (Eds.), *Diagnosis and treatment of senile dementia* (pp. 12–32). Berlin: Springer-Verlag.

Heston, L. L. (1977, April 15). Alzheimer's disease, trisomy 21, and myeloproliferative disorders: Associations suggesting a genetic diathesis. *Science, 196*, 322–323.

Heston, L. L., Mastri, A. R., Anderson, V. E., & White, J. (1981). Dementia of the Alzheimer type: Clinical genetics, natural history and associated conditions. *Archives of General Psychiatry, 38*, 1085–1090.

Hirst, C., Yee, I. M., & Sadovnick, A. D. (1994). Familial risks for Alzheimer disease from a population-based series. *Genetic Epidemiology, 11*, 365–374.

Hofman, A., Rocca, W. A., Brayne, C., Breteler, M. M., Clarke, M., Cooper, B., Copeland, J. R., Dartigues, J. F., da Silva-Droux, A., & Hagnell, O. (1991). The prevalence of dementia in Europe: A collaborative study of 1980–1990 findings: EURODEM Prevalence Research Group. *International Journal of Epidemiology, 20*, 736–748.

Homma, A., & Hasegawa, K. (1989). Recent developments in gerontopsychiatric research on age-associated dementia in Japan. *International Psychogeriatrics, 1*, 31–49.

Imai, Y., Homma, A., Hasegawa, K., Hirakawa, Y., Kosaka, A., Oikawa, K., & Shimogaki, H. (1994). An epidemiological study on dementia in Kanagawa prefecture (Japanese). *Japanese Journal of Geriatric Psychiatry, 5*, 855–862.

Ineichen, B. (1987). Measuring the rising tide. How many dementia cases will there be by 2001? *British Journal of Psychiatry, 150*, 193–200.

Johansson, B. B. (1994). Pathogenesis of vascular dementia: The possible role of hypertension. *Dementia, 5*, 174–176.

Jorm, A. F. (1991). Cross-national comparisons of the occurrence of Alzheimer's and vascular dementias. *European Archives of Psychiatry and Clinical Neuroscience, 240*, 218–222.

Jorm, A. F., Korten, A. E., & Henderson, A. S. (1987). The prevalence of dementia: A quantitative integration of the literature. *Acta Psychiatrica Scandinavica, 76*, 465–479.

Karasawa, A., Kawashima, K., & Kasahara, H. (1982). Epidemiological study of the senile in Tokyo metropolitan area. In *Proceedings of the World Psychiatric Association Regional Symposium* (pp. 285–289). Kyoto, Japan:

Karlinsky, H., Berg, J. M., Lennox, A., Ray, P. N., St. George-Hyslop, P., Farrer, L. A., Percy, M. E., Andrews, D. F., & Atack, E. A. (1992). Monozygotic twins concordant for late-onset probable Alzheimer disease with suspected Alzheimer disease in four sibs. *American Journal of Medical Genetics, 44*, 591–597.

Kase, C. S., Wolf, P. A., Chodosh, E. H., Zacher, H. B., Kelly-Hayes, M., Kannel, W. B., D'Agostino, R. B., & Scampini, L. (1989). Prevalence of silent stroke in patients presenting with initial stroke: The Framingham Study. *Stroke, 20*, 850–852.

Korczyn, A. D. (1986). Dementia in Parkinson's disease. In A. Fisher, I. Hanin, & C. Lachman (Eds.), *Alzheimer's and Parkinson's disease: Strategies for research and development* (pp. 177–189). New York: Plenum Press.

Larson, E. B., Kukull, W. A., & Katzman, R. L. (1992). Cognitive impairment: Dementia and Alzheimer's disease. *Annual Review of Public Health, 13*, 431–449.

Mayeux, R., Stern, Y., Ottman, R., Tatemichi, T. K., Tang, M. X., Maestre, G., Ngai, C., Tycko, B., & Ginsberg, H. (1993). The apolipoprotein epsilon 4 allele in patients with Alzheimer's disease. *Annals of Neurology, 34*, 752–754.

Molsa, P. K., Marttila, R. J., & Rinne, U. K. (1982). Epidemiology of dementia in a Finnish population. *Acta Neurologica Scandinavica, 65*, 541–552.

Park, J., Ko, H. J., Park, Y. N., & Jung, C. H. (1994). Dementia among the elderly in a rural Korean community. *British Journal of Psychiatry, 164*, 796–801.

Pfeffer, R. I., Afifi, A. A., & Chance, J. M. (1987). Prevalence of Alzheimer's disease in a retirement community. *American Journal of Epidemiology, 125*, 420–436.

Pittman, J., Andrews, H., Tatemichi, T., Link, B., Struening, E., Stern, Y., & Mayeux, R. (1992). Diagnosis of dementia in a heterogeneous population. A comparison of paradigm-based diagnosis and physician's diagnosis. *Archives of Neurology, 49*, 461–467.

Rocca, W. A., Bonaiuto, S., Lippi, A., Luciani, P., Turtu, F., Cavarzeran, F., & Amaducci, L. (1990). Prevalence of clinically diagnosed Alzheimer's disease and other dementing disorders: A door-to-door survey in Appignano, Macerata Province, Italy. *Neurology, 40*, 626–631.

St. George-Hyslop, P. H. (1994). The molecular genetic of Alzheimer disease. In R. D. Terry, R. Katzman, & K. L. Bick (Eds.), *Alzheimer disease* (pp. 345–352). New York: Raven Press.

Schneider, E. L., & Guralnik, J. M. (1990). The aging of America. Impact on health care costs. *Journal of the American Medical Association, 263*, 2354–2355.

Skoog, I., Nilsson, L., Palmertz, B., Andreasson, L. A., & Svanborg, A. (1993). A population-based study of dementia in 85-year-olds. *New England Journal of Medicine, 328*, 153–158.

Still, C. N., Jackson, K. L., Brandes, D. A., Abramson, R. K., & Macera, C. A. (1990). Distribution of major dementias by race and sex in South Carolina. *Journal of the South Carolina Medical Association, 86*, 453–456.

Sulkava, R., Wikstrom, J., Aromaa, A., Raitasalo, R., Lehtinen, V., Lahtela, K., & Palo, J. (1985). Prevalence of severe dementia in Finland. *Neurology, 35*, 1025–1029.

Taft, L. B.,, & Barkin, R. L. (1990). Drug abuse? Use and misuse of psychotropic drugs in Alzheimer's care. *Journal of Gerontological Nursing, 16*, 4–10.

Tatemichi, T. K., Sacktor, N., & Mayeux, R. (1994). Dementia associated with cerebrovascular disease, other degenerative disease, and metabolic disorders. In R. D. Terry, R. Katzman, & K. L. Bicks (Eds.), *Alzheimer disease*. New York: Raven Press.

Tatemichi, T. K., Paik, M., Bagiella, E., Desmond, D. W., Stern, Y., Sano, M., Hauser, W. A., & Mayeux, R. (1994). Risk of dementia after stroke in a hospitalized cohort: Results of a longitudinal study. *Neurology, 44*, 1885–1891.

Terry, R. D., & Katzman, R. (1983). Senile dementia of the Alzheimer's type: Defining a disease. In R. Katzman & R. D. Terry (Eds.), *The neurology of aging* (pp. 51–84). New York: FA Davis.

Terry, R. D., Masliah, E., & Hansen, L. A. (1994). Structural basis of the cognitive alterations in Alzheimer disease. In R. D. Terry, R. Katzman, & K. L. Bick (Eds.), *Alzheimer disease* (pp. 179–196). New York: Raven Press.

Tsai, M. S., Tangalos, E. G., Peterson, R. C., Smith, G. E., Schaid, D. J., Kokmen, E., Ivnik, R. J., & Thibodeau, S. N. (1994). Apolipoprotein E: Risk factor for Alzheimer disease. *American Journal of Human Genetics, 54*, 643–649.

Ueda, K., Kawano, H., Hasuo, Y., & Fujishima, M. (1992). Prevalence and etiology of dementia in a Japanese community. *Stroke, 23*, 798–803.

U.S. Department of Health and Human Services Advisory Panel on Alzheimer's Disease (1992). *4th annual report.* Bethesda, MD: Author.

Valle, R. (1994). Culture-fair behavioral symptom differential assessment and intervention in dementing illness. *Alzheimer's Disease and Associated Disorders, 8*, 21–45.

van Duijn, C. M., de Knijff, P., Cruts, M., Wehnert, A., Havekes, L. M., Hofman, A., & Van Broeckhoven, C. (1994). Apolipoprotein E4 allele in a population-based study of early-onset Alzheimer's disease. *Nature Genetics, 7*, 74–78.

Wallace, G. L. (1993). Neurological impairment among elderly African-American nursing home residents. *Journal of Health Care for the Poor and Underserved, 4*, 40–50.

Winblad, B., Aguero, H., Ericsson, K., Fratiglioni, L., & Nordberg, A. (1993). Alzheimer's disease: Caring and pharmacological treatment strategies in Sweden. In G. K. Wilcock (Ed.). *The management of Alzheimer's disease* (pp. 107–115). Kent, United Kingdom: Wrighson Biomedical.

Wolfe, N., Imai, Y., Otani, C., Nagatani, H., Hasegawa, K., Sugimoto, K., Tanaka, Y., Kuroda, Y., Glosser, G., & Albert, M. L. (1992). Criterion validity of the cross-cultural cognitive examination in Japan. *Journal of Gerontology, 47*, 289–291.

Wragg, R. E., & Jeste, D. V. (1989). Overview of depression and psychosis in Alzheimer's disease. *American Journal of Psychiatry, 146*, 577–587.

Zhang, M. Y., Katzman, R., Salmon, D., Jin, H., Cai, G. J., Wang, Z. Y., Qu, G. Y., Grant, I., Yu, E., & Levy, P. (1990). The prevalence of dementia and Alzheimer's disease in Shanghai, China: Impact of age, gender, and education. *Annals of Neurology, 27*, 428–437.

Chapter 3

Variations in Dementia Characteristics by Ethnic Category

Gwen Yeo
Dolores Gallagher-Thompson
Morton Lieberman

BACKGROUND

Although there has been little systematic research on types of dementia and other characteristics associated with the disease by ethnic minority category, the subject is of growing concern among providers of health and social services to the rapidly growing population of elders from diverse ethnic backgrounds and their family members. (See Chapter 1 for demographic projections by ethnic category.) The Advisory Panel on Alzheimer's Disease (1993) reviewed the information available related to Alzheimer's disease and related disorders and ethnic and cultural issues and recommended that "Alzheimer's disease research and health services delivery agendas should be broadened to reflect the wide cultural diversity encountered in our society'' (p. 29).

Studies funded by the National Institute on Aging and other agencies that will eventually help describe the variations in epidemiology and consequences of dementia are underway in a number of ethnic communities in the United States, but currently very little substantive data are available (Advisory Panel on Alzheimer's Disease, 1993). Developing and implementing well-designed, large-scale research efforts within the United States have been hampered by major difficulties, including the vast heterogeneity both within and between the ethnic minority categories, development of reliable assessments of cognitive performance applicable among culturally and educationally diverse groups, and access to small populations who tend to use clinical services where research is traditionally performed less often owing to a variety of barriers. In their review of the data available on dementia cross-nationally, Chang, Miller, and Lin (1993) found that the greatest problem was that the methods used to make diagnoses ranged from loose clinical criteria to neurospychological tests, many of which do not include the determination of type of dementia. Personnel with different training administered different tests using different diagnostic labels (Chang et al., 1993).

In the United States, a few studies with small samples in local settings have been reported that suggest that there may be differences in types of dementia by ethnic or racial background, or both (de la Monte, Hutchins, & Moore, 1989; Serby, Chou, & Franssen, 1987). (See Chapter 2.) Specifically, these studies suggested that multi-infarct dementia was more common in African American and Chinese samples than in the White samples with which they were compared. This finding among the African American population is in agreement with the hypothesis discussed by dementia scholars during the 1980s who predicted the higher rates of vascular-related dementia on the basis of the higher prevalence of hypertension (Folstein, Anthony, Parhard, Duffy, & Gruenberg, 1985). This trend was also confirmed in a comparison of 3,400 White and 2,600 African American cases from the South Carolina Statewide Alzheimer's Disease and Related Disorders Registry that found that the African Americans were more likely to be diagnosed with multi-infarct dementia, were younger, were more likely to be living with a caregiver who is not their spouse, and were less likely to be institutionalized (Cornman et al., 1994). As discussed by Baker in Chapter 6, "Issues in Assessing Dementia in African American Elders," assessment of cognitive status in some African American samples has been found to be influenced by the confound of education on performance on screening tests, according to some studies.

Although there are a number of widely referenced large-scale studies exploring the relationships between elders from various ethnic backgrounds and their family members (Cantor, 1975; Jackson, Chatters, & Taylor, 1991; Markides, Boldt, & Ray, 1986), until recently few investigated family relationships in the presence of dementia. From these and from census data, it is known that Hispanic and Asian/Pacific Islander elders are generally about twice as likely to live with their adult children as are older Americans who classify themselves as non-Hispanic Whites (American Association of Retired Persons, 1987). A few studies have also described patterns of family support among African American and Hispanic dementia patients and their families (Cox & Monk, 1990; Gonzales, Gitlin, & Lyons, 1995; Hinrichsen & Ramirez, 1992; Lawton, Rajagopal, Brody, & Kleban, 1992; Wykle & Segall, 1991). (See Part 3 of this book for more information.)

METHOD

Data from records of the nine Alzheimer's Disease Diagnostic and Treatment Centers (ADDTCs) funded by the California State Department of Health Services were analyzed to examine the identified ethnic background of the patients and the association between ethnicity and other characteristics, which included their diagnoses, severity of their dementia, comorbidity, living arrangements, and the relationship of the individuals with dementia to their primary caregivers.

Six of the ADDTCs were founded in 1986, and the remaining three were founded in 1989. They are located in metropolitan areas throughout the state. The referral, assessment, and data management systems used by the centers are coordinated through the California Department of Health Services. Some of the centers have specific outreach programs to provide ethnic-specific information and assessment for certain ethnic populations. All the cases in their centralized database through mid-1993 were used in the analyses reported in this chapter, which were based on information recorded at the time of the initial assessments.

Ethnicity was based on self-identification or medical records and categorized as American Indian or Alaska Native, Asian, Filipino, Pacific Islander, Black (not Hispanic), Hispanic origin, White (not Hispanic), or other. In this analysis, those reported as American Indian or Alaska Native were not included because there were only 10 reported cases; those classified as other or whose data on ethnic background were missing were also not included. The Filipino and Pacific Islander categories were combined with Asian to compose the Asian/Pacific Islander (Asian/PI) category because of small numbers and to make the category comparable to other data sources. Demographic data and relationship of caregivers to patients are based on information provided at the time of assessment.

Diagnoses were assigned on the basis of extensive assessment, which included neurological evaluation, neuropsychological testing, comprehensive history from family or other informants, and laboratory tests. In some cases magnetic resonance imaging (MRI) or computed tomography (CT) scans, positron emission tomography (PET) or single photon emission computed tomography (SPECT) scans, electroencephalogram (EEG), or lumbar puncture were performed or data were available from prior clinical assessments. The diagnosis of dementia was based on *Diagnostic and Statistical Manual of Mental Disorders* (3rd ed., rev., American Psychiatric Association, 1987) criteria; for the primary etiology of possible or probable Alzheimer's disease, National Institutes of Neurologic and Communicative Disorders and Stroke–Alzheimers Disease and Related Disorders Association criteria were used, and standardized ADDTC criteria were used for possible or probable ischemic vascular dementia. In this analysis, the possible and probable primary etiologies were combined.

Comorbidities were based on histories and laboratory assessments. Living arrangements and relationship of the patients to their primary caregivers were based on reports of the patient, family informant, or both. Severity of the disease was used as a construct to provide an approximate index of the level of demand placed on the family. It is a computed score based on the following assessments: (a) level of cognitive disturbance, as measured by the Mini-Mental State Exam (MMSE); (b) level of dementia, as measured by the Blessed-Roth Dementia Rating Scale (BRDRS); (c) number and intensity of psychiatric symptoms, based

Table 1   Comparison of Ethnic Category of Cases in California Alzheimer's Disease and Diagnostic Treatment Centers (ADDTCs), and Older Californians, 1990

Ethnic category	n	ADDTC Database, 1993 (N = 5,262; %)	California 65 +, 1990[a] (N = 3,136,000; %)
White (non-Hispanic)	4,026	76	75
Black	421	8	5
Hispanic	509	10	10
Asian/Pacific Islander[b]	198	4	6
Other	108	2	4

[a]Compiled from data from State of California State Census Data Center.
[b]Includes self-identified categories of Asian, Pacific Islander, and Filipino.

on clinic psychiatrists' rating of nine symptoms; (d) number of neurological signs and symptoms, based on clinic neurologists' rating of nine symptoms; (e) number of other health problems, based on clinic physicians' reports of number of major illnesses; and (f) number of years patient has exhibited dementia symptoms, based on interviews with family members.

Differences between the ethnic categories were tested for statistical significance by using chi-square statistics, unless otherwise noted.

RESULTS

Ethnic Distribution and Demographic Characteristics

At the time of the analysis, there were data on 5,262 individuals who had been referred and assessed in the nine ADDTC centers through the middle of 1993. Ethnic identification data indicated that 10% were Hispanic, 8% Black (non-Hispanic), and 4% Asian/PI. In comparison, the 65 + population in California in 1990 was 10% Hispanic, 5% Black, and 6% Asian/PI (see Table 1). On the basis of this analysis, Asian/PI is the only category that might be said to be underrepresented among the patients in the ADDTC program, if it is assumed that prevalence of dementia symptoms prompting referral is equally distributed in the ethnic categories.

Comparison of the demographic characteristics in the four ethnic categories revealed very similar age distributions, ranging from 73.4 years for Asian/PI to 75.2 years for Whites. There were about twice as many women as men in the study population, and about three times as many women as men among the Black patients. Mean number of years of school was 7.7 for Hispanics, 10.0 for Blacks, 12.4 for Asian/PI, and 12.7 for Whites. Whites had the highest mean income (in the $20,000–$25,000 range), followed by Asian/PIs, with Hispanics and Blacks reporting incomes about half those of Whites. White patients were one third as likely to be on Supplemental Security Income as those in any of the

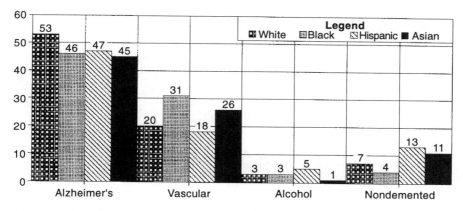

Figure 1 Type of dementia by ethnicity (percentage of cases in ethnic group) *Note. p* < .001, *N* = 4,875. For 271 (6%), the diagnosis was another type of dementia; for 325 (7%), amnestic syndromes; and for 244 (5%), the diagnosis was deferred.

three other categories. Fewer Black and Hispanics were married, more Blacks were widowed, and more Blacks and Hispanics were divorced.

Diagnoses

As indicated in Figure 1, significant differences were found between the percentage of individuals assigned to the various diagnostic categories by ethnicity. The major findings include the following: (a) More Whites than Blacks, Asian/PIs, or Hispanics were diagnosed as having Alzheimer's disease, (b) more Blacks and Asian/PIs than Whites and fewer Hispanics than Whites had vascular dementia, and (c) more Hispanics and Asian/PIs than Whites and Blacks were found to be non-demented.

Comorbidity

Patterns of comorbidity were compared in the four ethnic categories. As indicated in Table 2, significant differences among patients in the data set include the following: (a) Whites had much lower rates of diabetes than did all three other populations, (b) Blacks had higher rates of hypertension than did others, (c) depression was highest in Hispanics and lowest in Blacks, (d) heart disease and chronic obstructive pulmonary disease were highest among Whites and lowest among Asian/PIs, and (e) Whites had higher rates of thyroid disease than did the other three populations.

The combination of the patterns of comorbidity with the diagnoses reveals some interesting and somewhat unexpected relationships. The Hispanic dementia patients' higher rates of diabetes appear not to predispose them to higher rates of vascular dementia, as might be expected. Asian/PIs had higher rates of vas-

Table 2   Percentage of Patients Reporting History of Diseases by Ethnicity

Disease	White (n = 3,973)	Black (n = 414)	Hispanic (n = 500)	Asian (n = 195)
Diabetes	6	15	16	15
Thyroid disorder	14	9	7	6
Hypertension	34	52	32	37
Depression	22	16	28	19
Heart disease	26	23	19	16
COPD	8	6	4	3

Note. Only the diseases with significant differences reported. COPD = chronic obstructive pulmonary disease.

cular dementia in spite of lower rates of heart disease and chronic obstructive pulmonary disease and similar hypertension compared with those in other categories. The expected relationship between hypertension and vascular dementia was evident among the Black patients.

Severity of Illness

The computed scores for severity of illness were based on scores on measures of mental status (MMSE), level of dementia (BRDRS), psychiatric symptoms, neurological signs and symptoms, major illnesses, and length of time with dementia symptoms (Figure 2). After cases with missing data on one or more

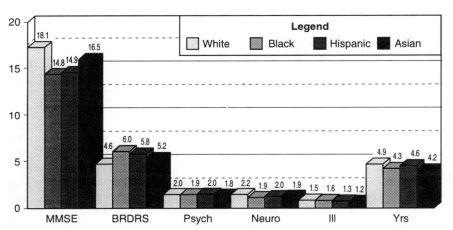

Figure 2   Severity of dementia by ethnicity (observed means on subscales) *Note.* Lower MMSE scores indicate greater severity; higher scores on all other measures denote greater severity. For the overall MANOVA, $p < .001$; MMSE, $p < .001$; BRDRS, $p < .01$; Psych, *ns*; Neuro, $p < .001$; Ill, $p < .001$; Yrs, $p < .05$; MMSE = Mini-Mental State Exam; BRDRS = Blessed-Roth Dementia Rating Scale; Psych = psychiatric symptoms; neuro = neurological signs and symptoms; ILL = major illnesses; Yrs = length of time with dementia symptoms.

Table 3 Living Arrangements (Percentage of Ethnic Patients)

Ethnicity	Alone	With spouse	With spouse and others	With other relatives	With nonrelatives	Health facility or group quarters
White	22	40	6	16	4	11
Black	22	18	7	40	5	6
Hispanic	21	22	13	33	4	5
Asian	16	32	19	22	2	9

Note. $p < .0001$.

measures were removed, 3,235 cases were entered in the multiple analysis of variance (MANOVA) that controlled for the number of years of schooling. Significant differences were found between ethnic categories in the composite MANOVA and in five of the six individual measures before adjustment for education. Black patients had more impairment in cognitive status, severity of dementia, and number of other major illnesses. Whites had less impairment in cognitive status and severity of dementia but more neurological symptoms and longer duration of illness. In four of the six measures, the Hispanic patients had the second highest severity, but some of the differences were slight. The composite index indicated that Black and Hispanic patients were at significantly greater risk for severity.

In view of the finding from prior studies that education may confound scores on the MMSE, the effect of the correction in scores for number of years of schooling is of particular interest. Observed versus adjusted mean scores for the MMSE (with 30 indicating no mistakes) were 18.2 versus 17.1, respectively, for Whites; 14.8 versus 15.1, respectively, for Blacks; 14.9 versus 16.3, respectively, for Hispanics (who had the least education in this sample); and 16.5 versus 15.9, respectively, for Asian/PIs.

Significant differences were found between the ethnic categories in a separate analysis of the number and intensity of problem behaviors exhibited by the patients based on data available from the clinical nurses' ratings after a home visit for 4,475 cases. Black families experienced an average of 1.7 problems, Whites, 1.6; Hispanic, 1.5; and Asian/PIs, 1.3.

Living Arrangements and Caregiver Relationships

About one fifth of all of the populations lived alone at the time of referral to the ADDTC, except among the Asian/PI category in which there were slightly fewer living alone (see Table 3). Living with one's spouse alone was the most common situation for Whites and Asian/PIs. The Black and Hispanic patients were more likely than those in the other categories to live with relatives other than their spouses. About half as many Black and Hispanic patients as White patients lived in health facilities or group quarters at the time of the referral.

Individuals designated as caregivers were more likely to be spouses for White and Asian/PI patients and daughters for Blacks and Hispanic patients (see

Table 4   Relationship of Caregivers to Patients by Ethnicity (Percentage of Ethnic Patients)

Ethnicity	Spouse	Son	Daughter	Other relative	Friend or neighbor
White (n = 4,020)	42	17	30	19	9
Black (n = 420)	22	15	40	36	10
Hispanic (n = 509)	32	20	42	27	6
Asian (n = 198)	47	24	32	21	2

Note. Percentages total more than 100 owing to identification of both primary and secondary caregivers by some patients.

Table 4). In all other categories, about half of the participants indicated that sons and daughters were caregivers, with Whites least likely and Hispanics most likely to have that indication. Although daughters are more likely than sons to be designated as caregivers in all ethnic categories, Asians were most likely to designate sons. More African American caregivers were relatives other than spouses.

CONCLUSION

One of the major findings of this analysis of more than 5,000 cases of older Californians assessed in a statewide system of centers designed to diagnose and treat patients with Alzheimer's disease is that ethnic minority populations are not underrepresented among those referred, with the exception of Asian/PIs, who had two-thirds as many cases as would be expected if dementia were equally distributed among the ethnic categories.

There were significant differences in the distribution of the types of dementia among the ethnic categories, with a higher percentage of White elders being diagnosed as having probable or possible Alzheimer's disease. More African American and Asian/PI elders were diagnosed as having vascular dementia, as has been observed in other studies, reviewed in Chapter 2. As expected, hypertension and diabetes were also found to be higher among Black elders than among Whites, although no specific analysis was performed to try to determine whether it was a specific predictor for vascular dementia. However, although the Asian/PI patients had high rates of diabetes, their rates of hypertension were only slightly higher than those of Whites, and they had the lowest rates of heart disease. Among Hispanics, there seemed to be no extra risk of vascular dementia even though diabetes was more common among them than among any of the other ethnic categories.

African Americans and Hispanic elders were more likely than White or Asian/PIs to live with relatives other than their spouses; more Hispanic caregivers are offspring, and more African American caregivers are other relatives. On the basis of the computed Severity of Illness Index, African American and Hispanic caregivers may be confronted with more problems.

The concerns that this analysis raises need to be addressed in future studies. As in any multicenter program that is designed primarily to provide assessment and treatment rather than to collect carefully controlled research data, one could wish for more uniformity in the availability of information about patient characteristics and measurement scores.

A major step forward in being able to sort out the different risk factors among elders of color would be to provide information on the specific ethnic background rather than the large ethnic categories, such as Asian or Hispanic. It is hoped that with the large number of Alzheimer's research centers now involved in dementia research, ethnicity will be included in a more systematic and careful way.

REFERENCES

Advisory Panel on Alzheimer's Disease. (1993). *Fourth Report of the Advisory Panel on Alzheimer's Disease, 1992* (NIH Pub. No. 93-3520). Washington, DC: U.S. Government Printing Office.

American Psychiatric Association. (1987). *Diagnostic and statistical manual of mental disorders* (3rd ed., rev.). Washington, DC: Author.

Cantor, M. (1975). Life space and the social support system of the inner city elderly of New York. *The Gerontologist, 15*, 23–27.

Chang, L., Miller, B. L., & Lin, K.-M. (1993). Clinical and epidemiological studies of dementias: Cross-ethnic perspectives. In K.-M. Lin, R. E. Poland, & G. Nakasaki (Eds.), *Psychopharmacology and psychobiology of ethnicity*. New York: American Psychiatric Press.

Cornman, C. B., Davis, D. R., Macera, C. A., Sharpe, P. A., Eleazer, G. P., & Zheng, D. (1994, November). *Ethnic differences between Whites and African-Americans with dementia*. Poster presented at the 47th annual scientific meeting of the Gerontological Society of America, Atlanta, GA.

Cox, C., & Monk, A. (1990). Minority caregiving of dementia victims: A comparison of Black and Hispanic families. *Journal of Applied Gerontology, 9*, 340–355.

de la Monte, S., Hutchins, G. M., & Moore, M. (1989). Racial differences in the etiology of dementia and frequency of Alzheimer lesions in the brain. *Journal of National Medical Association, 81*, 644–652.

Folstein, M., Anthony, J. C., Parhard, J., Duffy, B., & Gruenberg, E. M. (1985). The meaning of cognitive impairment in the elderly. *Journal of the American Geriatrics Society, 33*, 228–233.

Gonzales, E., Gitlin, L., & Lyons, K. J. (1995). Review of the literature on African American caregivers of individuals with dementia. *Journal of Cultural Diversity, 2*, 40–48.

Hinrichsen, G., & Ramirez, M. (1992). Black and White dementia caregivers: A comparison of their adaptation, adjustment, and service utilization. *Gerontologist, 32*, 375–381.

Jackson, J., Chatters, L., & Taylor, R. J. (1991). *Aging in Black America*. Newbury Park, CA: Sage.

Lawton, M. P., Rajagopal, D., Brody, E., & Kleban, M. H. (1992). The dynamics of caregiving for a demented elder among Black and White families. *Journal of Gerontology: Social Sciences, 47*, S156–S164.

Markides, K. S., Boldt, J. S., & Ray, L. A. (1986). Sources of helping and intergenerational solidarity: A three-generations study of Mexican Americans. *Journal of Gerontology, 41*, 506–511.

Serby, M., Chou, J. C.-Y., & Franssen, E. H. (1987). Dementia in an American-Chinese nursing home population. *American Journal of Psychiatry, 144*, 811–812.

State of California State Data Census Center. (1990). Summary of California Tape File 1: Complete Tables; U.S. Census of Population and Housing. Sacramento: Author.

Wykle, M., & Segall, M. A. (1991). A comparison of Black and White family caregivers' experience with dementia. *Journal of National Black Nurses' Association, 5*, 29–51.

Part 2

Assessment of Cognitive Status with Different Ethnic Populations

The challenges facing clinicians in providing appropriate dementia assessments vary both between and within the different ethnic minority categories. For example, the linguistic challenges are much different for populations who have immigrated during the past few decades, in which the older cohort is almost totally monolingual and non-English-speaking, as compared with those who speak some English or who speak it fluently. There are also major differences in educational and literacy levels, cohort experiences affecting trust and communication with providers, and explanatory models of illness and aging, all of which influence the assessment process and outcome.

In this section, four groups with experience in assessment with particular populations share their insights and techniques with readers.

Chapter 4

The Process of Development of Valid and Reliable Neuropsychological Assessment Measures for English- and Spanish-Speaking Elderly Persons

Dan Mungas

There has been a dramatic increase in the population of both minority and nonminority elderly persons in the United States in recent years. Data from the U.S. Bureau of the Census have indicated that the U.S. population of Hispanics aged 65 and older grew to a total of more than 1 million people between 1980 and 1990, a growth rate double that of older non-Hispanics. With this increase in the elderly population comes an associated increase in chronic illnesses associated with aging. Dementia, for which Alzheimer's disease is the most common etiology, is becoming an increasing problem in terms of quality of life for those with the disease and those who care for them and in terms of its economic impact. Estimates of the prevalence of dementia range from 1% to 3% for the 65–74 age range, from 7% to 18.7% for the 75–84 range, and from 25% to 47.2% for the 85+ population (Evans et al., 1989; U.S. Congress, Office of Technology Assessment, 1987).

On the basis of these prevalence estimates, the Alzheimer's Disease Program of the California Department of Health Services has estimated that there are

This project was supported by Grants AG10220 and AG10129 from the National Institute on Aging, Bethesda, MD, and by the California Department of Health Services Alzheimer's Disease Program, Contract 91-10344. Mary Haan and Bruce Reed made important contributions to study design and implementation. Minda deRussy and Sarah Marshall were responsible for study management and also contributed to study design and implementation. Salvador Santillán, Marisa Ramos, Antonia Olmos, Maria Velasco, Martha Rico, Esther Barajas, Andy Chen, Karima Harmon, Jaime Lizaragga, and Maria Ramirez were responsible for data collection.

between 166,596 and 393,585 patients with dementia residing in California. If one were to assume that prevalence rates for Hispanics match those of the population at large, one would estimate that there are between 18,325 and 43,294 elderly Hispanic individuals with dementia residing in the state of California. Assuming that the preferred language of 60% of these individuals is Spanish (Frerichs, Aneshensel, & Clark, 1981) suggests that there are between 11,000 and 26,000 demented elderly people who are Spanish speaking. These data indicate that cognitive impairment in both English- and Spanish-speaking elderly persons is a significant problem. For clinical reasons as well as for research on dementia in elderly persons, there is a definite need for objective test instruments to quantify cognitive functioning in this population.

Neuropsychological tests available for assessing cognitive functioning in elderly persons have a number of significant limitations. Widely used tests such as the Wechsler Adult Intelligence Scale—Revised (WAIS–R) and the Wechsler Memory Scale—Revised (WMS–R) were not specifically designed with neuro-psychological considerations in mind. Scales are not matched according to important psychometric characteristics like reliability and sensitivity to cognitive impairment (Chapman & Chapman, 1973), making it difficult to separate psychometric artifacts due to inherent psychometric characteristics of tests from valid variance in cognitive functioning. Available norms are also problematic. Although instruments like the WAIS–R and WMS–R have adequate norms for elderly individuals up to age 75, there are very few tests with adequate norms for elderly individuals over the age of 75.

Tests for assessing cognitive functioning in Hispanic elderly persons present more substantial problems. It is well-known that factors such as ethnic origin, language, and low levels of education can adversely affect performance on tests of cognitive functioning in elderly persons (Fillenbaum, Heyman, Williams, Prosnitz, & Burchett, 1990; Gurland, Wilder, Cross, Teresi, & Barrett, 1992; Murden, McRae, Kaner, & Bucknam, 1991). As a result of such factors, cognitive impairment may be overestimated in minorities and in individuals who have limited education and who do not speak English. Standardized psychological tests available for Spanish-language assessment have a number of limitations and may underestimate or overestimate cognitive functioning, depending on which normative group is used (López & Romero, 1988; López & Tausig, 1991). Normative data are particularly limited. The Spanish-language version of the WAIS, the *Escala de Inteligencia Wechsler para Adultos* (EIWA; Wechsler, 1968) has extensive and carefully collected population-based norms, but the normative sample was collected in Puerto Rico in the mid-1960s, and there is reason to question its current applicability within the continental United States (López & Romero, 1988). In addition, norms are not provided for individuals over the age of 65. Norms for other tests from other sources are generally derived from small samples that are not population based and provide very limited information regarding expected levels of functioning.

Because of limitations in available neuropsychological tests, a project is in progress at the University of California (UC), Davis, whose purpose is to develop and validate a battery of neuropsychological tests for English- and Spanish-speaking elderly persons. An important goal of this project is to create tests that are matched according to psychometric characteristics both across and within English- and Spanish-language versions. Tests of this nature will facilitate unbiased measurement of cognitive changes associated with aging in English- and Spanish-speaking elderly persons in both research and clinical settings. Psychometrically matched component scales will allow for identification of relative impairment in different areas of functioning, which will facilitate sensitive assessment of differential patterns of deficit associated with different etiologies for cognitive impairment. Finally, availability of age-corrected, population-based norms for the 60 + population will make a substantial contribution to the neuropsychological assessment of elderly persons.

METHODS FOR TEST DEVELOPMENT

This project is notably different from previous research on cross-cultural test development in that totally new test instruments are being created, as opposed to adapting existing English-language instruments to other languages and cultures. The intent is to develop a neuropsychological test battery that assesses a broad range of cognitive abilities that are neuropsychologically relevant for elderly persons. Both verbal and nonverbal measures are included, and all tests are nontimed. This test battery was designed to be composed of 12 separate scales. These scales include verbal and nonverbal measures in the domains of conceptual thinking, attention span, episodic memory, and semantic memory. In addition, there are separate tests of verbal expression, verbal comprehension, pattern recognition, and spatial judgment. Scales of the neuropsychological test battery are listed in Table 1.

Item Generation and Pilot Testing

For each scale, a large number of items were created. Items with verbal content and instructions for test administration were translated into Spanish. Item generation was guided by several goals. First, an attempt was made to create items that had face validity with respect to the domain of ability being assessed. Item generation was accomplished by neuropsychologists with broad experience in neuropsychological assessment and research. Second, an attempt was made to create items that did not have obvious language or cultural bias. This was a particularly challenging goal that was facilitated by having bilingual and bicultural members on the project team. However, an important feature of the plan for this project was to create three to five times the numbers of items that would be used in the final scales, so that empirical methods could be used to identify

Table 1   Domains of Ability Assessed by Neuropsychological Test Battery and Names of Component Scales

Domain of ability	Scale
Conceptual thinking	Verbal Conceptual Thinking
	Nonverbal Conceptual Thinking
Attention span	Verbal Attention Span
	Visual Attention Span
Episodic memory	Verbal List Learning
	Spatial Configuration Learning
Semantic memory	Verbal Semantic Memory—Object Naming
	Nonverbal Semantic Memory—Picture Association
Verbal abilities	Verbal Comprehension
	Verbal Expression
Visual–Spatial Abilities	Pattern Recognition
	Spatial Location

and eliminate biased items. Third, items were created to span a broad range of difficulty with the intent to include items that could be passed by demented elderly persons as well as items that high-functioning elderly persons would fail.

Participant Recruitment

Participants were recruited from two sources: UC, Davis, graduate students and community-dwelling elderly persons 60 years of age and older. Graduate students were used for pilot testing of scales. Three groups of graduate students were recruited: (a) Hispanic–Spanish test administration, (b) Hispanic–English test administration, and (c) Non-Hispanic–English test administration. Tests were administered in the participant's preferred language (either English or Spanish). A population-based community survey was used to identify elderly participants. A door-to-door survey was conducted, and all persons over the age of 60 were asked to complete a 45- to 60-minute interview. This interview was in either English or Spanish, depending on the participant's preference. Data collected included demographic and language information, information about health status, and measures of activities of daily living and instrumental activities of daily living. The Mini-Mental State Exam (MMSE) was administered, and several physical performance measures were obtained. Participants were eligible for testing if (a) they were 60 years of age or older, (b) English or Spanish was their primary language, and (c) they did not have physical or sensory limitations that would preclude their taking the tests.

From December 1992 through August 1994, the survey was conducted in Sacramento County census tracts selected on the basis of having relatively high percentages of Hispanic residents. During the period from October 1993 through August 1994, test administration was completed with 184 elderly participants recruited from the community survey, 105 tested in English (95 non-Hispanic,

Table 2   MMSE, Age, and Education Means and Standard Deviations for English and Spanish Test Administration Groups

Group	Age		Education		MMSE	
	m	SD	m	SD	m	SD
English (n = 105)	70.09	6.57	11.86	3.72	27.61	2.62
Spanish (n = 79)	68.94	7.28	5.49	4.09	24.72	3.88

Note. MMSE = Mini-Mental State Exam.

10 Hispanic) and 79 tested in Spanish (all Hispanic). These participants constituted the test development sample for subsequent analyses. Participants were allowed to self-select language of test administration subject to requirements that they be fluent in that language and use it on a daily basis. Means and standard deviations of the test development sample by English- and Spanish-language test administration for the variables age, education, and MMSE score are presented in Table 2. Group differences were statistically significant for education and MMSE score ($ps < .001$) but were not significant for age.

Forty additional participants—17 English-speaking (14 non-Hispanic, 3 Hispanic) and 23 Spanish-speaking (all Hispanic)—were recruited and tested from September 1994 through December 1994. These participants constituted the cross-validation sample used in subsequent analyses. Mean ages (English language, 70.2 years; Spanish language, 69.4 years) and education (English language, 11.3 years; Spanish language, 5.8 years) for these participants were quite similar to those of the test development sample.

Pilot Testing of Scales

Pilot testing of scales was first performed with the UC, Davis, graduate students. Ten participants in each of the three groups were tested. The purpose of testing these participants was to provide training and practical experience to staff administering the tests, to obtain data on high-end discrimination of test items, to obtain preliminary information regarding distribution of item difficulty, and to obtain empirical data by which items could be ordered according to increasing difficulty.

During October and November 1993, 21 English-speaking participants and 21 Spanish-speaking elderly participants were tested, and these data were used to evaluate the degree to which project goals were being met and to identify necessary changes in item content. On the basis of these data, distributions of item difficulty were calculated. The overall plan for test development was to include items that span the entire range of difficulty for the target population, following a relatively uniform distribution. Item difficulty distributions were found to be acceptable for all but three scales, and changes were made in format and item content of these scales.

Test Administration

For test administration to occur in either English or Spanish, the subject had to be fluent in that language and had to actively use that language. Bilingual participants were allowed to self-select their preferred language of administration. Test administration generally required 3–4 hours in one session. Participants were given breaks during testing, and an additional procedure was used to prevent participants from becoming overly fatigued. A maximum time limit of 4 hours was set for test administration, and administration was stopped after that time. As a result, all 12 scales were not administered to all participants. Three different orders of scale administration were used to distribute order and fatigue effects across scales and to ensure that the same scales were not the ones omitted because of time constraints.

Item Selection

Test item selection for each of the 12 scales followed a two-step process: First, items with language bias were eliminated, and second, items were selected from those remaining to match a desired distribution of item difficulty. A more detailed description of these steps follows.

Elimination of Items with Language Bias   The issue of test-item bias has received considerable attention in the psychometric literature, and several definitions of item bias have been proposed (Hulin, Drasgow, & Parsons, 1983). Hulin et al. proposed that item bias is present "when individuals with the same amount of an underlying trait from different subpopulations have different probabilities of responding to an item correctly" (p. 152). The operational definition of item bias used for this project was based on this definition. A broad definition of ability was used in which *ability* refers simply to the participant's capacity to successfully respond to test items. No assumptions were made about whether ability is an inherited characteristic, the result of experience, or both, and more specifically, no attempt was made to define ability as independent from other variables, most notably education, that might influence performance.

On the basis of the above considerations, the following two steps were used to determine item bias. First, items were identified that had similar item-total correlations (arbitrarily defined as both greater than .30 and within .20 of one another) for the English and the Spanish groups. This criterion operationalizes the measure of ability as the total score of the scale and identifies items that have a similar relationship to ability in both languages. Second, items meeting the first criterion were further assessed by means of a logistic regression analysis in which success or failure on a given item was regressed on language of test administration, age, and education. Items for which the language effect was nonsignificant ($p > .05$) were retained.

Selection of Unbiased Items for Scales From the subset of items for each scale that met criteria for being unbiased, a group of 20 items was selected in an attempt to establish a uniform distribution of item difficulty. The percentage of participants in each group who passed each item was calculated, and these two group percentages were then averaged to obtain an overall index of item difficulty. The model for item selection was to select 2 items (the same 2 items for the English and Spanish versions) to fall in each 10% range of the overall distribution of difficulty. That is, 2 items were passed by fewer than 10% of the sample, 2 were passed by between 10% and 20% of the sample, and so forth. This desired model was not met for all scales, but items were selected to match this model as closely as possible and to have a symmetrical distribution of difficulty around a mean value of .50.

RESULTS

Data from the participant sample described above are used to demonstrate the approach to test construction used in this project and to evaluate the extent to which project goals of developing psychometrically matched scales within and across English- and Spanish-language versions are being achieved.

Reliability and Validity of Scales

Internal Consistency Reliability Internal consistency reliability of the 20-item scales created in this manner was tested by using coefficient alpha. Cases with no missing data for all items for a given scale were used to calculate coefficient alphas. Results for several scales are based on substantially fewer cases. For scales modified after the initial pilot testing, results from the modified versions were used. Results from the entire sample were used for scales that were not modified. An additional factor influencing sample size for a given scale was the 4-hour test administration time limit previously described.

Alpha values and the sample sizes on which they are based are shown in Table 3. Values ranged from a low of .807 for Nonverbal Conceptual Thinking to a high of .936 for Visual Configuration Learning and Spatial Localization. Seven of the 12 scales had overall alpha values falling between .85 and .90, and 3 had alphas greater than .90. Absolute differences between coefficient alpha values for English and Spanish versions of the scales ranged from .000 to .099 ($M = .036$, $SD = .041$). These results indicate a high level of internal consistency reliability in using 20-item scales and show very good stability of these estimates across scales and across English- and Spanish-language versions.

Assessment of Reproducibility of Results It is widely known in psychometric research that individual-item statistics can be unstable when the ratio of participants to items is small. Because the approach to item selection relied

Table 3   Internal Consistency (Coefficient Alphas) of Scales in Two Samples

| Scale | Development sample | | | | Cross-validation sample | | | |
| | English | | Spanish | | English | | Spanish | |
	α	n	α	n	α	n	α	n
Verbal Conceptual	.83	101	.87	70	.87	16	.88	22
Nonverbal Conceptual	.74	97	.84	70	.79	15	.75	21
Verbal Attention Span	.91	99	.87	69	.88	12	.80	22
Visual Attention Span	.87	84	.88	65	.87	16	.84	22
Object Naming	.87	61	.88	33	.84	15	.90	22
Picture Association	.89	89	.88	70	.88	15	.92	21
Verbal List Learning	.82	80	.83	50	.90	17	.80	23
Visual Configuration Learning	.91	55	.88	29	.82	13	.92	19
Verbal Comprehension	.82	36	.90	18	.74	15	.91	22
Verbal Expression	.85	61	.83	32	.85	10	.76	16
Pattern Recognition	.87	94	.87	67	.79	13	.89	20
Spatial Localization	.93	97	.93	71	.86	15	.93	21

heavily on individual-item statistics, an additional analysis was performed to assess stability of results at the level of the total scale score. The cross-validation sample was used to test the reproducibility of the results from the test development sample. Internal consistency reliabilities of the 20-item scales created with the test development sample were calculated by using the cross-validation sample. Coefficient alpha values for this sample are also included in Table 3. Results again show alpha values that were primarily in .80s and .90s for both samples, that were similar to values from the test development sample, and that were similar for English- and Spanish-language versions.

Scale Validity   Means and standard deviations of each scale (in terms of percentage correct) by English and Spanish test administration are presented in Table 4. Scores were consistently higher for English versions of scales than for Spanish versions. Group differences were statistically significant ($p < .05$) for all scales except Visual Configuration Learning. However, mean differences in raw score were expected owing to the large group differences in mean education (11.9 years vs. 5.5 years). A more salient evaluation of the degree to which goals for this project are being met would address the question of whether language-group differences are present after education and age are controlled for and whether scales are differentially sensitive to cognitive impairment in English- and Spanish-language versions. Analyses relevant to these questions were performed for each scale in the following manner. First, participants were dichotomized into a cognitively impaired group and a cognitively intact group. Second, an analysis of covariance was performed that included language of test admin-

Table 4 Means and Standard Deviations of Percentage Correct of Scales

Scale	English		Spanish		Combined	
	m	*SD*	*m*	*SD*	*m*	*SD*
Verbal Conceptual	591	192	415	212	519	218
Nonverbal Conceptual	545	171	444	218	502	199
Verbal Attention	630	236	354	200	516	260
Visual Attention	542	213	459	226	506	222
Object Naming	579	214	433	217	528	226
Picture Association	579	214	405	230	503	238
Verbal List Learning	574	221	437	226	521	233
Visual Configuration Learning	530	312	467	307	508	312
Verbal Comprehension	582	202	472	271	545	234
Verbal Expression	560	211	433	213	516	220
Pattern Recognition	583	225	419	233	515	242
Spatial Localization	590	288	408	288	513	301

Note. Decimal points omitted.

istration and cognitive impairment as crossed between-groups factors and education and age as covariates.

Identification of cognitively impaired participants was performed by using a measure that represented a statistical adjustment of the MMSE for the effects of age and education (Mungas, Marshall, Weldon, Haan, & Reed, in press). Briefly, results from the community survey data ($N = 590$, 315 English-speaking–non-Hispanic, 111 English-speaking–Hispanic, 164 Spanish-speaking–Hispanic) revealed highly significant group differences on the MMSE. However, group differences were no longer statistically significant after controlling for effects of education and age. Linear regression methods were then used to create an adjustment of the MMSE for education and age. This resulted in the following adjusted MMSE score:

$$MMSEAdj = \text{raw } MMSE - \{[.471 * (education - 12)]$$
$$+ [.131 * (age - 70)]\}.$$

This formula adjusts the obtained MMSE score to correspond to what would be expected if the individual was 70 years of age and had received 12 years of education. The values of 12 years of education and 70 years of age are arbitrary. The three groups from the community survey did not significantly differ on *MMSEAdj*. The validity of this measure as a screening instrument for identifying dementia was tested on an independent sample of 2,983 patients who received comprehensive clinical evaluations through the California Alzheimer's Disease Diagnostic and Treatment Centers between 1985 and 1992. The MMSEAdj measure, using a cutoff value of 23–24, had overall diagnostic sensitivity for

Table 5   Relationship of Scale Scores to Education, Age, Language of Administration, and Cognitive Impairment (p values)

Scale	Education	Age	Language	Impairment	Language × Impairment
Verbal Conceptual	001	056	*	001	*
Nonverbal Conceptual	018	005	*	018	235
Verbal Attention Span	001	159	057	007	*
Visual Attention Span	011	010	*	001	*
Object Naming	001	003	249	030	264
Picture Association	001	001	313	001	*
Verbal List Learning	008	001	*	009	*
Visual Configuration Learning	002	090	*	001	*
Verbal Comprehension	137	287	*	126	114
Verbal Expression	001	144	*	151	*
Pattern Recognition	001	002	*	010	*
Spatial Localization	001	001	*	007	*

Note. Decimal points omitted.
*$F < 1.0$.

dementia of 84.5% and specificity of 87.4%. More important, this measure yielded stable results across low- and high-education groups and across non-Hispanic Whites and Hispanics, in marked contrast to the MMSE, which showed very striking differences in sensitivity and specificity across education and ethnic groups. These results indicated that MMSEAdj is as effective as the uncorrected MMSE in a general sample, but produces much more stable results in minority and low education individuals.

Participants in the test development sample were operationally defined as cognitively impaired if they attained a MMSEAdj score of 23 or less and were considered cognitively intact if they attained a MMSEAdj score of 24 or greater. The numbers of cognitively impaired participants were relatively small, ranging from 6 (3 English-speaking and 3 Spanish-speaking) for Verbal Comprehension to 19 (7 English-speaking and 12 Spanish-speaking) for Verbal Attention Span and Pattern Recognition.

Results of the analyses of covariance involving language of administration, cognitive impairment, age, and education are presented in Table 5. All scales except Verbal Comprehension were significantly related to education. Seven of the 12 scales were significantly related to age. All scales except Verbal Comprehension and Verbal Expression were significantly affected by cognitive impairment. Only Verbal Attention Span approached significance in terms of language of administration differences, and the interaction between language of administration and cognitive impairment was nonsignificant for all scales. Although statistical power for this interaction effect is low, it is noteworthy that this effect did not even approach statistical significance for 11 of the 12 scales. The lack of significant findings for the language of administration effect cannot be attributed to low statistical power as group sizes on which this effect were based were relatively large, and even for the Verbal Comprehension scale the available sample would have a statistical power of greater than 80% for identifying a between-group difference of one standard deviation. Even though statistical power for the cognitive impairment effect is somewhat limited, highly significant results were found for most scales.

CONCLUSION

Results to date provide very favorable evidence that the goals of this project are being met. First, very respectable levels of reliability were found in the development and cross-validation samples for all scales, using only 20 items per scale. The obtained reliabilities compare very favorably with those of the WAIS–R and the EIWA, in which the majority of subtests have reliability coefficients in the .80s and a few have reliability coefficients in the .90s, but some have reliability coefficients in the .60s and .70s. Second, using the development sample, all but two scales showed high levels of correspondence of reliability between English- and Spanish-language versions, and for the remaining two scales, reliabilities were within .10 of one another. In the cross-validation sample, only one scale had an English–Spanish reliability difference greater than .10. Third, scale scores did not demonstrate language group bias independent of effects of age and education. Fourth, the available data indicated that scale scores were sensitive to impaired cognitive functioning, and the effect of cognitive impairment on scales was the same for English- and Spanish-language versions.

The approach to test construction used in this project deliberately did not attempt to eliminate effects of education and thereby control test score differences between English and Spanish versions of the test. A primary role of education is to promote cognitive functioning and a major purpose for neuropsychological testing with elderly individuals is to determine if there has been a decline in cognitive functioning in neuropsychologically relevant areas. To measure only abilities that are not influenced by education would eliminate a number of areas of cognitive functioning that are important for neuropsychological assessment of elderly persons. The approach used in this study may not meet with universal agreement, but ultimately its validity is an empirical question. Data indicating that the English- and Spanish-language versions of the test battery have similar measurement characteristics and have similar sensitivity to cognitive impairment indicate that this is a viable approach to multilingual and cross-cultural test development.

An important element of the approach to test construction in this project was an emphasis on using empirical data to identify and eliminate biased items. This does not negate the importance of cultural awareness and sensitivity in the test development process. Indeed, knowledge of culture and language can be very valuable, particularly in the item-generation phase of test construction where cultural awareness can maximize the percentage of items that will not be biased.

However, cultural sensitivity alone is not a sufficient guarantee that bias will not be present, as even knowledgeable experts cannot always anticipate empirical relationships in data. For this reason, it is important that characteristics of items be directly tested. Combining a priori knowledge and experience with rigorous empirical methods is likely to maximize the advantages of both approaches, yielding an efficient and effective test development process.

A final aspect of the approach used in this project that merits discussion is the emphasis on psychometric matching of scales. Chapman and Chapman (1973, 1988) have argued forcefully that scales have to be psychometrically matched in order to reach valid conclusions about the presence of differential deficits of one ability in comparison with another. This principle has obvious relevance to neuropsychology, where deficit measurement is a central issue; however, in current practice different neuropsychological tests are rarely matched according to psychometric characteristics. Unfortunately, this introduces an element of judgment into the evaluation process because the examiner must take into consideration information, often based on personal experience with the tests, regarding relative sensitivity to different disorders. Using available methodology to construct psychometrically matched tests of different abilities will contribute to the overall fidelity of the neuropsychological assessment process by eliminating one significant source of examiner judgment. Another definite advantage of the psychometric matching approach is that it lends itself very well to cross-cultural test development. The same methodology that can be used to match scales within one language or culture can be used to match scales across languages or cultures. This study illustrates a cross-cultural application of this psychometric methodology that may well have value for other cross-cultural test development.

The research described in this chapter is a work in progress, and results are presented as an interim evaluation of this approach to test development rather than as a final outcome. Several additional steps need to be completed before final neuropsychological test instruments can be created. First, subject recruitment continues, with a goal of obtaining a sample of 200 English-language test administration participants and 200 Spanish-language test administration participants. Second, English- and Spanish-speaking participants with clinical diagnoses of dementia are being recruited and tested to directly assess sensitivity to cognitive impairment. Third, item-response theory methods (Baker, 1985; Hambleton & Swaminathan, 1985; Hulin, Drasgow, & Parsons, 1983; Lord, 1980) will also be used in the process of item selection, and results will be compared with results using methods based on classical psychometric theory, as described in this chapter. Item-response theory presents advantages in that item and participant parameters are sample independent if assumptions are met, but presents disadvantages in that assumptions can be restrictive and relatively large samples are needed to produce stable results. Finally, provisional scale norms will be calculated for the final scale versions based on cognitively normal participants participating in the test development process. A goal for future research will be to obtain population-based norms for the final versions of each scale. This work underscores the importance of differentiating between genuine cognitive impairment and a lack of comprehension due to language difficulties and incompatibilities. By using the information provided in this chapter, professionals can begin to address the challenge of correctly assessing ethnic elders.

REFERENCES

Baker, F. B. (1985). *The basics of item response theory*. Portsmouth, NH: Heineman.

Chapman, L. C., & Chapman, J. C. (1973). *Disordered thought in schizophrenia*. New York: Appleton-Century-Crofts.

Chapman, L. C., & Chapman, J. C. (1988). Artifactual and genuine relationships of lateral difference scores to overall accuracy in studies of laterality. *Psychological Bulletin, 104*, 127–136.

Evans, D. A., Funkenstein, H. H., Albert, M. S., Scherr, P. A., Cook, N. R., Chown, M. J., Hebert, L. E., Hennekens, C. H., & Taylor, J. O. (1989). Prevalence of Alzheimer's disease in a community population of older persons. *Journal of the American Medical Association, 262*, 2551–2556.

Fillenbaum, G., Heyman, A., Williams, K., Prosnitz, B., & Burchett, B. (1990). Sensitivity and specificity of standardized screens of cognitive impairment and dementia among elderly Blacks and White community residents. *Journal of Clinical Epidemiology, 43*, 651–660.

Frerichs, P. R., Aneshensel, C. S., & Clark, V. A. (1981). Prevalence of depression in Los Angeles County. *American Journal of Epidemiology, 113*, 691–699.

Gurland, B. J., Wilder, D. E., Cross, P., Teresi, J., & Barrett V. W. (1992). Screening scales for dementia: Toward reconciliation of conflicting cross-cultural findings. *International Journal of Geriatric Psychiatry, 7*, 105–113.

Hambleton, R. K., & Swaminathan, H. (1985). *Item response theory: Principles and applications*. Boston: Kluwer-Nijhoff.

Hulin, C. L., Drasgow, F., & Parsons, C. K. (1983). *Item response theory: Application to psychological measurement*. Homewood, IL: Dow Jones-Irwin.

López, S., & Romero, A. (1988). Assessing the intellectual functioning of Spanish-speaking adults: Comparison of the EIWA and the WAIS. *Professional Psychology: Research and Practice, 19*, 263–270.

López, S. R., & Tausig, I. M. (1991). Cognitive-intellectual functioning of Spanish-speaking impaired and nonimpaired elderly: Implications for culturally sensitive assessment. *Psychological Assessment: A Journal of Consulting and Clinical Psychology, 3*, 448–454.

Lord, F. M. (1980). *Applications of item response theory to practical testing: Problems*. Hillsdale, NJ: Erlbaum.

Mungas, D., Marshall, S. C., Weldon, M., Haan, M., & Reed, B. R. (in press). Age and education correction of Mini-Mental State Examination for English- and Spanish-speaking elderly. *Neurology*.

Murden, R. A., McRae, T. D., Kaner, S., & Bucknam, M. I. (1991). Mini-Mental Status Exam scores with education in Blacks and Whites. *Journal of the American Geriatric Society, 39*, 149–155.

U.S. Congress, Office of Technology Assessment. (1987). *Losing a million minds: Confronting the tragedy of Alzheimer's disease and other dementias* (Publication OTABA-323). Washington, DC: Government Printing Office.

Wechsler, D. (1968). *Escala de Inteligencia Wechsler para Adultos* (Wechsler Adult Intelligence Scale). New York: Psychological Corporation.

Chapter 5

Issues in Neuropsychological Assessment for Hispanic Older Adults: Cultural and Linguistic Factors

I. Maribel Taussig
Marcel Pontón

The purpose of this chapter is twofold: (a) to address cultural and linguistic issues that may interfere in the assessment of the cognitive functioning of Hispanic older adults and (b) to highlight the pros and cons of existing neuropsychological tests to assess cognitive impairments of Hispanic elderly persons.

The issue of neuropsychological assessment of an older adult suggests some concern regarding organic brain disorders and possible serious damage to the structure of the brain. When reasonable suspicion exists that a patient is functioning at a lower level than previous capacity, the assessment or evaluation can establish the presence or absence of cognitive and behavioral dysfunction and be a guide to both the health professional and the family. For the professional, such evaluation allows or helps to differentiate between normal aging changes and dementia; for families, the explanation and validation of what they have observed in terms of cognitive impairments can make families more understanding, as progressive cognitive impairment will incapacitate and disrupt the life of the patient and his or her family.

DIAGNOSIS OF DEMENTIA

The diagnosis of dementia according to the *Diagnostic and Statistical Manual of Mental Disorders* (4th ed.; American Psychiatric Association, 1994) is characterized by the development of multiple cognitive deficits with sufficient severity to interfere or cause impairment in occupational or social functioning. Memory impairment and at least one of the following cognitive disturbances must be present to make a diagnosis of dementia: apraxia, agnosia, or a disturbance in cognitive functioning (American Psychiatric Association, 1994, p. 134). Although dementia has common symptoms in its presentation, its etiology may differ, and its prevalence varies according to epidemiological studies and the type of procedure used (screening vs. complete medical and neuropsychological evaluation). Because the number of older adults residing in the United States whose language and culture varies from that of White English-speaking older adults is not known, it is difficult to properly estimate the number of those suffering from a dementia. Other problems associated with estimating the number of older adults with dementia in the United States are the shortage of well-trained professionals proficient in other languages and, equally important, culturally sensitive and language-appropriate tests. Regardless of barriers and difficulties epidemiologists may face, however, the number of older adults with a progressive and incurable dementia is steadily rising in the United States, thus creating a tremendous burden on families and social services alike.

CAUSES OF DEMENTIA

The causes of dementia are many; however, the most frequent cause is Alzheimer's disease (Henderson & Finch, 1989) The prevalence of Alzheimer's disease is approximately 4% to 10% in older adults in persons aged 65 years and as much as 47% in those surpassing age 85. The criteria to establish a diagnosis of Alzheimer's disease are well defined by several entities, including the Consortium to Establish a Registry for Alzheimer's Disease (CERAD, 1986); many professionals (if not a sufficient number of professionals) are well trained to provide a diagnosis; and many neuropsychometric tools are available to establish the patterns of cognitive impairment. However, what needs to be considered when an older adult suspected of having cognitive deficits is Hispanic? Are there any specific issues to be considered?

DEFINITION OF *HISPANIC*

To be able to address such questions one should first consider the definition of *Hispanic*. What is Hispanic? Can it be defined through race, culture, religion, or language?

The terms *Hispanic* or *Latino* are often used to described a person of Latin American origin living in the United States. The 1990 Census considered this population as Hispanics, and when individuals of Latin American or Spanish background are asked how they like to be identified, the answer varies, suggesting a preference more than a rule. Therefore and for the purpose of uniformity, the authors of this chapter defined this group as Hispanics.

Race

Defining *Hispanic* by race is difficult because of the multiple races that are considered Hispanic. For example, Whites, Blacks, Indians from the Americas, and every combination of these races are considered Hispanic. Therefore, race is a poor indicator for this population.

Culture

Although certain traits can be found in older Hispanics residing in the United States, the 21 Spanish-speaking countries offer a great variation in cultures, especially if culture can be defined as "a way of the people," which should include beliefs and behaviors. It is well-known that each Spanish-speaking country has its own unique characteristics. One's socioeconomic status also dictates beliefs and behaviors. If one takes into consideration acculturation of those older adults residing in the United States, one also needs to account for various degrees of difference, in terms of degrees of acculturation and assimilation into U.S. norms. Such degrees can be associated with (a) number of generations in the United States; (b) number of years residing in the United States; and (c) degree of integration, based on lifestyle, such as place of employment (i.e., all Hispanics), social activity, and housing (neighborhood), among others. For example, an older adult who has resided in the United States for 20 years, speaks only Spanish, spent his or her working years in factories or similar working environments surrounded by other Spanish speakers, watched TV and movies in Spanish, and attended social and religious activities among his or her own may not have had the opportunity to learn about the American way.

Therefore, multiculturalism (the many differences found among Spanish-speaking countries and the possible variation within each country, plus degrees in the levels of acculturation to the American way) makes it virtually impossible to define Hispanics by culture.

Religion

Religion is often considered a uniform variable in the Hispanic population, specifically Catholicism. Although a very large proportion of Hispanics are Catholic, Protestant churches such as the Seventh-day Adventist, Mormon, Pentecostal, and so forth have a large number of Hispanics in their congregations. Therefore, religion is also not the best identifiable factor of this population.

Language

Out of all the possible variables that could identify older Hispanics as a group, language could be the most useful one. The literature suggests that 60% of the Hispanic population 65 years and older residing in the United States are monolingual in Spanish (Cubillo & Prieto, 1987), and 70% to 90% prefer to speak Spanish to express sentiments and needs (Lopez-Aquires, Kemp, Plopper, Staples, & Brummel-Smith, 1984). At the same time, depending on the number of generations in the United States, there are Hispanic elderly people able to communicate in both English and Spanish, but whose verbal abilities are more toward English, with great limitations in Spanish, and those who speak only English.

Many researchers have expressed great concern regarding whether the Spanish language can vary so greatly from country to country as to became another language. It is a fact that the meanings of specific words differ from one Spanish-speaking country to another; for example, a word commonly used in one country may be meaningless or offensive in another, or it may exist but be used only in a specific manner (i.e., colloquialism). However, grammatically speaking, there are no major differences between Spanish-speaking countries. Therefore, gero-neuropsychologists servicing Spanish-speaking older adults residing in the United States must be aware of and knowledgeable concerning a word's meaning and how verbal expressions can differ from country to country, especially when translating and validating tests to measure cognitive functioning.

Another area of concern when addressing older Hispanics residing in the United States is the great difference in the years of formal school attainment. It is well-known that older Hispanics have on average 6 years of formal education, and many never attended any school. Many of the latter have, however, learned to read and write on their own, and although they have never attended formal school, they cannot be considered illiterate.

In general, older Hispanics residing in the United States vary in terms of race, cultural background, religion, language proficiency, and levels of education. Therefore, it can be said that the definition of Hispanic in terms of specifics is difficult to grasp, although often Hispanics are treated as a homogeneous group.

CAVEATS FOR RESEARCHERS TO ADDRESS

In this section, the authors look at some of the important caveats that researchers should address while pursuing research with this population, and they offer future directions in the assessment of and ongoing research with Hispanic elderly persons.

Research with Hispanic elderly persons requires a paradigmatic shift. First, psychometric assumptions about cognitive assessment of the Hispanic population need to be reviewed. Although there are at present multiple efforts in the area of test translation (Brislin, Lanner, & Thorndike, 1973; Karno, Burman, Escobar, & Eaton, 1983), the emphasis should shift to test development (e.g., Pontón et al., 1992). Development and adaptation of tests is labor intensive and requires structured clinical validation protocols (LaRue & Markee, 1995), making it less appealing to researchers interested in large-scale funding. "Good translations" may be easier to accomplish, and may be "equivalent" to the English-language measures; however, they may not be measuring the same thing. For instance, a perfect translation of CERAD and Alzheimer's Disease Assessment Scale items will convey the original intent of the question to the family or the patient, but the content of the question may be so culturally irrelevant that its only usefulness is as an index of how far Hispanics are from the Anglo standard.

Second, neuropsychological research with this population needs to focus on the kinds of tests being developed. Paper-and-pencil tasks are of only limited value, particularly when less educated persons are evaluated. There ought to be a shift toward the development of tests with ecological validity and that address functional aspects of behavior. This should be accompanied by a change of attitude in looking for the "perfect normals." Elderly people who have chronic illnesses that are medically managed should be included in normative research studies. The reason is simple: They are representative of the real world.

This approach is not new. Ivnik and colleagues (1992) used participants with controlled chronic medical conditions in their Mayo's Older Americans Normative Studies. They found that medical condition had minimal impact on test performance. Research with Hispanic elderly persons should include participants with controlled medical conditions in normative studies.

Development of Norms

As noted above, the issues affecting the appropriate assessment of Hispanic elderly people are multiple and complex. The heterogeneity of this population and the interplay between these variables make the issues of differentiation in the assessment of dementia particularly challenging. Although not all variables can be controlled for or addressed exhaustively in any viable research study, at least two variables of interest merit critical attention with the Hispanic population: education and language.

Education   Perhaps the most daunting element affecting neuropsychological research with Hispanic elderly persons appears to be the issue of education. Ardila and colleagues (Ardila, 1993a, 1993b; Ardila, Rosselli, & Puente, 1994; Ardila, Rosselli, & Rosas, 1989) have reported in a convincing manner that less educated individuals or those who are functionally illiterate tend to score on neuropsychological measures much like brain-injured individuals. This issue of the "Ardila effect" has been borne out by multiple findings in the literature. In a recent article, Taussig (in press) reported that even on global measures of cognitive status (such as the Mini-Mental State Examination or the Mental Status Questionnaire), education made a significant difference in the performance of Spanish-speaking individuals.

Similarly, Pontón et al. (1996) found that participants with fewer than 6 years of education tended to perform up to 2 standard deviations below individuals with 16 years of education or more, and Taussig, Henderson, and Mack (1992) had similar results. The data overwhelmingly support the notion that education needs to be carefully measured and classified when assessing the Hispanic population, and more so when assessing Hispanic elderly persons. Education may contribute significantly to the cohort effect found among Hispanic elderly persons from rural backgrounds, while producing equivocal results with urban participants.

Socioeconomic status may be confounded with education, as more distinct social classes were evident throughout Latin America during the first half of this century, and socioeconomic status was inextricably webbed with ethnicity. How socioeconomic status is assessed and classified is also of importance. The Hollingshead (1958) paradigm may now be obsolete and culturally irrelevant.

The classification of education can be complex. Although the most basic classification is the actual number of years of formal education, there are several dichotomies that should also be considered. For instance, those from rural backgrounds have a different quality of education than those from urban backgrounds and therefore perform differently on cognitive tests. Similarly, private versus public education may affect test performance. However, even if a more meticulous approach is used in measuring education, informal education (i.e., learning of trades) is difficult to measure accurately. How can a carpenter's learning be qualified, if the carpenter acquired his or her skills as an apprentice or from a family business? How can the successful business skills of a person who runs the neighborhood store be coded when she or he had only 3 years of formal schooling? These formally acquired skills that facilitated success will most certainly affect test performance, yet they could go unrecorded and unstudied.

Education then needs to be coded and analyzed rigorously. It needs to be studied as a significant contributor to neuropsychological test performance and should be an intricate part of research design when assessing Hispanic elderly persons. The authors offer the following suggestions for the consideration of education in assessment:

1 Any study should consider at least four levels of education, including 6 or fewer years, 7–10 years, 11–15 years, and 16+ years of education.
2 Education should also be, as much as possible, rated in the dichotomies of rural versus urban, and if possible data should be collected on private versus public education.
3 Country of origin will be significant, as different countries experience varying rates of exposure to technological and industrial development in the 20th century, contributing to different cohort effects.

The fact that education could play such an important role in the cognitive performance of this population speaks to the strong need to develop tests differentially for various educational groups. This will represent a significant dilemma for standardized research; however, the issue of floor and ceiling effects with either easy or difficult tasks for people from different educational backgrounds diminishes the relevance of research if the measures are not used.

Language   The language of the instruments used to assess participants may be either too technical or too culturally inappropriate, or may use vocabulary, expressions, or concepts alien to a particular age group. This is certainly true in the United States's adult Anglo population, where normative data that were collected for measures decades ago may be significantly irrelevant for those who are elderly now and those who will be in their 60s in the decades ahead. This is quite clearly the case in the Hispanic population, as their understanding of social mores, the stressors faced in young adulthood, and the different ways in which they learn will affect their performance in cognitive measures.

These issues will affect the assessment of what is understood to be proper psychosocial functioning as well as independent functioning. Cultural expectations of gender roles as well as family expectations will play a role in how researchers understand Hispanics' social adaptability and their ability to cope with different stressors that they face as a result of the dementing process.

Language is a critical factor in the evaluation of Hispanic elderly persons. Although as much as 90% of the elderly cohort (Lopez-Aquires et al., 1984) identified Spanish as their language of preference for testing, bilingualism needs to be addressed systematically and accurately.

To research individuals who are primarily Spanish-speaking, researchers are faced with the issue of translating the current measures, adapting those measures through a process of research that would make the measures more culturally appropriate, or developing measures of their own. At any rate, clinicians are faced with the important yet time-consuming process of validating the instruments with clinical populations for their reliability and validity.

Tests will also have to be revised for colloquial terms or items that would penalize people from different countries of origin or different degrees of bilingualism. The issue of bilingualism is an important and thorny one. As the Hispanic population ages, their degree of bilingualism will be directly tied to their level of acculturation into this society, contributing even further to measurement error. Ardila et al. (1994) have pointed out that patients with aphasias in Spanish will not have problems with grammatical construction, as the Spanish language is more flexible than English, but will instead present with significant difficulties in the semantic aspects of language. This problem will be compounded when a bilingual individual is tested and he or she presents with a multilingual aphasia. The patient experiencing insidious decline in one language may mix the grammatical rules of the second language with those of his or her primary language. One does not, however, need to be concerned with aphasias in bilingualism to appreciate the problem. Hispanic people who will be elderly in the year 2000 and beyond will have been in this country for long periods of time, will have significant elements of ''Spanglish'' in their vocabulary, and will have developed concepts that have a functional meaning for their cognitive experience of the American culture, but that have no equivalent term in formal Spanish. In what language should these people be properly assessed? Formal Spanish may in fact penalize their performance because it is functionally removed from their experience.

How should researchers know which language to test patients in and what numbers of bilingual or monolingual responses are acceptable for different test items? This may appear to be a simple question; however, as far as the issue of standardized assessment and systematic research is concerned, mixed or ambiguous responses in Spanglish can confound test results.

A totally unexplored area of research is what happens to the cognitive functioning of aging bilingual persons and what the areas of cognitive decline are. What happens to language, for instance, with the onset of dementia or any other complicating factors in neuropsychological assessment? Longitudinal studies need to address the issues of cognitive changes in individuals with bilingual backgrounds and the impact of this understudied and potentially fascinating variable to aging. Satz's (1993) cognitive reserve theory suggests that individuals with a large reservoir (i.e., education) may have more tools to adapt to changes in aging, changes brought about by brain insults, or both because they have more resources to cope with the changes and compensate for their newly acquired deficits. It will be important to study whether bilingualism contributes to the cognitive reservoir of an individual's language functioning.

The following strategies can be used to address the language issue in the assessment of Hispanic elderly persons:

1 Measure bilingualism and level of Spanish-language mastery.
2 Use acculturation scales (Marín & Marín, 1991) to determine the degree to which a person has personalized the values of the dominant culture, including language.
3 Develop tests using universal Spanish for instructions and items, but that allow for multiple responses according to regional differences or usages of Spanish.
4 Develop decision trees—rules for which language to assess bilingual patients in.

To summarize, the issues about language that affect neuropsychological assessment include the most obvious: (a) availability of measures in the Spanish language and (b) standardized assessment of level of bilingualism. Significant research effort is currently underway (Ardila et al., 1994; Lopez & Taussig, 1991; Rey, Feldman, Rivas-Vazquez, & Levin, 1994; Pontón et al., 1996; Taussig, Mack, & Henderson, in press; Taussig et al., 1992) to develop appropriate norms for Spanish-speaking individuals residing in the United States. The neuropsychological community should make the effort to standardize these tests, to study the clinical population, and then to validate them so as to have the most appropriate norms. This issue obviously affects not only the Hispanic community, as other neuropsychological measures need to be revised and adapted for a newer generation of elderly persons who will become a significant proportion of the U.S. population by the year 2015.

SUGGESTIONS AND CONCLUSION

Suggestions for the neuropsychological assessment of Hispanics, then, are the following:

- standardization of multiple batteries currently available that have already been translated, adapted, or both (Loewenstein, Arguelles, Barker, & Duara, 1993; Pontón et al., in press; Taussig, 1994; Taussig et al., 1992, in press)
- study of vascular dementia, which appears to be of high incidence and prevalence in the Hispanic population
- addressing changes in health issues and studying populations with high risk for cardiovascular problems, diabetes, and toxic exposure
- the establishment of the research community's credibility within the Hispanic community. Much research has focused on taking things away or benefiting from this community but has offered little in return, and as such has created a problem for future research, as well as a strong sense of suspicion between Hispanic communities and university-based clinical trials.
- multisite, multicenter studies will be important, as Hispanics from different cultures and countries of origin need to be studied. Hispanics in Florida are widely different from those in Los Angeles, New York, and Chicago because of their differences in their ethnicity, as well as their degree of education, mastery of language, and so forth. There is already interest and support from federal funding that mandates the inclusion of minorities and women, when appropriate.
- measures that assess practical intelligence or wisdom as a measure of intellectual competence, as opposed to models of intelligence traditionally known in the Anglo community that can underestimate cognitive functioning (Lopez & Taussig, 1991)
- development of short-term, short batteries suitable for research

Although the issue of cognitive assessment of Hispanic elderly persons residing in the United States is complex, researchers must go forth and use present and existing batteries of tests, but must interpret the findings cautiously. After all, the profile of a neuropsychological battery of tests assists the multidisciplinary team in the diagnosis. Listed in the Appendix to this chapter are tests that can be used with a degree of confidence, keeping in mind that the patient's level of education and life experience will greatly affect the final scores.

REFERENCES

American Psychiatric Association. (1994). *Diagnostic and statistical manual of mental disorders* (4th ed.). Washington, DC: Author.

Ardila, A. (1993a). Future directions in the research and practice of cross-cultural neuropsychology. *Journal of Clinical and Experimental Neuropsychology, 15*(1), 19.

Ardila, A. (1993b). Historical evaluation of spatial abilities. *Behavioral Neuropsychology, 6,* 83–87.

Ardila, A., Rosselli, M., & Puente, A. E. (1994). *Neuropsychological evaluation of the Spanish speaker.* New York: Plenum Press.

Ardila, A., Rosselli, M., & Rosas, P. (1989). Neuropsychological assessment of illiterates: Visuospatial and memory abilities. *Brain and Cognition, 11*(2), 147–166.

Benton, A. L., & Hamsher, K. (1983). *Multilingual Aphasia Examination.* Iowa City: AJA Associates.

Blessed, G., Tomlinson, B. E., & Roth, M. (1968). The association between quantitative measures of dementia and of senile changes in the cerebral grey matter of elderly subjects. *British Journal of Psychiatry, 114,* 797–811.

Bornstein, T. A. (1985). Normative data on selected neuropsychological measures from a nonclinical sample. *Journal of Clinical Psychology, 41,* 651–659.

Brislin, R. W., Lanner, W. J., & Thorndike, R. M. (1973). Cross-cultural research methods. New York: Wiley.

Consortium to Establish a Registry for Alzheimer's Disease, Duke University Medical Center. (1987). Durham, NC: Author.

Cubillo, H. L., & Prieto, M. M. (1987). The Hispanic elderly: A demographic profile. Washington, DC: Policy Analysis Center, Office of la Raza, Advocacy and Legislation, National Council of La Raza.

Folstein, M. F., Folstein, S. E., & McHugh, P. R. (1975). Mini-Mental State: A practical method for grading the cognitive state of patients for clinicians. *Journal of Psychiatric Research, 12,* 189–198.

Fuld, P. A. (1980). Guaranteed stimulus-processing in the evaluation of memory and learning. *Cortex, 16,* 255–271.

Goodglass, H., & Kaplan, E. (1983). The assessment of aphasia and related disorders (2nd ed.). Philadelphia: Lea & Febiger.

Green, R. F., & Martinez, J. N. (1968). *Manual para la Escala de Inteligencia Wechsler para Adultos* (Manual for the Wechsler Adult Intelligence Scale). New York: Psychological Corporation.

Henderson, W. V., & Finch, C. E. (1989). The neurology of Alzheimer's disease. *Journal of Neurosurgery, 70,* 335–353.

Hollingshead, A. (1958). Two factor index of social position. New Haven, CT: Yale University Press.

Ivnik, R. J., Malec, J. F., Smith, G. E., Tangalos, E. G., Petersen, R. C., Kokment, E., & Krukland, L. T. (1992). Mayo's older Americans normative studies: WAIS-R norms for ages 59–90. *Clinical Neuropsychologist, 6*(Suppl.), 1–30.

Kahn, R. L., Goldfarb, A. L., Pollack, M., & Peck, A. (1960). Brief objective measures for the determination of mental status in the aged. *American Journal of Psychiatry, 117,* 326–328.

Karno, M., Burman, M. A., Escobar, J. I., & Eaton, W. W. (1993). Development of the Spanish-language version of the National Institute of Mental Health diagnostic interview schedule. *Archives of General Psychiatry, 40,* 1183–1188.

LaRue, A., & Markee, T. (1995). Clinical assessment research with older adults. *Psychological Assessment, 7,* 376–386.

Lopez-Aquires, J. N., Kemp, B., Plopper, M., Staples, F. R., & Brummel-Smith, K. (1984). Health needs of the Hispanic elderly. *Journal of the American Geriatric Society, 32*, 191–197.

Lopez, S. R., & Taussig, I. M. (1991). Cognitive-intellectual functioning of Spanish-speaking impaired and nonimpaired elderly: Implications for psychological assessments. *Journal of Consulting and Clinical Psychology, 3*, 448–454.

Lowenstein, D. A., Arguelles, T., Barker, W. W., & Duara, R. (1993). A comparison analysis of neuropsychological test performance of Spanish-speaking and English-speaking patients with Alzheimer's disease. *Journal of Gerontology, 48*(3), 142–149.

Mattis, S. (1976). Mental status examination for organic mental syndrome in the elderly patient. In L. Bellack & T. B. Karasu (Eds.), *Geriatric psychiatry*. New York: Grune & Stratton.

Mohs, R. C., & Cohen, L. (1988). Alzheimer's Disease Assessment Scale (ADAS). *Psychopharmacology Bulletin, 24*, 627–628.

Pontón, M. O., Satz, P., Herrera, L., Urrutia, C. P., Ortiz, F., Young, R., D'Elia, L., Furst, C., & Namerow, N. (1996). Normative data stratified by age and education for the Neuropsychological Screening Battery for Hispanics (NesSBHIS): A standardization report. *Journal of International Neuropsychological Society, 2*, 96–104.

Ponton, M. O., Satz, P., Herrera, L., Young, R., Ortiz, F., D'Elia, L., Furst, C., & Namerow, N. (1992). Modified Spanish version of the Boston Naming Test. *The Clinical Neuropsychologist, 6*(3), 334.

Rey, G. J., Feldman, E., Rivas-Vazquez, R., & Levin, B. E. (1994). Current trends and future of neuropsychological research with Hispanics. *The Clinical Neuropsychologist, 8*(3), 351.

Satz, P. (1993). Brain reserve capacity on symptoms onset after brain injury: A formulation and review of evidence for threshold theory. *Neuropsychology, 7*(3), 273–295.

Taussig, I. M. (1994). Cuadro clínico y neuropsicológico de la enfermedad de Alzheimer [Clinical and neuropsychological features of Alzheimer's disease]. *Monografías Psiquiátricas, IV*(3),15–22.

Taussig, I. M., Dick, M., Teng, E., & Kempler, D. (1993). *The Taussig Cross-Cultural Memory Test*. (Available from Andrus Gerontology Center, University of Southern California, Los Angeles, CA 90089-0191)

Taussig, I. M., Henderson, V. W., & Mack, W. (1992). Spanish translation and validation of a neuropsychological battery: Performance of Spanish- and English-speaking Alzheimer's disease patients and normal comparison subjects. *Clinical Gerontologist, 11*, 95–108.

Taussig, I. M., Mack, W., & Henderson, V. W. (in press). Concurrent validity of Spanish-language versions of the Mini-Mental State Examination, Mental Status Questionnaire, Information-Memory-Concentration Test and Orientation-Memory-Concentration Test: Alzheimer's disease patients and nondemented elderly subjects. *Journal of International Neuropsychological Society*.

Wechsler, D. (1981). *Wechsler Adult Intelligence Scale—Revised*. New York: Psychological Corporation/Harcourt Brace Jovanovich.

Yesavage, J. A., Brink, T., Rose, T. L., & Lum, O. (1983). Development and validation of a Geriatric Depression Scale: A preliminary report. *Journal of Psychiatric Research, 17*, 37–49.

Appendix   Suggested List of Tests Used at the Spanish-Speaking Alzheimer's Disease Research Program (ADRC) at the University of Southern California

Tests	Original authors
1. Mental Status Questionnaire	Kahn, Goldfarb, Pollack, and Peck (1960)
2. Mini-Mental Status Examination	Folstein, Folstein, and McHugh (1975)
3. Blessed-Roth Dementia Rating Scale	Blessed, Tomlinson, and Roth (1968)
4. Mattis Dementia Rating Scale	Mattis (1976)
5. Boston Naming Test	Goodglass and Kaplan (1983)
6. Parietal Lobe (Clock-House)	Goodglass and Kaplan (1983)
7. WAIS (Similarities, Digit Span, Vocabulary, Block Design)	Wechsler (1981)
EIWA (same scales)	Green and Martinez (1968)
8. Basic Mathematics	Taussig et al. (1992)
9. FAS (Control Word Association)	Benton and Hamsher (1983)
10. Word List Generation (Animal/ Supermarket)	Benton and Hamsher (1983)
11. Trails A and B	Bornstein (1985)
12. Fuld Object Memory Test	Fuld (1980)
13. CERAD Memory Word List	CERAD, Duke University Medical Center (1987)
14. The Taussig Cross-Cultural Memory Test	Taussig, Dick, Teng, and Kempler (1993)
15. The Geriatric Depression Scale	Yesavage, Brink, Rose, and Lum (1983)

Chapter 6

Issues in Assessing Dementia in African American Elders

F. M. Baker

To provide a context for discussing the issues involved in the assessment of dementia in older African Americans, it is important to review the current knowledge of the risk factors for the development of dementing illness, the genetics of dementia, and the existing knowledge of dementia among African Americans. This chapter begins with an overview of recent research in dementia in which the current research findings are reviewed. The second section, titled Psychosocial Considerations for Studies of Dementia in African Americans, reviews the specific demographic characteristics and economic concerns that will affect epidemiologic studies of this population. The third section of this chapter, Epidemiologic Studies of Dementia in African Americans, is divided into two parts, Methodological Concerns and Screening Instruments. Methodological Concerns addresses the impact of education on screening for the presence of cognitive impairment in African American elders. Screening Instruments describes the specific instruments that can be used to screen for the presence of cognitive impairment and addresses the specific advantages and disadvantages of these instruments in older African Americans. Screening African American Elders for the Presence of Cognitive Impairment, the fourth section of this chapter, reviews

The author acknowledges the contribution of funding from the Mental Disorders of the Aging Research Branch of the National Institute of Mental Health (Grant 2 KO7 MH00816-02) and the Fogarty International Research Center, funding the Minority International Research Training Grant (TW00027).

the experience of using various screening instruments to identify the presence of cognitive impairment in African American elders and describes a two-stage strategy to identify the etiology of the cognitive impairment identified. The major points of these sections are summarized in the Conclusion.

OVERVIEW OF RECENT RESEARCH IN DEMENTIA

After the initial warning of Plum (1979) of an epidemic of dementia with the increasing aging of the world population, the past decade has seen a significant expansion of the research into Alzheimer's disease (AD) and other dementing illnesses (Baker, 1991; Baker, Kokman, Chandra, & Schoenberg, 1991; Baker, Robinson, & Stewart, 1993b; Ballard, Nash, Raiford, & Harrell, 1993; Breteler, Claus, van Duijn, Launer, & Hofman, 1992; Cummings, 1985; Evans et al., 1989; Folstein, Anthony, Parhard, Duffy, & Gruenberg, 1985; Folstein, Bassett, Anthony, Romanoski, & Nestadt, 1991; Gurland et al., 1995; Hofman, 1991; Holzer, Tischler, Leaf, & Myers, 1984; Jorm et al., 1991; Kokmen, Chandra, & Schoenberg, 1985; Launer, 1992; Rocca, Amducci, & Schoenberg, 1985; Sulkava, Wikstrom, & Aromaa, 1985). Epidemiologic studies of multiracial and multicultural populations provided specific information about the differences in the prevalence of various dementing illnesses in these populations (Folstein, et al., 1985; Folstein et al., 1991; Fukunishi, Hayabara, & Hosokawa, 1991; Gurland et al., 1995; Haerer, Anderson, & Schoenberg, 1987; Hasegawa, Homma, & Imai, 1986; Heyman et al., 1991; Li et al., 1989, 1991; Schoenberg, Anderson, & Haerer, 1985; Soldo & Agree, 1988). The prevalence of multi-infarct dementia (MID) was found to be twice that of AD in Chinese and Japanese populations (Fukunishi et al., 1991; Hasegawa et al., 1986; Kua, 1991; Li et al., 1989, 1991). In U.S. studies, African Americans have been found to have a higher prevalence rate of MID as well as a higher prevalence of AD in comparison to Whites in the few studies completed of African American elders (Folstein et al., 1985, 1991; Gurland et al., 1995; Haerer et al., 1987; Heyman et al., 1991; Schoenberg et al., 1985).

The reanalysis of case-control studies completed in Europe and the United States by European Studies of Dementia (EURODEM), an international collaborative project (Van Duijn, Stijnen, & Hofman, 1991a) has identified increasing age and a family history of dementia as clear risk factors for the development of AD. Other factors found to be associated with AD are a positive family history of Parkinson's disease or Down's syndrome (Van Duijn et al., 1991b), a maternal age of 40 years and older suggestively associated with a higher risk of AD among sporadic (late onset) cases of AD (Rocca et al., 1991), a history of head trauma within 1 year or more of the onset of AD (Mortimer et al., 1991), and a history of depression 10 years or more before the onset of AD (Jorm et al., 1991).

Interestingly, some medical illnesses (Breteler et al., 1991) have been found to increase the risk of developing AD. A history of hypothyroidism was increased among AD cases, but severe headache and migraine were inversely related to AD, suggesting that they may have some protective effect against the development of AD. An increased rate of tobacco consumption by cigarette smoking was associated with a decreased risk across four studies (Graves et al., 1991), and no excess risk was found for any level of alcohol consumption (Graves et al., 1991). The majority of cases of dementia (50%–60%) were found to be due to AD (Breteler et al., 1991).

The neuroanatomic studies of postmortem brain tissue from patients with AD demonstrated the loss of neurons in the frontal and parietal cortex with the resulting enlargement of brain sulci as characteristic features of the disease (Miller, Cheong, Oropilla, & Mena, 1994). Neuroimaging techniques have been useful in demonstrating these changes in the cerebral tissues (Morihisa, 1991). The loss of cholinergic neurons in these areas of the brain provides at least a partial explanation for the loss of memory. The encoding of a memory trace is mediated by the neurotransmitter, acetylcholine, which is produced by cholinergic neurons in those areas (Bartus, Dean, Beer, & Lippa, 1982, Read, 1991; Wisniewski, Wisniewski, & Wen, 1985).

The recent advances by geneticists and cell biologists have produced further excitement in the field. These genetic studies are helping to clarify the characteristics and genetic basis of early onset or familial AD and late onset or sporadic AD. The initial report of St. George-Hyslop et al. (1987) identified a locus on the proximal long arm of chromosome 21 as involved in AD. The finding that a mutation of the amyloid precursor protein gene was responsible for some cases of early onset (familiar AD) and the accumulation of protein found in the neurofibrillary tangles and plaques has been confirmed by other investigators (Goate et al., 1989; Tanzi et al., 1992). An additional locus on chromosome 19 has been shown to be associated with the excess production of the protein found in congophilic angiopathy among early onset (familial) cases of AD (Van Duijn et al., 1991a, 1994). Recent studies have identified another location on chromosome 14 that is associated with familial cases of AD (Chartier-Harlin et al., 1991; Schellenberg et al., 1992; Van Duijn et al., 1994).

Although the specific mechanisms that result in the neuroanatomic changes characteristic of AD have yet to be described, an abnormality in microtubular production has been hypothesized as the etiology of these changes (Matsuyama & Jarvik, 1989), on the basis of the work of Grundke-Iqbal et al. (1986). The development of neuroimaging and DNA transcriptase as well as gene-splicing technology has enabled investigators in clinical epidemiology, cellular biology, and medical genetics to pursue studies to define the basic mechanisms underlying AD and to study the genetic determinants of AD (Valluri et al., 1994; van Duijn et al., 1994). The work of these investigators has provided additional information on the genetic basis of familial AD occurring before the age of 55 and on risk factors for the sporadic cases of AD occurring after age 60 and increasing with increasing age (Valluri et al., 1994). With this background concerning the development of knowledge concerning AD, let us turn to a consideration of the psychosocial considerations affecting older African Americans and their effect on studies of dementia in this population.

PSYCHOSOCIAL CONSIDERATIONS FOR STUDIES OF DEMENTIA IN AFRICAN AMERICANS

Only within the past 10 years has there been an interest in the study of dementing illness among African Americans. Studies of the patterns of caregiving among Black American families have appeared only in the past 5 years (Hartung, 1994; Henderson, Gutierrez-Mayka, Garcia, & Boyd, 1993; Lawton, Rajagopal, Brody, & Kleban, 1992; Valle, 1988). Lack of access to a community-based sample of African Americans, reliability of screening instruments in older Black Americans, and interest in completing such investigations are some of the factors contributing to the earlier absence of such studies. Additional concerns included the willingness of older African Americans to participate in a research study. Black elders familiar with earlier, uncontrolled research studies may have been reluctant to participate in "research." The Tuskegee research study of the natural course of syphilis withheld effective treatment from Black male study subjects for more than 40 years (Baker, 1991; Benedek, 1978; Brandt, 1978; Edgar, 1992; Jones, 1981, 1992; King, 1992; Roy, 1995) in order to provide a continual source of sera to develop improved tests for syphilis (Roy, 1995). The revelation of the conduct of this study contributed to the reluctance of Black Americans to participate in research studies. Although the establishment of required informed consent and institutional review boards resulted from the Tuskegee Study and provides protection for all persons who are approached concerning participating in research studies, a negative attitude toward research remains among some members of the Black community.

Another factor affecting the enrollment of African American elders in research studies involves the signing of informed consent. To protect older African Americans from attempts to steal any financial resources (e.g., Social Security checks or retirement payments), Black elders have been instructed by their adult children and their ministers "not to sign anything!" Informed consent without signature that is witnessed by a third party (e.g., a nurse, family member, or friend) and the willing participation of the African American elder are alternatives acceptable to both institutional review boards and participating African American elders.

Economic resources are an important concern in the screening of African American elders for the presence of dementia. The unique history of the current cohort of African Americans age 65 and older has been detailed in several publications (Baker, 1982, 1991, 1994; Baker, Lavizzo-Mourey, & Jones, 1993a; Baker & Lightfoot, 1993). Born and growing to young adulthood in a society with legalized segregation, the opportunities for many Black families in the 1900s were limited. Segregated health care and segregated schools restricted the amount of formal education and the availability and accessibility of health care. Employment opportunities were restricted for many to service occupations, regardless of educational attainment (i.e., housework, live-in maid, live-in child care). Although some 20% of the current cohort of older African American have completed high school and 10% have completed college, the majority of older African Americans in the 1990s have restricted income because of limited educational attainment and restricted employment opportunities in their working years (Baker, 1994; Baker & Lightfoot, 1993). In 1986, 60% of Black women age 65 and older not living with their families had incomes below the poverty level (Soldo & Agree, 1988).

Decreased economic resources, limited access to health care, and restricted economic resources as a result of legalized segregation during their developmental years combined to leave many older Black Americans with poverty-level incomes (varying by city) and multiple medical problems of hypertension, osteoarthritis, diabetes, and glaucoma (Baker et al., 1993a). Decreased economic resources limit the intake of fresh fruits and vegetables and protein because of their cost and may result in an abnormal threshold level of B_{12}, B_6, and folic acid. Serum levels of protein and albumin may be borderline or abnormal in older persons unable to afford the frequent purchase of meat or fish. Eating alone may further compromise their diet. Thus, a determination of income level (Gottlieb, 1991) and a review of medical records for current laboratory results for evidence of anemia, vitamin deficiencies, or inadequate protein stores, if available, are important baseline data for the determination of cognitive impairment among older African Americans. This database will enable the investigator to evaluate specific factors known to influence the results of screening tests for cognitive impairment (Baker, Velli, Friedman, & Wiley, 1995b). Older Black Americans screening positive for cognitive impairment who have abnormal B_{12} levels, abnormal levels of vitamins, and evidence of protein deprivation require vitamin supplements and a referral to Meals on Wheels or an "eat-together" site. In this case, the observed cognitive impairment may be based on a reversible physical condition that is due to a diet restricted by income, not to a dementing process.

Although the majority of the current cohort of older Americans have not completed college (Baker et al., 1993a) and have not taught at the college level, some 10% of older African Americans have completed college and more than 2% have taught at the college level (Baker & Lightfoot, 1993). Therefore, it is important to ask all elders about the formal education that they completed and their work history and to avoid making assumptions. From this information and the language the Black elder uses to respond to the questions, the interviewer will be able to determine the most appropriate approach to use in screening the African American elder for the presence of cognitive impairment. The investigator must be sensitive to African American elders' historical context and how their history can affect their current living conditions (Baker, 1994; Baker & Lightfoot, 1993). This knowledge should influence the specific instruments selected to screen for cognitive impairment and should influence the specific base-line information that is obtained.

The importance of providing a meaningful context for the screening questions and making it meaningful to the older person will facilitate obtaining the Black elder's cooperation in the process. An example of an explanation of the benefits to the Black elder of participating in a study of dementia that proved successful in enlisting older African Americans into a study follows:

> Answering these questions will help us to find out how well you can remember and think. With your OK, we will let your doctor know the results. You and your doctor can talk about whether you are fine or whether you may need some help with your memory.

EPIDEMIOLOGIC STUDIES OF DEMENTIA IN AFRICAN AMERICANS

Methodological Concerns

Fewer than 8 years of formal education (Anthony, Niaz, LeResche, Von Korff, & Folstein, 1982) has been shown to be associated with an increased rate of false positives for the Mini-Mental State Examination (MMSE; Folstein, Folstein, & McHugh, 1975), one frequently used screening test for cognitive impairment. Investigators have attempted to clarify the factors that affect MMSE results among older Black Americans. Berkman (1986) felt strongly that the increased cognitive impairment found among persons with fewer than 8 years of formal education reflected actual deficits. This was consistent with the hypothesis that more formal education was protective in preventing significant cognitive decline as assessed by screening instruments. In contrast to the earlier study by Anthony et al. (1982) of a biracial hospital population that found that Black patients with fewer than 8 years of education were more likely to have MMSE scores consistent with cognitive impairment, Jorm, Scott, Henderson, and Kay (1988) found no bias in a homogeneous sample of elderly White community residents with primary and secondary education. Jorm et al. compared the MMSE with the Activities of Daily Living (ADL) scale in 269 Hobart, PA, community residents and found that persons with better education had higher MMSE scores and ADL scores with a smaller standard deviation, but found no evidence of a difference in the validity or reliability of the MMSE in persons with more education as compared with persons with less education.

In a study from the Epidemiologic Catchment Area Piedmont Health Survey in North Carolina, 1,681 community residents (604 of whom were African American elders) were evaluated with the MMSE (Fillenbaum, Hughes, Heyman, George, & Blazer, 1988). Additional data included the Diagnostic Interview Scale, Instrumental Activities of Daily Living (IADL; Katz, 1983), information on the number of days of limited activity in the past 3 months, adequacy of hearing and vision, and the presence and impact of 12 chronic medical illnesses or conditions (Fillenbaum et al., 1988). When age, sex, race, and education were considered in a regression analysis as factors identified as influencing the MMSE, education was the most important in explaining 20.6% of the MMSE score. When the remaining four health variables were considered, only the IADL was statistically significant, explaining 23.3% of the variance in MMSE score. The conclusion of this study of Black and White elderly persons in North Carolina was that education, age, race, and the performance of ADL and IADL influenced the MMSE score (Fillenbaum et al., 1988). Thus, clarification of the educational level reported by the older African American, confirming the person's current reading level, and the person's ability to perform on the ADL and IADL are important baseline data to obtain (Baker, Johnson, Velli, & Wiley, 1996; Baker, Parker, Wiley, Velli, & Johnson, 1995a).

Screening Instruments

Although there are several screening tests (Baker, 1989) for cognitive impairment (Table 1), only one instrument, the Short Portable Mental Status Questionnaire (SPMSQ), has an adjustment for age and race (Pfeiffer, 1975). Developed specifically to determine the presence of cognitive impairment in rural southern African American elderly people, the SPMSQ may be particularly useful in this population (Fillenbaum, Heyman, Wilkinson, & Haynes, 1987; Fillenbaum, Heyman, Williams, Prosnit, & Burchett, 1990). When the MMSE was used to screen persons with less than an eighth-grade education for the presence of cognitive impairment (Table 2), many older persons who had fewer than 8 years of education screened positive, but did not have dementia, delirium, or any cause of cognitive impairment on formal psychiatric assessment (Baker et al., 1993b).

Because the MMSE has become one of the international standard instruments for the assessment of cognitive impairment, it is important to be aware of its limitations. It may be important to use the MMSE in combination with another screening instrument for cognitive impairment that has adjustment for education or an instrument that has been shown to be reliable in persons with 8 years or less of formal education, such as the SPMSQ.

When the sensitivity and specificity of seven screening instruments for cognitive impairment were assessed in a sample of 164 older persons drawn from the Established Population for Epidemiologic Studies of the Elderly at Duke University, the SPMSQ had a higher specificity than the MMSE (Fillenbaum et al., 1990; see Table 2). Inclusion of an instrument assessing ADL and IADL performance is also an important consideration in planning a study to assess cognitive impairment among older African Americans (Katz, 1983).

Table 1   Summary of Characteristics of Five Mental Status Screening Instruments[a]

	Mini-Mental State[b]	Short Portable Mental Status[c]	Mental Status	Cognitive Capacity Screening	Dementia Rating Scale
Community sample					
Urban	x	—	x	x	x
Rural	—	x	—	—	—
Inpatients					
Psychiatric	x	x	x	x	x
Medical	x	—	x	x	—
Neurological	x	—	—	x	x
Skilled nursing	—	x	x	—	x
Other[d]	—	—	—	x	—
Qualities measured					
Orientation	x	x	x	x	x
Attention and registration	x	—	x	—	x
Cognitive processing	x	x	x	x	x
Memory (recall)					
Immediate	x	—	x	x	x
Recent	x	x	x	x	x
Past	—	x	x	—	x
Remove	—	x	—	—	x
Language	x	—	—	x	x
Three-step praxis	x	—	—	—	—
Visuomotor function	x	—	—	—	x
Sensitivity	.83	.55–.88	.55–.96	.73	.84
Specificity	.99	.72–.96	—	.90	—

Note. From "Screening Tests for Cognitive Impairment," by F. M. Baker, 1989, Hospital and Community Psychiatry, 40, p. 340. Copyright © 1989 by Hospital and Community Psychiatry. Reprinted with permission.

[a]Use with specific population groups and qualities measured are indicated by x.
[b]Results affected by race and education.
[c]Adjusts for race and education.
[d]Hospital staff used.

SCREENING AFRICAN AMERICAN ELDERS FOR THE PRESENCE OF COGNITIVE IMPAIRMENT

Table 2 summarizes the studies that have screened various samples of older African Americans for the presence of cognitive impairment. Where available, the sensitivity and specificity of the instrument used have been included. Both studies included a second-stage diagnostic assessment of those who screened positive to determine the etiology of the cognitive impairment. The *Diagnostic and Statistical Manual of Mental Disorders* (4th ed., or *DSM–IV*; American Psychiatric Association, 1994) contains the most frequently used diagnostic criteria, along with the National Institute of Neurologic and Communicative Disorders and Stroke–Alzheimer's Disease and Related Disorders Association (NINCDS-ADRDA) Criteria to Establish a Diagnosis of AD developed in a Consensus Conference (McKhann et al., 1984; Tierney et al., 1988).

Table 2 Sensitivity and Specificity of Screening Instruments for Cognitive Impairment Reported in African American Populations

Study	Screening questionnaire	Sensitivity (%)	Specificity (%)
Fillenbaum et al. (1990, *N* = 164, Black = 83): Probability sample of community residents in 5 counties in North Carolina	MMSE SPMSQ MSQ	100.0 89.6 100.0	58.4 89.9 70.5
Baker et al. (1993b; *N* = 55, Black = 55): Community residents in senior citizen housing and eat-together site	MMSE	70.0	93.0

Note. MMSE = Mini-Mental State Examination; SPMSQ = Short Portable Mental Status Questionnaire; MSQ = Mental Status Questionnaire.

As shown in Table 2, the MMSE has been the most frequently used screening instrument. Its usefulness in older Black Americans was found to be limited because of its decreased reliability and increased number of false positives with education levels of less than 8th grade. The SPMSQ is useful in this population because it contains adjustments for race and education of less than 8th grade (Table 1), but it does not contain items that access hemispheric function or visual spatial orientation (Baker, 1989). As shown in Table 2, in comparison with the Mental Status Questionnaire (MSQ; Kahn, Goldfarb, & Pollack, 1960) and SPMSQ, the specificity of the MMSE was significantly less than that of the SPMSQ.

Recently, investigators in New York (Gurland et al., 1995) compiled an instrument composed of five screening tests for cognitive impairment. The compendium instrument was organized to minimize redundancies between similar measures and to facilitate the instrument's smooth flow. The Kahn Goldfarb Mental Status Questionnaire (Kahn, Goldfarb, & Pollack, 1960), the SPMSQ (Pfeiffer, 1975), the Comprehensive Assessment and Referral Interview (CARE) Cognitive Scale (Dementia Version; Golden, Teresi, & Gurland, 1984), the Blessed Memory Information-Concentration Test (Katzman et al., 1983), and the MMSE (Folstein et al., 1975) were the screening instruments that were combined. The threshold score for the identification of cognitive impairment was set so that each of the five instruments had a sensitivity of 90% or greater without losing specificity. Using these criteria, the CARE instrument had the lowest false-positive rate of the instruments studied. Using a varying definition of a case of dementia, lower education (0–4 years vs. 5–11 years) among Black Americans was associated with increased rates of dementia. The effect of education was greater than the effect of age in this study of a sample of older African Americans, Santo Domingans, and non-Hispanic Whites in upper Manhattan (Gurland et al., 1995). The total time required to administer the CARE instrument must be considered in deciding on its use in a specific study.

In studies that have followed a Stage 1 screening with a Stage 2 diagnostic assessment, African American elders were found to have higher rates of AD among persons age 75 and older and higher rates of MID (Folstein et al., 1985, 1991; Gurland et al., 1995; Haerer et al., 1987; Heyman et al., 1991; Schoenberg et al., 1985; see Table 3). Because of the higher prevalence of hypertension and diabetes among African American elders (Baker et al., 1993a; Task Force on Black & Minority Health, 1985), these findings are consistent with the presence of these risk factors. A study of community-resident, elderly Black Americans living in San Antonio who screened positive on the MMSE found depression, adjustment disorder, and no psychiatric illness among Black elders at the Stage 2 diagnostic assessment (Baker et al., 1993b).

Table 4 summarizes the main points to consider in screening African Americans for the presence of cognitive impairment. In the studies published to date of dementing illness, both AD and MID are a concern in older Black populations studied in several regions of the United States. In published studies, sporadic cases of AD were more predominant in Black populations as compared with White populations and the rates of MID were higher among Black Americans than those reported in studies of White Americans. Although the rate of dementia associated with alcoholism was hypothesized to be higher among older African American men (Baker, 1991), this has not been assessed in the majority of the published studies. Only one study to date has addressed this issue. Fillenbaum et al. (1990) did not find a higher rate of alcoholic dementia in their sample of older African Americans.

CONCLUSION

The screening of older African American populations for the presence of cognitive impairment is the first stage of the two-stage epidemiologic determination of the prevalence of dementia. The second-stage evaluation, the diagnostic assessment, determines the cause of the cognitive impairment. The importance of using standardized criteria (either *DSM–IV* or the NINCDS-ADRDA, or both) must be underscored for comparability with the existing literature (McKhann et al., 1984; Tierney et al., 1988). The limitation of screening instruments must be considered, and false positives due to lower education (MMSE) and the influence of education, age, race, activities of daily living (ADL), and instrumental activities of daily living (IADL) on MMSE scores as well as the presence of depression (Rabins, Merchant, & Nestadt, 1984) must be remembered in designing the screening battery. The role of protein malnutrition and inadequate diet as a result of poverty-level incomes producing vitamin deficiencies or borderline levels of nutrients must be evaluated through medical records or through current determinations with serum levels. African American elders who screen positive for the presence of cognitive impairment may do so because of the presence of multiple chronic medical problems and associated dysphoric symptoms or the presence of a major depressive disorder (Anthony et al., 1982; Baker et al., 1993a, 1995a; Rabins et al., 1984).

Table 3 Prevalence of Dementia among African Americans Age 60 and Older: Data from Published Studies 1985–1991

Study	Sample	N	Screening instrument	Age	Illness	Blacks Men	Blacks Women	Whites Men	Whites Women
Schoenberg et al. (1985)	Probability sample from Copiah County, MS; community residents and institutions	4,503 (1,823 Blacks, 2,680 Whites)	MMSE	60–69		0.72	0.00	0.53	0.27
				70–79		0.02	2.55	1.27	1.40
				80–89		3.26	9.45	7.25	7.25
				Age adjusted		1.00		1.00	
Heyman et al. (1991)	Probability sample of 5 counties in North Carolina, community residents	164 (19 Blacks, 7 Whites)	SPMSQ	65+	Hypertension[a]	3.9 (SE=1.6)		—	
					Diabetes[a]	27.8		14.0	
					Stroke[a]	26.3		14.0	
Folstein et al. (1991)	Stratified probability sample of catchment areas of 3 community mental health centers in eastern Baltimore, MD	923 (210 Blacks, 713 Whites)	MMSE		AD	3.9 (SE=1.60)		1.6 (SE=0.06)	
					MID	2.7 (SE=1.30)		1.8 (SE=1.40)	
					Mixed dementia	0.6 (SE=0.60)		0.4 (SE=0.30)	
					All dementia	7.2 (SE=2.10)		3.8 (SE=1.50)	

Note. MMSE = Mini-Mental State Examination; SPMSQ = Short Portable Mental Status Questionnaire; AD = Alzheimer's disease; MID = multi-infarct dementia.
[a]Medical illnesses with a higher incidence among demented elderly persons.

Table 4   Factors to Consider in Screening Older African Americans for the Presence of Cognitive Impairment

Preparation	Review of the literature
	Review of the history of current cohort of African American elders
	Consider 2 or 3 focus groups meetings in the areas you will be sampling to gain a sense of the daily lives and concerns of the people you will be studying
Baseline information in screening form	Age, education, income, current reading level
	Nutrition status (Does the elder's diet contain adequate protein, vitamins, and minerals?)
	Recent laboratory studies of albumin, total protein, vitamin B_{12}, vitamin B_6, and folate
Functional assessment	Instrumental Activities of Daily Living and Activities of Daily Living
Select criteria for case definition of dementia	*DSM–IV* or NINCDS-ADRDA criteria, or both
Two-stage design	
Stage 1	Screening for cognitive impairment with combined instrument
	Consider use of CARE Cognitive Scale (Dementia version)
	MMSE comparability with the literature
	SPMSQ effective for persons with <8 years of education and comparability with the literature
Stage 2	Diagnostic assessment of those screening positive and a percentage of those screening negative
	Use of a structured clinical interview to determine psychiatric disorders present (DIS or SCID)
	Careful evaluation for depressive symptoms or major depressive disorder

Note. DSM–IV = Diagnostic and Statistical Manual of Mental Disorders (4th ed.); NINCDS-ADRDA = National Institute of Neurologic and Commmunicative Disorders and Stroke–Alzhemer's Disease and Related Disorders Association; CARE = Comprehensive Assessment and Referral Interview; MMSE = Mini-mental State Examination; SPMSQ = Short Portable Mental Status Questionnaire; DIS = Diagnostic Interview Scale; SCID = Structured Clinical Interview for DSM–IV.

The importance of establishing the education attainment, work history, and current economic resources of African American elders has been emphasized as an indicator of their risk for psychosocial stress and nutritional deficiencies. With these baseline data from a pilot study of the population of interest, the most appropriate instruments to use to screen the population for cognitive impairment can be determined. The use of more than one screening instrument in a combined instrument (e.g., the MMSE and the SPMSQ) will enable the investigators to address the diversity observed within the current cohort of African American elders.

REFERENCES

American Psychiatric Association. (1994). *Diagnostic and statistical manual of mental disorders*. Washington DC: Author.

Anthony J. C., Niaz, U., LeResche, L. A., Von Korff, M. R., & Folstein, M. F. (1982). Limits of the 'Mini-Mental State' as a screening test for dementia and delirium among hospitalized patients. *Psychological Medicine, 12*, 397–408.

Baker, F. M. (1982). The Black elderly: Biopsychosocial perspective within an age cohort and adult development context. *Journal of Geriatric Psychiatry, 15*, 225–239.

Baker, F. M. (1989). Screening tests for cognitive impairment. *Hospital and Community Psychiatry, 40*, 339–340.

Baker, F. M. (1991). Dementing illness in African American populations: Evaluation and management for the primary physician. *Journal of Geriatric Psychiatry, 24*, 73–91.

Baker, F. M. (1994). Psychiatric treatment of older African Americans. *Hospital and Community Psychiatry, 45*, 32–37.

Baker, F. M., Johnson, J. T., Velli, S. A., & Wiley, C. (1996). Congruence between education and reading levels of older persons. *Psychiatric Services, 47*, 194–196.

Baker, F. M., Kokmen, E., Chandra, V., & Schoenberg, B. S. (1991). Psychiatric symptoms in cases of clinically diagnosed Alzheimer's disease. *Journal of Geriatric Psychiatry and Neurology, 4*, 71–78.

Baker, F. M., Lavizzo-Mourey, R., & Jones, B. E. (1993a). Acute care of the African American elder. *Journal of Geriatric Psychiatry, 6*, 66–71.

Baker, F. M., & Lightfoot, O. B. (1993). Psychiatric care of ethnic elders. In A. C. Gaw (Ed.), *Culture, ethnicity & mental illness* (pp. 517–552). Washington, DC: American Psychiatric Press.

Baker, F. M., Parker, D. A., Wiley, C., Velli, S. A., & Johnson, J. T. (1995a). Depressive symptoms in African American medical patients. *International Journal of Geriatric Psychiatry, 10*, 9–14.

Baker, F. M., Robinson, B. H., & Stewart (1993b). Use of the Mini-Mental State Examination in African American elders. *Clinical Gerontology, 14*, 5–13.

Baker, F. M., Velli, S. A., Friedman, J., & Wiley, C. (1995b). Screening tests for depression in older Black and White patients. *American Journal of Geriatric Psychiatry, 3*, 43–51.

Ballard, E. L., Nash, F., Raiford, K., & Harrell, L. E. (1993). Recruitment of Black elderly for clinical research studies of dementia: The CERAD experience. *The Gerontologist, 33*, 561–565.

Bartus, R. T., Dean, R. L., Beer, B., & Lippa, A. S. (1982). The cholinergic hypothesis of geriatric memory dysfunction. *Science, 217*, 408–417.

Benedek, T. G. (1978). The Tuskegee Study of Syphilis: Analysis of moral versus methodological aspects. *Journal of Chronic Disease, 31*, 335–350.

Berkman, L. K. (1986). The association between educational attainment and mental status examination: Of etiologic significance for senile dementia or not? *Journal of Chronic Disease, 39*, 171–175.

Brandt, T. A. M. (1978). Racism and research: The case of the Tuskegee Syphilis Study. *Hastings Center Report, 8*(6), 21–29.

Breteler, M. M. B., Claus, J. J., van Duijn, C. M., Launer, L. J., & Hofman, A. (1992). Epidemiology of Alzheimer's Disease. *Epidemiologic Reviews, 14,* 59–82.

Breteler, M. M. B., Van Duijn, C. M., Chandra, V., Fratiglioni, L., Graves, A. B., Heyman, A., Jorm, A. F., Kokmen, E., Kondo, K., Mortimer, J. A., Rocca, Q. A., Shalat, S. L., Soininen, H., & Hofman, A. (1991). Medical history and the risk of Alzheimer's disease: A collaborative reanalysis of case-control studies. *International Journal of Epidemiology, 20,* S36–S42.

Chartier-Harlin, M. C., Crawford, F., Houldlen, H., Warren, A., Hughes, D., Fidani, L., Goate, A., Rossor, M., Roques, P., Hardy, J., & Mullan, M. (1991). Early onset Alzheimer's Disease by mutation at codon 17 of the beta-amyloid precursor protein gene. *Nature, 353,* 844–846.

Cummings, J. L. (1985). Dementia. In *Clinical neuropsychiatry* (pp. 75–94). Boston: Grune & Stratton.

Edgar, H. (1992). Outside the community. *Hastings Center Report, 22,* 32–35.

Evans, D. A., Fundenstein, H. J. H., Albert, M. S., Schert, P. A., Cook, N. R., Chown, M. J., Herbert, L. E., Hennekens, C. H., & Taylor, J. O. (1989). Prevalence of Alzheimer's disease in a community population of older persons higher than previously reported. *Journal of the American Medical Association, 262,* 2551–2556.

Fillenbaum, G. G., Heyman, A., Wilkinson, W. E., & Haynes, C. S. (1987). Comparison of two screening tests of Alzheimer's disease: The correlation and reliability of the Mini-Mental State examination and the modified Blessing Test. *Archives of Neurology, 44,* 924–927.

Fillenbaum, G., Heyman, A., Williams, K., Prosnit, B., & Burchett, B. (1990). Sensitivity and specificity of standardized screens for cognitive impairment and dementia among elderly Black and White community residents. *Journal of Clinical Epidemiology, 43,* 651–660.

Fillenbaum, G. G., Hughes, D. C., Heyman, A., George, L. K., & Blazer, D. G. (1988). Relationship of health and demographic characteristics to Mini-Mental State Examination Score among community residents. *Psychological Medicine, 18,* 719–726.

Folstein, M., Anthony, J. C., Parhard, J., Duffy, B., & Gruenberg, E. M. (1985). The meaning of cognitive impairment in the elderly. *Journal of the American Geriatric Society, 33,* 228–233.

Folstein, M. F., Bassett, S. S., Anthony, J. C., Romanoski, A. J., & Nestadt, G. R. (1991). Dementia: Case ascertainment in a community survey. *Journal of Gerontology, 46,* M132–M138.

Folstein, M. F., Folstein, S. E., & McHugh, P. R. (1975). Mini-Mental State: A practical method for grading the cognitive state of patients for the clinician. *Journal of Psychiatric Research, 12,* 189–198.

Fukunishi, I., Hayabara, T., & Hosokawa, K. (1991). Epidemiologic survey of senile dementia in Japan. *Journal of Social Psychiatry, 37,* 51–56.

Goate, A. M., Haynes, A. R., Owens, M. J., Farrall, M., James, L. A., Lai, Y. C., Mullan, M. S., Roques, P., Rossor, M. N., Williamson, R., & Hardy, J. A. (1989). Predisposition for Alzheimer's disease on chromosome 21. *Lancet, 1,* 352–355.

Golden, R. B., Teresi, J. A., & Gurland, B. J. (1984). Development of indicator scales for the Comprehensive Assessment and Referral Evaluation (CARE) interview schedule. *Journal of Gerontology, 39,* 138–146.

Gottlieb, G. L. (1991). Financial issues. In J. Sadavoy, L. W. Lazaraus, & L. F. Jarvik (Eds.), *Comprehensive review of geriatric psychiatry* (pp. 667–686). Washington, DC: American Psychiatric Press.

Graves, A. B., Van Duijn, C. M., Chandra, V., Fratiglioni, L., Heyman, A., Jorm, A. F., Kokmen, E., Kondo, K., Mortimer, J. A., Rocca, W. A., Shalat, S. L., Soininen, H., & Hofman, A. (1991). Alcohol and tobacco consumption as risk factors for Alzheimer's disease: A collaborative re-analysis of case-control studies. *International Journal of Epidemiology, 20*, S48–S57.

Grundke-Iqbal, J., Iqbal, K., Quinlan, M., Tung, Y.-C., Zatch, M. S., & Wisniewski, H. M. (1986). Microtubule-associated protein Tau. *Journal of Biological Chemistry, 261*, 6084–6089.

Gurland, B., Wilder, D., Cross, P., Lantigua, R., Teresi, J., Barrett, V., Stern, Y., & Mayeux, P. (1995). Relative rates of dementia by multiple case definitions, over two prevalence periods, in three socio-cultural groups. *American Journal of Geriatric Psychiatry, 3*, 6–20.

Haerer, A. F., Anderson, D. W., & Schoenberg, B. S. (1987). Survey of major neurologic disorders in a biracial United States population: The Copiah County Study. *Southern Medical Journal, 80*, 339–343.

Hartung, R. (1994). On Black burden and becoming noveau poor. *Journal of Gerontology, 48*, 533–534.

Hasegawa, K., Homma, A., & Imai, Y. (1986). An epidemiological study of age-related dementia in the community. *International Journal of Geriatric Psychiatry, 1*, 45–55.

Henderson, J. N., Gutierrez-Mayka, M., Garcia, J., & Boyd, S. (1993). A model for Alzheimer's Disease support group development in African American and Hispanic populations. *The Gerontologist, 33*, 409–414.

Heyman, A., Fillenbaum, G., Prosnitz, B., Raiford, K., Burchett, B., & Clark, C. (1991). Estimating prevalence of dementia among elderly Black and White community residents. *Archives of Neurology, 48*, 594–598.

Hofman, A. (1991). Epilogue. Risk factors for Alzheimer's disease: A collaborative reanalysis of case-control studies. *International Journal of Epidemiology, 20*(Suppl. 2), S72–S73.

Holzer, C. E., Tischler, G. L., Leaf, P. L., & Myers, J. K. (1984). An epidemiologic assessment of cognitive impairment in a community population. *Research in Community and Mental Health, 4*, 3–32.

Jones, J. H. (1981). *Bad blood: The Tuskegee syphilis experiment. A tragedy of race and medicine.* New York: Free Press.

Jones, J. H. (1992). The Tuskegee legacy: AIDS and the Black community. *Hastings Center Report, 22*, 38–40.

Jorm, A. F., Scott, R., Henderson, A. S., & Kay, D. W. K. (1988). Educational level differences on the Mini-Mental State: The role of test bias. *Psychological Medicine, 18*, 727–731.

Jorm, A. F., Van Duijn, C. M., Chandra, V., Fratiglioni, L., Graves, A. B., Heyman, A., Kokmen, E., Kondo, K., Mortimer, J. A., Rocca, W. A., Shalat, S. L., Soininen, H., & Homan, A. (1991). Psychiatric history and related exposures as risk factors for Alzheimer's disease: A collaborative re-analysis of case-control studies. *International Journal of Epidemiology, 20*, S43–S47.

Kahn, R. I., Goldfarb, A. I., & Pollack, M. (1960). Brief objective measure for the determination of mental status in the aged. *American Journal of Psychiatry, 117,* 326–328.

Katz, S. (1983). Assessing self-maintenance: Activities of daily living, mobility, and instrumental activities of daily living. *Journal of the American Geriatrics Society, 31,* 721–727.

Katzman, R., Brown, T., Fuld, P., Peck, A., Schechter, R., & Schimmel, H. (1983). Validation of a short, orientation-memory-concentration test of cognitive impairment. *American Journal of Psychiatry, 140,* 734–738.

King, P. A. (1992). The dangers of difference. *Hastings Center Report, 22,* 35–38.

Kokmen, E., Chandra, V., & Schoenberg, B. S. (1985). Trends in the incidence of dementing illness in Rochester, Minnesota in three quinquennial periods, 1960-1974. *Neurology, 38,* 975–980.

Kua, E. H. (1991). The prevalence of dementia in elderly Chinese. *Acta Psychiatrica Scandinavica, 83,* 350–352.

Launer, L. (Ed.). (1992). European studies on the incidence of dementing diseases. *Neuroepidemiology, 11* (Suppl. 1), 1–122.

Lawton, M. P., Rajagopal, D. L., Brody, E., & Kleban, M. H. (1992). The dynamics of caregiving for the demented elder among Black and White families. *Journal of Gerontology, 47,* S158–S164.

Li, G., Shen, Y. C., Chen, C. H., Zhao, W., Li, S. R., & Lu, M. (1989). An epidemiological survey of age related dementia in an urban area of Beijing. *Acta Psychiatrica Scandinavica, 79,* 557–563.

Li, G., Shen, Y. C., Chen, C. H., Zhao, W., Li, S. R., & Lu, M. (1991). A three-year follow-up study of age-related dementia in an urban area of Beijing. *Acta Psychiatrica Scandinavica, 83,* 99–104.

Matsuyama, S. S., & Jarvik, L. F. (1989). Hypothesis: Microtubules, a key to Alzheimer disease. *Proceedings of the National Academy of Science, 86,* 8152–8156.

McKhann, G., Drachman, D., Folstein, M., Katzman, R., Price, D., & Stadian, E. M. (1984). Clinical diagnosis of Alzheimer's disease: A report of the NINCDS-ADRDA Work Group. *Neurology, 34,* 939–944.

Miller, B. L., Cheong, L., Oropilla, G., & Mena, I. (1994). Alzheimer's disease and frontal lobe dementia. In C. E. Coffey & J. L. Cummings (Eds.)., *Textbook of geriatric neuropsychiatry* (pp. 390–404). Washington, DC: American Psychiatric Press.

Morihisa, J. M. (1991). Advances in neuroimaging technologies. In A. L. Stoudemire & B.S. Fogel (Eds.)., *Medical psychiatric practice* (Vol. 1, pp. 3–28). Washington, DC: American Psychiatric Press.

Mortimer, J. A., Van Duijn, C. M., Chandra, V., Fratiglioni, L., Graves, A. B., Heyman, A., Jorm, A. F., Kokman, E., Kondo, K., Rocca, W. A., Shalat, S. L., Soininen, H., & Hofman, A. (1991). Head trauma as a risk factor for Alzheimer's disease: A collaborative re-analysis of case-control studies. *International Journal of Epidemiology, 20,* S28–S35.

Pfeiffer, E. (1975). A short portable mental status questionnaire for the assessment of organic brain deficits in elderly patients. *Journal of the American Geriatrics Society, 23,* 433–441.

Plum, F. (1979). Dementia: An approaching epidemic. *Nature, 279,* 372–373.

Rabins, P. V., Merchant, A., & Nestadt, G. (1984). Criteria for diagnosing reversible dementia caused by depression: Validation by 2-year follow-up. *British Journal of Psychiatry, 144,* 488–492.

Read, S. (1991). The dementias. In J. Sadovy, L. W. Lazarus, & L. F. Jarvik (Eds.), *Comprehensive review of geriatric psychiatry* (pp. 287–309). Washington, DC: American Psychiatric Press.

Rocca, W. A., Amducci, L. A., & Schoenberg, B. S. (1985). Epidemiology of clinically diagnosed Alzheimer's disease. *Annals of Neurology, 19,* 415–424.

Rocca, W. A., Van Duijn, C. M., Clayton, D., Chandra, V., Fratiglioni, L., Graves, A. B., Heyman, A., Jorm, A. F., Kokmen, E., Kondo, K., Mortimer, J. A., Shalat, S. L., Soininen, H., & Hofman, A. (1991). Maternal age and Alzheimer's disease: A collaborative re-analysis of case-control studies. *International Journal of Epidemiology, 20,* S21–S27.

Roy, B. (1995). The Tuskegee syphilis experiment: Biotechnology and the administrative state. *Journal of the National Medical Association, 87*(1), 56–67.

Schellenberg, G. D., Bird, T. D., Wijsman, E. M., Orr, H. T., Anderson, L., Nemens, E., White, J. A., Bonnycastle, L., Weber, J. L., Alonso, M. E., Potter, H., Heston, L. L., & Martin, G. M. (1992). Genetic linkage evidence for a familial Alzheimer's disease locus on chromosome 14. *Science, 258,* 668–671.

Schoenberg, B. S., Anderson, D. W., & Haerer, A. F. (1985). Severe dementia: Prevalence and clinical features in a biracial U.S. population. *Archives of Neurology, 42,* 740–743.

Soldo, B. J., & Agree, E. M. (1988). America's elderly population. *Population Bulletin, 43,* 1–53.

St. George-Hyslop, P. H., Tanzi, R. E., Polinsky, R. J., Haines, J. I., Nee, L., Watkins, P. C., Myers, R. H., Feldman, R. G., Pollen, D., Drachman, D., Growdon, J., Bruni, A., Foncin, J. F., Salmon, D., Frommell, P., Amaducci, L., Sorbi, S., Piacentin, S., Stewart, G. D., Hobbs, W. J., Conneally, P. M., & Gusella, J. F. (1987). The genetic defect causing familial Alzheimer's disease maps on chromosome 21. *Science, 235,* 885–890.

Sulkava, R., Wikstrom, H., & Aromaa, A. (1985). Prevalence of severe dementia in Finland. *Neurology, 35,* 1025–1029.

Tanzi, R. E., Vaula, G., Romano, D. M., Mortilla, M., Huang, T. L., Tupler, R. G., Wasco, W., Hyman, B. T., Haines, J. L., Jenkins, B. J., Kalaitidaki, M. K., Warren, A. C., McInnis, M. C., Antonarakis, S. E., Karlinsky, H., Percy, M. E., Connor, L., Growden, J., Crapper-McIachian, D. R., Gusella, J. F., & St. George-Hyslop, P. H. (1992). Assessment of amyloid beta-protein precursor gene mutations in a large set of familial and sporadic Alzheimer's disease cases. *American Journal of Human Genetics, 51,* 272–282.

Task Force on Black and Minority Health. (1985). *Report of the Secretary's Task Force on Black and Minority Health. Volume I: Executive summary.* Washington, DC: Department of Health and Human Services.

Tierney, M. C., Fisher, R. H., Lewis, A. J., McKhann, G., Drachman, D., & Folstein, M. (1988). The NINCDS-ADRDA Work Group criteria for the clinical diagnosis of probable Alzheimer's disease: A clinicopathologic study of 57 cases. *Neurology, 38,* 359–364.

Valle, R. (1988). *U.S. ethnic minority groups access to long-term care*. In T. Meyers (Ed.), *International long term care* (pp. 339–366). New York: McGraw-Hill.

Valluri, S. R., van Duijn, C. M., Connor-Lacke, L., Cupples, L. A., Growdon, J. H., & Farrer, L. A. (1994). Multiple etiologies for Alzheimer's disease are revealed by segregation analysis. *American Journal of Human Genetics, 55,* 991–1000.

Van Duijn, C. M., Clayton, D., Chandra, V., Fratiglioni, L., Graves, A. V., Heyman, A., Jorm, A. F., Kokmen, E., Kondo, K., Mortimer, J. A., Rocca, W. A., Shalat, S. L., Soininen, H., & Hofman, A. (1991b). Familial aggregation of Alzheimer's disease and related disorders: A collaborative re-analysis of case-control studies. *International Journal of Epidemiology, 20,* S13–S20.

Van Duijn, C. M., Hendriks, L. E., Farrer, L. A., Backhovens, H., Cruts, M., Wehnert, A., Hogman, A., & Van Broeckhoven, C. (1994). A population based study of familial Alzheimer's disease: Linkage to chromosome 14, 19, and 21. *American Journal of Human Genetics, 55,* 714–727.

Van Duijn, C. M., Stijnen, T., & Hofman, A. (1991a). Risk factors for Alzheimer's disease: Overview of the EURODEM collaborative reanalysis of case-control studies. *International Journal of Epidemiology, 20,* S4–S11.

Wisniewski, K. E., Wisniewski, H. M., & Wen, G. Y. (1985) Occurrence of neuropathological changes and dementia of the Alzheimer type in Down's syndrome. *Annals of Neurology, 7,* 278–282.

Chapter 7

Cross-Cultural Testing and the Cognitive Abilities Screening Instrument

Evelyn Lee Teng

The development of cross-culturally applicable tests for dementia is important for two reasons. First, such tests are needed to serve the increasing number of aging ethnic minorities in the United States (see Chapter 1). Second, their international application can facilitate closer comparison of data from different parts of the world and can aid global health care planning.

This chapter is divided into three sections. The first section considers some general issues in cross-cultural testing. The second section describes a recently developed test that has been designed for easier cross-cultural adaptability. The third section provides an example of how to modify the test, which was originally designed for an educated, English-speaking population, for use with a population of predominantly illiterate Chinese elders.

GENERAL CONSIDERATIONS IN CROSS-CULTURAL TESTING

Language

When a test originally designed for one language group is adapted for another language group, current common practice is to have it translated into the second language. This step is usually followed with back-translation to check the accuracy of translation. When certain words or phrases in one language do not have counterparts in another language, translation is obviously impossible. For example, in the Visual Naming subtest of the Multilingual Aphasia Examination Battery (Benton & Hamsher, 1978), one stimulus plate shows the drawing of a lower limb, and the subject is asked to name *shin, instep*, and some other parts. In the Chinese language, however, there are no words for these body parts. In Chinese, different words are used to denote various relatives depending on whether they are from the mother's side or from the father's side, but no such distinctions are made in English. As another example, the expression "no ifs, ands, or buts" used in the Mini-Mental State Examination (MMSE; Folstein, Folstein, & McHugh, 1975) probably cannot be translated into any other language.

A more subtle but no less troublesome situation is when easy and accurate translation between two languages nevertheless results in items of quite different difficulty levels. For example, reciting the months of the year is a much easier task in Chinese than in English, because in Chinese the 12 months are simply named Month 1, Month 2, Month 3, and so forth. As another example, when the Digit Span subtest of the Wechsler Adult Intelligence Scale—Revised (Wechsler, 1981) was administered to four groups of participants who were comparable in age and education, but who spoke Chinese, English, Spanish, and Vietnamese, respectively, the Chinese and the Vietnamese groups scored the highest and the Spanish-speaking group scored the lowest (Dick, Taussig, Teng, & Kempler, 1995; Teng, Dick, Kempler, & Taussig, 1995). A reasonable cause for the observed differences is that all digits from 1 to 9 are monosyllabic in Chinese and Vietnamese, only the numeral 7 has two syllables in English, but six of the nine digits have two syllables in Spanish.

Education

Many older individuals from developing countries have had little or no formal schooling. It is easy to understand that illiterate individuals will fail on test items that require reading and writing. It is perhaps more surprising to learn that they also have trouble copying geometric designs such as the cube shown in Figure 1. Close observation of their performance on this task reveals that they seem to have difficulty both in perceptual analysis and in manual control.

For individuals who have studied geometry, the cube is an easily identified meaningful unit; when asked to copy the cube, they hardly need to take a second look at it because they can make use of their background knowledge about a cube's characteristics in their production. For individuals who have not studied geometry, the same model may appear to be a meaningless juxtaposition of line segments or two-dimensional shapes; they need to look at the model repeatedly to inspect and copy line segments and angles one at a time, and often miss part of the model in their production.

People who have never used a pen or pencil before tend to hold the instrument in an awkward manner and appear to have trouble drawing lines toward

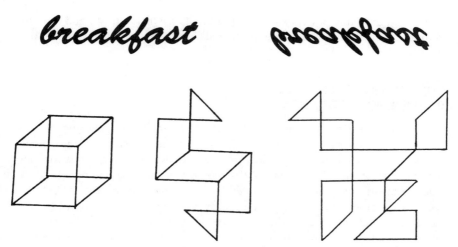

Figure 1 The top row shows the word *breakfast* and its reflection. In the bottom row, the middle design is created by rearranging the 12 lines of the cube, and the design on the right is created by rearranging the seven two-dimensional pieces of the cube.

intended directions. Their difficulty with this seemingly simple task becomes more understandable if one imagines oneself being asked to put on a pair of skates to trace a figure 8 on ice. Even if one has a perfectly healthy body and has used it daily and adroitly in a variety of activities, even if one knows perfectly what a figure 8 ought to look like, the first time one tries to skate it on ice, one will miss by a wide margin—and would be lucky to not fall.

Education not only teaches specific knowledge and skills, but also enhances information-processing proficiency and test-taking skills in general. It is reasonable to expect that, as long as a cognitive test covers a broad range of difficulty levels and the participants differ widely in their educational background, test performance will show an association with education.

Ecological Relevance of Test Items

Cognitive tests are typically designed by academicians whose life experiences and lifestyles can be drastically different from those of some of the people to whom their tests will be administered. For example, an illiterate grandmother in a developing country probably has never taken a test in the manner an academician in this country is used to, and being asked by a stranger to perform a variety of tasks that are foreign and meaningless to her is likely to be a very stressful experience. She may not know the day of the month or the day of the week not because she has dementia, but because her life has never been regulated by appointment books. Her role in life may emphasize interpersonal nurturing skills more than the ability to process large amounts of abstract information. She may excel at cooking, sewing, raising children, growing vegetables, and getting along with members of her extended family, all of which reflect good cognitive abilities, yet she may score in the "impaired" range on the tests commonly used for dementia.

THE COGNITIVE ABILITIES SCREENING INSTRUMENT

The previous section showed that when a test originally designed for one kind of population is used with another kind of population, accuracy of translation is but one of many factors to consider. However, to design a unique test for every particular study population not only is too costly, but also hampers between-study comparisons. The Cognitive Abilities Screening Instrument (CASI) is a recently developed test designed for easier cross-cultural adaptability but that strives to maintain some continuity across different studies. Its items cover 10 cognitive domains commonly assessed in dementia research, but users of the CASI are encouraged to devise alternative items to assess the specified domains in order to better suit their participants' backgrounds. An example of this approach is provided in the third section of this chapter.

Thus, the CASI is a generic term for a family of more or less similar tests. To distinguish the various versions of the CASI, each CASI will have a version code in the format of L-N1.N2, where *L* represents a letter and *N1* and *N2* represent two numerals. The letter is used to indicate the language the version is in (e.g., *E* for English, *C* for Chinese, *J* for Japanese, *S* for Spanish). *N1* is used to distinguish major versions in each language that have been developed to suit major differences in educational background or some other factor. *N2* is used to distinguish minor variations, including future improvements, of each major version. The following are common characteristics of all versions of the CASI.

Short and Easy

The CASI takes approximately 15–20 minutes to administer. Its brevity is intended to make it practical when time or resources are limited. Some of its items have time limits or other discontinuation rules to avoid causing the participants excessive fatigue or stress.

Broad Coverage and Modular Composition

Individual CASI items are classified under 10 domains: attention, concentration, orientation, short-term memory, long-term memory, language abilities, constructional praxis, list-generating fluency, abstraction, and judgment. Most of the domains have a score range of 0–10. This modular composition provides the flexibility of selective assessment of, and comparison across groups on, individual domains. The CASI total score has a range of 0–100.

Multiple Uses

The CASI has been designed to serve three main functions: A small number of its items can be used to screen for dementia. Its domain scores can be used to plot ability profiles to reveal individual strengths and weaknesses. Its total score is probably the most reliable measure for tracking within-individual changes over time.

Linkage to Other Studies

Most of the CASI items are taken or modified from the MMSE (Folstein et al., 1983), the Modified Mini-Mental State Test (Teng & Chui, 1987), and the Hasegawa Dementia Screening Scale (Hasegawa, 1983). Therefore, scores from subsets of CASI items can be used to yield approximated scores on the MMSE, the Modified Mini-Mental State, and the Hasegawa Dementia Screening Scale to provide continuity with the large number of studies that use these tests.

Item modification may involve either item content or its scoring, or both. For example, the MMSE item of "no ifs, ands, or buts" has been a problematic one even for English-speaking participants: It is easy for individuals who happen to be familiar with this idiomatic expression, but difficult for those who are not, especially if they have some hearing loss from normal aging or other causes. The counterpart of this MMSE item in CASI is classified under the domain of attention. For this purpose, a sentence is devised that is composed of common words, but the combination of the words is novel, so that the participant can hardly respond correctly unless careful attention is paid to every word. The participant is asked to repeat "This yellow circle | is heavier than | blue square" and is given 1 point for correct repetition of each of the three segments. A full 3 points on this item yields 1 point for the estimated MMSE score, and fewer than 3 points will yield an estimated MMSE item score of zero.

Although many of the items in the CASI E-1.0 have undergone considerable modification from their MMSE counterparts in order to improve their reliability and validity, the MMSE score estimated from CASI E-1.0 items has been found to be remarkably close to the score obtained from an independently administered MMSE. On the basis of a sample of 57 dementia patients and 88 normal control participants, the means and standard deviations were 23.21 and 7.04, respectively, for CASI-estimated MMSE scores and 23.30 and 7.78, respectively, for true MMSE scores; the two types of scores had a correlation of .92 (Graves, Larson, Kukull, White, & Teng, 1993).

Training Aids for Users

CASI seeks to obtain a maximum amount of information in a minimal amount of time with limited stress to the participants. Many of its items have discontinuation rules. Many of the participants' responses are scored in a graded manner.

To aid the training of its users, a detailed manual on its administration and scoring, plus a training video that shows the administration of it to 3 participants of different ability levels (normal, mild to moderate dementia, moderate to severe dementia), have been made for its prototype version, CASI E-1.0. In addition, two parallel forms of a 30-item multiple-choice quiz have been prepared to qualify the user of the CASI. Potential users are asked to study the manual, watch the training tape, and then take the quiz. Comparable training materials are available for a Chinese version, the CASI C-2.0. The use of the quiz is highly recommended because experience has shown that providing a manual and conducting a workshop are no guarantee of accurate administration and scoring of even simpler tests such as the MMSE.

ADAPTATIONS FROM CASI E-1.0 TO CASI C-2.0 FOR USE WITH A PREDOMINANTLY ILLITERATE CHINESE POPULATION

The prototype version of the CASI, CASI E-1.0, has been designed for English-speaking participants in North America who have had at least some high school education. More detailed descriptions of it, and findings from its pilot testing (along with that of CASI J-1.0) in coordinated studies conducted in the United States and Japan, have been reported elsewhere (Teng et al., 1992; Teng, Hasegawa, et al., 1994). Other versions of the CASI now in existence include CASI E-2.0 (for studying dementia among the Chamorros on Guam; Waring et al., 1994) and CASI C-2.0 (for studying dementia among Chinese elders in Kinmen and Taiwan; Liu et al., 1994). Additional versions of the CASI in Vietnamese and Spanish are under development (Dick et al., 1995; Teng et al., 1995).

CASI C-2.0 was modified from CASI E-1.0 for use with Chinese elders of low educational backgrounds. Some of the differences between CASI E-1.0 and CASI C-2.0 are now presented to illustrate the reasons for and ways of item modification.

Attention

One of the CASI E-1.0 items for assessing attention is asking the participant to repeat "This yellow circle is heavier than blue square." The abstract nouns *circle* and *square* are rarely used in the daily lives of illiterate Chinese elders; therefore, this item was modified to be "This yellow cup is heavier than red rice bowl."

Concentration

One of the CASI E-1.0 items for concentration is serial subtractions of 3s from 100. In CASI C-2.0, this item was made more concrete: Participants are asked how many dollars are left if they started with $100 and spent $3, and so forth.

Temporal Orientation

For reporting the current year, the Chinese participants can answer according to any one of three commonly used calendar systems (Western, national, or the folk system with cycles of 12 animals). Instead of the season, the Chinese participants are asked about the time of the day and are provided with four choices: morning, noon, afternoon, and evening. The reason for this substitution is that CASI C-2.0 was to be used in an epidemiological study in Kinmen, which is a subtropical island with indistinct seasonal variations.

Long-Term Memory

CASI E-1.0 includes an item on the date of birth to assess long-term memory. However, the intended subjects of CASI C-2.0 were born in an era of no official birth records; most of them do not celebrate their birthdays regularly, and throughout their lives they have rarely been requested to report their date of birth. In addition, some of them deliberately registered false dates of birth with the government many years ago for personal reasons such as avoiding the draft. Therefore, reporting dates of birth is a harder task for the Chinese elders than for their American counterparts, and the answers they do provide are difficult to verify. For these reasons, in CASI C-2.0 this item is replaced with questions about popular folk festivals.

Short-Term Memory

CASI E-1.0 asks the person to remember three words, one of which is an abstract noun, *honesty*. Although this word poses no difficulty for educated persons, it is not in the common vocabulary of poorly educated persons and is difficult for them to grasp when it is presented. In CASI C-2.0 *honesty* is replaced with a common word, *child*.

Language Abilities

To yield an estimated MMSE score, the reading and writing items are retained in CASI C-2.0 even though many of the intended participants are illiterate. However, whereas reading and writing count for 4 points in CASI E-1.0, they count for only 2 points in CASI-2.0, and the participants are asked to write only very simple and common Chinese characters. To make up for the lost points, more weight is given to naming abilities.

CONCLUSION

Cross-cultural assessment involves much more than accurate translation of test items between languages. To adapt a test originally designed for one type of population for another type of population, one needs to know not only the languages involved but also the life experiences and life circumstances of both populations. Careful consultation with local professionals and residents will help detect potential difficulties and obtain suggestions to get around them. Extensive pilot testing is needed to help select replacement items from various alternatives. Still, some of the shortcomings will not become apparent until large sets of data have been collected and analyzed.

The CASI does not solve all the problems of cross-cultural testing, but it offers a practical compromise among various considerations. Each of its versions can be improved from accumulated experience and data, through modifications in either item content or item scoring. It is encouraging to note that the four CASI items of repeating three words, temporal orientation, list-generating fluency, and recalling three words have already been found to be as good as or better than the MMSE as a screening tool for dementia for American, Japanese (Teng, Hasegawa, et al., 1994), and Chinese (Teng et al., 1994) participants. These four items do not involve reading, writing, calculations, or the use of a pen or pencil and they can even be administered over the telephone; therefore, they seem particularly suitable for cross-cultural epidemiological studies.

REFERENCES

Benton, A. L., & Hamsher, K. (1978). *Multilingual aphasia examination.* Iowa City: University of Iowa Hospitals.
Dick, M., Taussig, I. M., Teng, E. L., & Kempler, D. (1995). The Cross-Cultural Neuropsychological Assessment Battery. *The Clinical Neuropsychologist, 9,* 249. (Abstract)
Folstein, M. F., Folstein, S. E., & McHugh, P. R. (1975). "Mini-Mental State": A practical method for grading the cognitive state of patients for the clinician. *Journal of Psychiatric Research, 12,* 189–198.
Graves, A. B., Larson, E. B., Kukull, W. A., White, L.R., & Teng, E. L. (1993). Screening for dementia in the community in cross-national studies: Comparison between the Cognitive Abilities Screening Instrument and the Mini-Mental State Examination. In B. Corain, K. Iqbal, M. Nicolini, B. Winblad, H. Wisniewski, & P. Zatta (Eds.), *Alzheimer's disease: Advances in clinical and basic research* (pp. 113–119). New York: Wiley.
Hasegawa, K. (1983). The clinical assessment of dementia in the aged: A dementia screening scale for psychogeriatric patients. In M. Bergener, U. Lehr, E. Lang, & R. Schmitz-Scherzer (Eds.), *Aging in the eighties and beyond* (pp. 207–218). New York: Springer.
Liu, H. C., Chou, P., Lin, K. N., Wang, S. J., Fuh, J. L., Lin, H. C., Liu, C. Y., Wu, G. S., Larson, E. B., White, L. R., Graves, A. B., & Teng, E. L. (1994). Assessing cognitive abilities and dementia in a predominantly illiterate population of older individuals in Kinmen. *Psychological Medicine, 24,* 763–770.
Teng, E. L., & Chui, H. C. (1987). The Modified Mini-Mental State (3MS) Examination. *Journal of Clinical Psychiatry, 48,* 314–318.

Teng, E. L., Dick, M., Kempler, D., & Taussig, M. (1995). The Cross-Cultural Neuro-psychological Test Battery (CCNB): Effects of education, age, and language on performance. *The Gerontologist, 35*, 219. (Abstract)

Teng, E. L., Hasegawa, K., Homma, A., Imai, Y., Larson, E., Graves, A., Sugimoto, K., Yamaguchi, T., Sasaki, H, Chiu, D., & White, L. R. (1994). The Cognitive Abilities Screening Instrument (CASI): A practical test for cross-cultural epidemio-logical studies of dementia. *International Psychogeriatrics, 6*, 45–58.

Teng, E. L., Hasegawa, K., Homma, A., Imai, Y., Larson, E., Sasaki, H., & White, L. R. (1992). A practical test for cross-cultural epidemiological studies of dementia: The Cognitive Abilities Screening Instrument (CASI). In H. Orimo, Y. Fukuchi, K. Kuramoto, & M. Iriki (Eds.), *New horizons in aging science* (pp. 326–327). Tokyo: University of Tokyo Press.

Teng, E. L., Lin, K. N., Chou, P., Fuh, J. L., Wang, S. J., & Liu, H. C. (1994). The Cognitive Abilities Screening Instrument (CASI) and its Chinese version C-2.0. *Chinese Journal of Clinical Psychology, 2*, 69–73. (Written in Chinese)

Waring, S. C., Esteban-Santillan, C., Teng, E., Petersen, R. C., O'Brien, P. C., & Kurland, L. T. (1994). Evaluation of a modified version of the Cognitive Abilities Screening Instrument (CASI) for assessment of dementia in elderly Chamorros on Guam. *Neurobiology of Aging, 15*(Suppl. 1), S43. (Abstract)

Wechsler, D. (1981) *Wechsler Adult Intelligence Scale—Revised*. San Antonio, TX: The Psychological Corporation.

Part 3

Working with Families of Dementia Patients from Different Ethnic Populations

Ethnic minority families provide even more of the care for dementia patients than do non-Hispanic White families who themselves provide most of the care. It follows, then, that an important skill in cultural competence needed by geriatric health care providers is working with family caregivers.

All of the groups of authors in this section include professionals from the ethnic backgrounds of the families about whom they are writing. They and their coauthors share their research, their professional experience, and the insights they have gained from observing and participating in their own culture.

Chapter 8

Working with Chinese Families in the Context of Dementia

Kathryn Sabrena Elliott
Mariann Di Minno
Darrick Lam
Alicia Mei Tu

The goal of this chapter is to present strategies for working with Chinese patients and their families. The intention is to provide a conceptual basis, as well as to provide health care and social service providers tools with which to apply these concepts in everyday practice. These strategies and the clinical vignettes provided were culled primarily from a National Institute on Aging–funded research project to study outreach strategies to the Chinese community, as well as a collaborative project and professional partnership between the Memory Clinic and Alzheimer's Center (MC&AC) of the University of California, San Francisco (UCSF; a tertiary care medical center), and Self Help for the Elderly (SHE; a Chinese community-based agency) in San Francisco to provide on-site dementia evaluations in San Francisco's Chinatown.

The collaborative project between UCSF MC&AC and SHE represents a unique attempt to provide services to monolingual elderly Chinese patients and their families. Both UCSF MC&AC and SHE recognized the need to provide diagnostic and social services to elderly monolingual Chinese patients presenting with symptoms of memory loss and possible dementia. SHE provided linkage to two other key organizations in Chinatown: Chinese Hospital, the community-based hospital serving the Chinese community, and District Health Center 4, the major community health center within Chinatown. As a result of all four agencies working together and pooling resources, a successful project ensued, providing on-site dementia evaluations in Chinatown. UCSF MC&AC provided the clinical

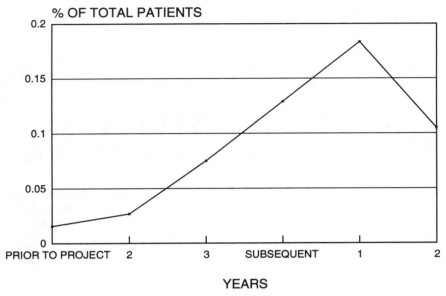

Figure 1   The success of reaching Chinese patients and families before the collaborative project and afterward.

team to conduct the evaluations; SHE identified, through their networks, patients requiring an evaluation and the social services and case coordination needed; District Health Center 4 provided clinic space in their building; and Chinese Hospital provided a referral source for diagnostic tests and scans, as well as a source for ongoing primary care as required. Figure 1 illustrates the success of reaching Chinese patients and families before the collaborative project and afterwards.

Alicia Mei Tu, one of the coauthors of this chapter, drew on her experience working for yet another agency serving the San Francisco Bay Area, the Family Caregiver Alliance, in its efforts to assist caregivers of brain-impaired adults through education, research, services, and advocacy and to extend those efforts to the Chinese-speaking population. In her work, she has helped Chinese caregivers to understand the diagnosis, develop care plans, locate community resources, increase family support, and gain emotional support.

All of the authors are intimately involved in the development and running of programs directed toward monolingual Chinese elderly persons and their families in the San Francisco Bay area. All have developed strategies for dealing with the interface of Western biomedical models and patients embedded in the context of Chinese culture.

CONCEPTUAL MODELS

Three conceptual models underlie the chapter discussion of strategies developed. The classic model of service utilization was originally suggested by Anderson and Newman (1975), who postulated three classes of predictors of use of health services: (a) perceived need for the service, (b) perceived ability of the service to alleviate the problem, and (c) enabling conditions such as income, availability of services, and knowledge of availability and willingness to use services.

The second model is one developed by Valle (1989). Although much of Valle's work has focused on the Hispanic community and culture, applications of key concepts, with some adaptations, can be made across cultural lines for delivering care and developing services in other ethnic communities. Valle (1981) emphasized the importance of confidence building, which he regarded as an ongoing process that must be attended to, particularly when professionals from the majority culture are attempting to make inroads into an ethnic community. Valle (1989) has also strongly recommended that professionals learn about the ethnic culture and such concepts as the acculturation continuum before attempting to work within the community. He suggested, as well, that more professional partnerships be developed across ethnicities to accomplish this goal.

Valle (1989), Brownlee (1978), and Green (1982) also emphasized the need for identifying linkages to the ethnic community's natural helpers and endogenous organizations. It is critical to identify the family or kinship networks, aggregate networks, "linkpersons," and community and social service broker networks, all of which provide the community context for the ethnic patient and family.

The third model that underlies the material presented in this chapter is Kleinman's (1980, 1986a) explanatory model (EM). Kleinman (1980) defined EMs as ideas "about an episode of sickness and its treatment that are employed by all those engaged in the clinical process" (p. 105).

Kleinman (1986a) viewed medical systems as both cultural and social systems, emphasizing that the health care system articulates illness in a cultural idiom, linking beliefs about disease etiology, experience of symptoms, and patterns of illness behavior, such as treatment alternatives, therapeutic practices, and the evaluation of treatment outcomes, together. Kleinman specified that most health care systems consist of three arenas: the popular arena, the professional arena, and the folk arena. Most illness is managed solely in the domain of the popular arena, where beliefs about when to seek aid, when to consult healers, whether to comply, and lay evaluation of treatment efficacy all take place. The professional arena includes the professional, scientific, Western biomedical model traditions of healing. The folk arena includes nonprofessional healing specialists. All of these domains influence two aspects of the healing process: (a) the effective control of the disease and (b) the personal and social meaning and experience of the illness.

Practitioners frequently have EMs about the etiology, course, and proper treatment of a sickness that are very different from those of patients and families. Although EMs draw on general cultural beliefs about health and sickness, they are "formed and employed to cope with a specific health problem" (Kleinman, 1980, p. 106).

Understanding that Chinese have very different EMs for dementia from the one used by Western researchers and practitioners is of critical importance, because in some cases these EMs preclude even the use of Western biomedicine from a patient's or family's point of view. In other cases, divergent EMs can lead to misunderstanding or disagreement during clinical encounters between Chinese-speaking patients and families on the one hand and practitioners on the other.

To appreciate fully the nature of the difference between Chinese patient and family EMs of dementia and the biologically based EM used by Western biomedical practitioners, readers need to understand the distinction made by Kleinman (1980) between disease and illness: "*Disease* refers to a malfunctioning of biological and/or psychological processes, while *illness* refers to the psychosocial experience and meaning of perceived disease" (p. 72). Thus, although *disease* refers to processes gone awry within the individual, *illness* is "created by personal, social, and cultural reactions to disease" (p. 72).

All three models underscore the strategies developed and discussed within this chapter. The issues of perceived need, enabling conditions, professional partnerships, EMs, and linkpersons or link agencies form the basis for many of the problems outlined in the next section, Barriers to Care, and the Strategies section.

BARRIERS TO CARE

In this section, barriers to care are viewed from two perspectives: (a) beliefs (EMs) as barriers and (b) family caregiver views of responsibility, obligation, and illness as barriers to successful interventions. As discussed below, the reader should note that patients and families differ as to where on the acculturation continuum they fall and the degree of commitment they may feel to traditional Chinese values.

Chinese Beliefs About Dementia and Alzheimer's Disease

In writing this section, all four coauthors have drawn on their combined experience in providing health and social services to Chinese dementia patients and their families. In addition, the two ethnic Chinese coauthors, both of whom were born and raised in the Chinese-speaking world (Hong Kong and Canton, respectively) have drawn on their own knowledge, as cultural "natives," of widely shared Chinese beliefs about health, illness, and aging. Beliefs about dementia that are commonly encountered in Chinese-speaking communities in the United States are specific expressions of these broader, widely shared Chinese beliefs. These beliefs, in turn, reflect the Chinese cosmological view that an individual's life and well-being are closely intertwined with features of the social, natural, and supernatural worlds.

Normalization of Illness

One of the most common Chinese responses to memory problems and associated behaviors in elderly people is to see these as a normal consequence of growing old. Terms used for dementia in Chinese include ones that translate into English as "stupid and silly" or "less smart." Many Chinese families may not seek services because they do not perceive dementia as an illness, or they may seek services much later in the disease process. This perception may even be reinforced by a Western-trained primary care physician who is him- or herself ethnically Chinese and who shares this perception of aging.

Dementia as Mental Illness

Alternatively, Chinese persons very often interpret the signs and symptoms of dementia as indicative of a mental disorder, especially because dementia manifests symptoms of hallucinations, paranoia, suspiciousness, delusion, catatonia, and disorientation, which are also found in persons with mental disorders like schizophrenia. As a consequence, dementia has also been translated by using two Chinese characters, the first of which means "crazy" and the second "catatonic."

This view of dementia is persistent. For example, during a White House Mini-Conference on Aging held in February 1995 in San Francisco's Chinatown, an informational lecture was presented in Cantonese on dementia symptoms and the disease processes underlying them. Of the 134 Chinese attendees who completed an evaluation instrument, 35% marked the statement "Alzheimer's disease is a form of insanity" as true, while answering four other basic, informational questions about Alzheimer's disease correctly. This suggests that Chinese persons may categorize dementia primarily by the irrational behavior of persons suffering from this illness and the disruptive social and interpersonal consequences it shares with mental disorders. Knowing about the visible, biological pathology of brain cells that underlies the way Western biomedicine categorizes this disease may be irrelevant to their own way of categorizing "behavioral" illnesses.

In any case, this perception of dementia will trigger a strong negative response among Chinese families and will often inhibit their seeking diagnosis and assistance. Mental illness is extremely stigmatizing and considered shameful in Chinese culture (Kleinman, 1986b; Lee, 1982; Phillips, 1993). This, in combination with the cultural admonition that "bad deeds that happen in a family are not to be disclosed to outsiders" because this will bring shame to the family, makes it very unlikely that traditional Chinese caregivers coping with what they believe to be a mental illness will seek outside services, preferring instead to hide both the demented elder and the problem within the family.

Chinese EMs for Dementia Etiology Differ from the Western Biomedical Model

When traditionally oriented Chinese persons do perceive dementia as an illness, they may explain its cause in ways that contrast sharply with the EM for dementia used by Western biomedicine. They may interpret dementia as retribution for the sins of one's ancestors or family misdeeds; the result of the afflicted person's being possessed by supernatural or evil spirits; fate; an imbalance between opposing forms of energy ("yin" and "yang") in the body; or the improper alignment of a house, the grave of an ancestor, or another physical site important to the family's welfare with the forces of nature and other objects in its physical environment.

If a Chinese family believes that the cause of an elder's dementia is one of the above, the family will seek the help of traditional Chinese healers, or of experts within the Chinese community who specialize in such matters as exorcism or geomancy. Herbalists and acupuncturists who perceive dementia symptoms as the result of an imbalance of yin and yang or a blockage of the flow of energy or "chi" within the body believe that their treatments will cure or alleviate these symptoms. In such cases, the family will simply not see Western health care providers as having the kind of expertise needed to heal the afflicted elder and will not seek help from the practitioners of Western biomedicine. If a family believes that the dementia is caused by fate, they may accept the hand that they have been dealt because they do not believe it is possible to change fate.

The Obligation to Care for Elders Within the Family

Family is the important unit in caring for dementia patients with respect to service use (see Lieberman & Fisher, 1994). Thus, knowing about the Chinese family is critical. Although the discussion below focuses on the ways in which Chinese family structure and beliefs can become barriers to care, the reader should remember that they can also be important positive resources in providing care to demented Chinese elders.

The Importance of Family   The family, rather than the individual, is the most important unit of social organization in Chinese culture. Traditionally, the family's goals and interests take precedence over the goals and interests of any individual family member. This helps to maintain harmony within the family, which is highly valued in Chinese culture.

Traditional cultural and Confucian ethical values specifically mandate that the eldest son and his wife care for his parents in their old age. Even when there is no son, or the eldest son is not able to fulfill this role, elderly parents will still expect one of their other children to care for them. In immigrant families in which the adult children have assimilated to mainstream American values, the traditional expectations of an elderly parent frequently conflict with the values and preferences of their adult children. This can lead to intergenerational disagreements and much disappointment for a Chinese elder. This, in turn, can have an impact on patient and family compliance with health care recommendations. Such recommendations may not be followed, for example, because there is conflict within the family as to who is responsible for carrying them out.

Nonetheless, many first-and second-generation Chinese still feel strongly that taking care of their family members within the family, regardless of age, is solely their own physical and moral responsibility. This may have an impact on decisions related to the use of day care, paid aides, and placement in a nursing home or board-and-care facility.

The Importance of the Chinese-Speaking Community   Because the Chinese-speaking community remains the primary cultural and social environment for many Chinese Americans, service providers should not underestimate its influence in judging and sanctioning the behavior of individuals and families (Lee, 1982, pp. 539–540). Although virtually overwhelmed by caring for a demented elder, family caregivers may also be very concerned with what other people will think if the obligation to care for one's own family member is not met. In this situation, inability to provide such care may bring shame and loss of face to the individual caregiver and to the family as a whole, a very serious consequence within the context of traditional Chinese values and interpersonal relationships.

Practitioners must collaborate with Chinese families in devising treatment and care plans that will not cause shame or other difficulties vis-à-vis the Chinese community in which they live. For example, consider the case of the eldest son and daughter-in-law of a demented Chinese woman who have taken on the entire burden of his mother's care, having her live with them and making all decisions about her care with only minimal physical help and decision-making input from this woman's three married daughters. This may conflict with a non-Chinese professional care provider's values about "shared burden" within the family and with his or her belief that an important intervention would be advising all family members to share responsibility for this elderly mother.

Health care and social service providers should recognize this care arrangement as consistent with the traditional Chinese pattern in which (a) the eldest son and his wife are the family members with the culturally mandated responsibility of caring for an elderly parent and (b) a daughter marries into another family, with the responsibility of taking care of her in-laws if married to an eldest son, and is therefore not considered to be part of her natal family. In this traditional pattern, it is inappropriate for daughters (such as the three mentioned in the case above) to come back and intervene in what is now someone else's family. Doing so would also communicate to others in the Chinese community that the eldest son and his wife are unable, or unwilling, to care properly for their parent. Thus, by intervening the daughters could cause their brother and sister-in-law to lose face vis-à-vis a traditionally oriented Chinese community.

In such a case, polite inquiries can be made about whether the daughters have participated in their mother's care at all, but it would be inappropriate for providers to dictate to the eldest son that he should share the burden of care with his sisters or to suggest in any way that the sisters' lack of involvement indicates that there is something "dysfunctional" about the family. Doing this is, in essence, imposing mainstream American family patterns and values on a family whose culture supports and morally values a different care arrangement. Recommendations in this case should be made with the goal of supporting the care arrangement preferred by the family (which can differ from family to family) and providing respite, if desired, for the culturally designated caregivers.

Western professional care providers need to realize that many Chinese American families are socially and culturally embedded in their broader Chinese community. Therefore, working with the broader Chinese community in providing dementia education and services cannot be completely separated from working with individual families. Good services provided to one family may lead to personalized word-of-mouth referrals of other families in this community to such services. Successful community outreach and Alzheimer's education may also change some of the shared ideas in the community about what dementia is and the options that are appropriate in coping with it.

Western professional care providers also need to assess where a particular Chinese family is on the continuum with respect to these issues. As adult children adapt to mainstream American culture, they may hold views about these issues that conflict with those of others in the family.

Avoiding Misfortune in the Future   Belief systems about the causes of misfortune influence a family's motivation and endurance in providing care to a demented elder. For example, failure to care for an elder could bring misfortune in the caregiver's next life, or in the lives of his or her descendants. Caregivers may also fear retribution in this life, in which they may find themselves bereft of family care in old age. In contrast, bearing heavy burdens and enduring harsh conditions will have the opposite effect, as is reflected in the Chinese saying, "The more one suffers in this life, the more blessings will be granted in the next life."

In attempting to intervene, service providers should realize, therefore, that Chinese family caregivers who are clearly stressed and overburdened in caring for a demented elder solely within the family may have profoundly compelling motivations for continuing to do so despite extreme hardship. These are motivations that have deep personal meaning derived from cultural tradition and that are also buttressed by powerful social sanctions within the Chinese community.

Help-Seeking Patterns Among Chinese Immigrants

This section focuses on the ways in which help-seeking patterns can create barriers to care. However, as in the discussion of family structure and beliefs presented above, the reader should remember that these help-seeking patterns can also function as a positive resource for demented Chinese elders and their families. Length of time spent in the United States influences help-seeking patterns among Chinese immigrants. Among Chinese who have arrived recently, older immigrants may seek help in more traditionally Chinese ways, such as praying to their gods, burning incense, having their fortunes regarding an illness told at a temple, using herbal medicines, and going to practitioners of traditional Chinese medicine. Younger immigrants may be more willing to seek help in a mainstream American way, by going to Western-style service agencies and Western-trained medical personnel. However, in many cases, both older and younger immigrants may seek help from a variety of traditional Chinese sources as well as from Western-style agencies.

Immigrants who have been in the United States for some time show help-seeking patterns similar to those of more recently arrived immigrants, although such patterns will vary according to the degree to which the individuals involved have acculturated to mainstream American patterns. Individual immigrants have also been influenced by sociopolitical events in China, such as the Cultural Revolution, and, as such, may have beliefs that are less traditional.

Help-seeking patterns among families that Lee (1982, p. 531) has designated "immigrant-American" can be quite complex and may lead to disagreement between generations in a family with regard to seeking help. In these families, the parents are foreign born and the children American born. The parents, depending on their education, profession, and where they were born and raised, may use a combination of traditional Chinese and mainstream American approaches in seeking help. In contrast, their American-born children will usually use mainstream American approaches. At the far end of this continuum are "immigrant-descendent" families (Lee, 1982, p. 534) in which all family members are American born and will probably seek help in ways that are consistent with mainstream American patterns.

It is very important to determine not only where families are along this continuum, but also where along the continuum various individuals within the same kin network may be located. In fact, individuals within a kin network may differ in ways that invert a service provider's assumptions about the relative importance of the variables discussed above.

In one case, the very recently immigrated husband of a Chinese patient was in serious conflict with his wife's siblings about the appropriateness of bringing her to Western biomedical practitioners in the first place. The husband, a well-educated professional, believed in Western biomedicine and insisted on bringing his wife for a dementia evaluation despite the strenuous—and, for the husband, emotionally painful—disapproval of her siblings. The siblings had lived for many years in the Chinese American community, seeking the help of traditional Chinese healers practicing within this community in times of illness. They simply did not believe in Western biomedicine, despite their long-term residence in the United States.

STRATEGIES FOR PRACTITIONERS WORKING WITH CHINESE: LEARNING TO IDENTIFY WHERE YOUR PATIENT IS ON THE CONTINUUM

There is a great deal of variation within the Chinese-speaking population in the United States. Effectively applying generalized knowledge of Chinese beliefs and family structure to specific clinical cases requires taking this variation into account in a very concrete and practical way. Individuals and families will vary along several different continuua, including the degree of commitment to traditional Chinese values. Practitioners must also use strategies in interacting with clients that accommodate Chinese values and perspectives while also enabling the practitioner to accomplish the goals set by the clinical encounter itself.

Be Knowledgeable About Your Patient

Determine the Patient's Country of Origin and Other Significant Aspects of His or Her Background   Chinese Americans are often mistaken by mainstream Americans as coming from only one part of the world. In fact, members of this ethnic group have come to the United States not only from mainland China or Taiwan, but also from such places as Hong Kong, Singapore, Vietnam, and other Southeast Asian countries. The political, social, and economic characteristics of a patient's country of origin can be significant in determining the kinds of services that are needed by, and appropriate for, him or her and expectations of what constitutes care. Urban-rural and class differences are also important to consider. Life in a rural Taiwanese village is very different from that in the center of Taipei, Taiwan's crowded and industrial capital.

Determine the Language or Dialect Spoken by the Patient and the Patient's Family   Chinese is not one language, but a family of languages and dialects, although the written characters are the same. The most common Chinese dialects spoken among Chinese immigrants in the United States are Cantonese, Toishanese, and Mandarin. If one is using interpreters to provide service, it is critical to have one who speaks the correct dialect.

Determine the Immigration History of the Patient and the Impact It Has Had on the Availability of a Kin Network in Old Age   Immigration exclusion acts that were passed in the United States (including the Chinese Exclusion Act of 1882 and the National Origins Quota Act in 1924) severely restricted Chinese immigration, prevented immigrant Chinese men from bringing their families over to join them, and banned the immigration of Chinese women in general (Gould-Martin & Ngin, 1981; Nee & Nee, 1973). War and successive political upheaval in China also prevented men from returning home to settle or to find wives. As a result, many Chinese men remained single and childless or lived for decades as "married singles" separated from wives and children left behind in China. This has resulted in a large number of elderly Chinese men residing in American Chinatowns who have no family members to care for them in their old age and who therefore comprise a unique subpopulation with special needs within the Chinese American elderly population as a whole.

In contrast, the liberalization of U.S. immigration policy in 1965 resulted in an increase in the number of Chinese allowed to immigrate to the United States and permitted Chinese women and family members of already-resident Chinese to enter the country as well (Gould-Martin & Ngin, 1981; Nee & Nee, 1973). This has allowed other Chinese to grow old in the United States with spouses and kinship networks in place.

It is important, therefore, for service providers to determine the immigration history of an elderly Chinese person and whether a spouse or kinship network even exists in a particular elder's case, instead of assuming that all Chinese elders will, as a matter of course, have family members available to provide assistance and support.

Be Knowledgeable About Chinese Family Structure and Decision Making

Identify the Decision Maker in the Family and Consult with This Individual   The hierarchical structure of traditionally oriented Chinese families can have a great deal of impact on if, when, and how assistance may be sought from outside of the family. The decision maker in a Chinese family is usually the husband or the oldest male or female in the household. This traditional hierarchy, based on age and gender, is explicitly sanctioned by Confucian ethics, which have been practiced widely in one form or another for more than 2,000 years in the Chinese-speaking world and define what is considered to be morally proper behavior within the family. Failure to adhere to these moral standards can be very disruptive in traditionally oriented families.

When they encounter this kind of hierarchical family structure in Chinese families, service providers should respect its considerable social, cultural, and moral strength and its consequent impact on decision making about a demented elder. The existence of this traditionally oriented family decision-making pattern in any particular family does not necessarily preclude a successful intervention. However, it will be necessary to consult with the culturally sanctioned decision maker before any decision is made in order to avoid open conflict and disharmony within the family and to decrease further barriers to health interventions.

Service providers should identify the decision maker and try to use this individual as a leverage point in implementing a treatment plan, utilizing services, and addressing the needs of a patient, recognizing that in some cases this may be the only chance for success. However, practitioners must also recognize that success—from the Western biomedical–social service perspective, at any rate—may not be achieved, despite the use of culturally appropriate strategies that can, in fact, work with other Chinese families.

In one case, for example, the demented father in a traditionally oriented Chinese family had become physically violent toward other family members, particularly his wife. Because family members were in danger of being injured during these violent outbursts, and because there were other serious difficulties in caring for him and preventing him from wandering, the clinical team strongly recommended the family consider placing the father in an institution. The eldest son, however, refused to consider this option, explaining that Chinese do not give their elders over to the care of people outside the family. He could not repay his debt of gratitude to his father by abandoning him in this way.

However, behind the scenes in this family, the matter was not so clear-cut. During a home visit conducted as part of a 6-month reevaluation, the distraught mother of the family confided to a Chinese nurse that she very much wanted the father to be institutionalized, that he constantly attacked her, and that she was afraid for her own physical safety. The younger sons in this family—all adults like their older brother—concurred with the mother. At this point, in fact, the oldest son had moved away for business reasons, having delegated the physical care of his father to his mother and brothers, all of whom continued to live in the same household with the demented father.

Despite their serious concerns about the physical safety of everyone involved, both the mother and younger sons stated to members of the clinical team that they had no choice other than to submit to the authority of the eldest son, the designated decision maker. Clinical team members found this willingness to obey the eldest son extremely difficult to understand under the circumstances, and initially encouraged the mother and sons to assert themselves in a way consistent with the more democratic family structure found in American mainstream culture. Both mother and sons refused to do this, saying that things could be resolved only if the eldest son changed his mind. This, and a cultural explanation of Chinese family structure and decision making, convinced the clinical team that the eldest son should be made the primary target for education and persuasion. A concerted effort was then made by the clinical team to change the eldest son's mind about institutionalizing his father, an effort that, unfortunately, was unsuccessful.

Working with Clients Who Combine Western and Chinese Treatments

Many Chinese rely heavily on traditional Chinese healing practices and treatments. They may, for example, combine Western medications with Chinese herbal medicine without telling anyone. Kathryn Sabrena Elliott, an author of this chapter and a medical anthropologist and sociocultural gerontologist, has accompanied the home visiting nurse on visits to Chinese dementia patients. She quickly discovered that Chinese family members would bring out all the Western medicines prescribed when the nurse asked to see the patient's medications. Matters would end there unless the medical anthropologist politely asked, in the context of discussing medications in general, whether the patient was also using any Chinese herbal medicines. Inevitably, family members would pull out a drawer full of such medicines and willingly explain the purpose and proper use of each.

Clinicians should always ask Chinese-speaking patients if they are currently using treatment options other than Western biomedicine and whether they are experiencing any problems in doing so. If the clinician asks this in the context of gathering information on all the medicines and treatments that a patient is using, Chinese patients will probably be less likely to feel that their use of Chinese medicine is being singled out for possible negative scrutiny by a Westerner. A clinician who works frequently with Chinese dementia patients and their families should make the effort to learn enough about traditional Chinese medicine to assure the patient that he or she understands and accepts that these are legitimate and frequently used options in the Chinese community.

If providers have any concerns about the mix of Western and Chinese medicines, unusual symptoms, or drug reactions, consultation can be sought from those knowledgeable about Chinese medicines in the community, through a university-based school of pharmacy, or a pharmacist.

Establishing Personal Relationships of Trust and Reciprocity as a Prerequisite to Doing Alzheimer's Outreach and Clinical Practice in Ethnic Chinese Communities

Service providers and others working with the Chinese-speaking community must recognize the profound influence of culture and individuals' perceptions of the degree to which they are embedded in personal relationships of reciprocal dependency and intimate connectedness in shaping the social world of the Chinese. Establishing personal relationships of trust and reciprocity, or *guanxi,* is a core value in Chinese culture.

The importance for service providers of taking the time and making the effort to cultivate guanxi connections in the Chinese community in general, and with Chinese dementia patients and their families in particular, cannot be overemphasized. Doing so is a critical prerequisite for carrying out successful Alzheimer's outreach with ethnic Chinese service providers and family caregivers. Carefully and deliberately cultivating such personal connections contrasts with the more impersonal style of professional practice in American society and may, in fact, seem to constitute unprofessional behavior from the cultural perspective of mainstream American service providers.

Nonetheless, such personal relationships of trust and reciprocity are seen "by Chinese everywhere" to have "primacy and binding power . . . in meeting the needs and desires of everyday life" (Yang, 1994, p. 6). Pursuing and cultivating guanxi is the Chinese way of getting many things done, of opening doors that would otherwise remain closed. Because Western practitioners will be knocking on many of these doors in the Chinese community, they must use the right key or be locked out.

Developing Chinese User-Friendly Services: The Role of Chinese Legitimation in Service Delivery and Connecting with Respected Agencies for Program Development and the Role of Professional Partnerships and Link Persons

Ethnic Chinese service agencies and health facilities are often quite insulated from the non-Chinese community and are frequently culturally self-sufficient. This is very much the case in San Francisco's Chinese community, for example, where a sophisticated infrastructure of ethnic social service agencies and health care facilities is firmly in place. Because of this insularity and self-sufficiency, mainstream practitioners wishing to provide services to Chinese persons must cultivate personal links with the individuals who run the well-known and important ethnic agencies in the Chinese community and with other community leaders who are trusted, respected, and well-known in the community as a whole. These individuals are legitimizing gatekeepers vis-à-vis outside service agencies and health care facilities. Mainstream service providers simply must acquire the cooperation and assistance of these linkage persons in order to gain legitimacy, credibility, and trust within the Chinese community.

How can such links be cultivated? Outside service providers should make overtures to linkage persons over a period of time with the initial goal of introducing themselves personally and building collegial friendships; in this way linkage persons come to know the outside practitioners as persons and know that they share some personal experiences and professional goals. Once such personal rapport and trust have been established, they can be built on incrementally by offering ideas about potentially fruitful collaboration and resources to facilitate this collaboration. Service providers must realize that this is a delicate negotiation that can take a long time. They may be creating barriers by initially introducing themselves to linkage persons and then immediately suggesting a large-scale collaboration. This is most likely to be seen as an attempted intrusion by strangers who know little about the Chinese community and its ways and whose motives for wishing to serve the community are unknown, and possibly even suspect.

This latter point is an extremely important one. Practitioners must remember the egregious history of discrimination against the Chinese by mainstream American institutions and that the Chinese created their own mutual aid associations and service agencies in part to protect themselves from this discrimination. One of the roles of gatekeeping linkage persons or linkage agencies is to continue to protect the community from possible mainstream discrimination and from non-Chinese strangers pressuring for access to the community.

The first, critical phase in which personal social links are established and cultivated can take several years, and the timeline for an overall outreach effort must allow for this. For example, it took Mariann Di Minno, the second author of this chapter, 3 years to develop the critical social relationships within the Chinese service community before the successful collaborative project could even begin.

Hiring bilingual and bicultural staff members is also highly recommended in doing outreach with the Chinese community—with, however, one important caveat. Ethnic Chinese professionals representing an agency outside of the Chinese service network who are themselves new to that particular Chinese community must also be given time to establish critical guanxi social connections within that community. As ethnic bilingual Chinese, these staff members will not be seen as strangers to Chinese culture and custom. They will, however, be seen as personal strangers to the individuals already in the Chinese service community and as representing a ''stranger'' service agency.

This is demonstrated well by the experience of Alicia Mei Tu in initially establishing herself in San Francisco's Chinese service community. Despite the fact that she is herself Chinese and Chinese-speaking, she was new to this community and had no preestablished relationships. She also worked for a highly respected agency, but one that had not yet been legitimated within the Chinese service community. As a result, many ethnic Chinese service providers were not interested in working with her, telling her that they had never heard of the agency for which she worked, even though this agency is located only half a block from the gate of San Francisco's Chinatown. It took her 3 months to cultivate the guanxi connections that allowed her to function well within this community, and she continues to cultivate such social connections within and outside of San Francisco as an important component of functioning professionally.

Developing Personal Rapport with Patients and Families

Establishing Personal Rapport with Chinese in Clinical Settings Is Important Because establishing guanxi is a core value in Chinese culture, it is only natural from the Chinese perspective for Chinese-speaking elderly patients and their families to bring this cultural emphasis on personal relationships of trust and reciprocity directly into clinical encounters with them as they seek dementia-related help. Indeed, doctors of traditional Chinese medicine frequently establish personal rapport as part of their clinical practice, in which ''there is (ideally) a sense of partnership between doctor and patient in perceiving and managing the illness's characteristics and course'' (Farquhar, 1994, p. 45). Therefore, many patients are likely to expect this from Western service providers as well. Chinese-speaking patients and their families who are inexperienced with the more impersonal style of Western medical practitioners and other Western service providers may consequently judge these individuals as being less competent professionally than the Chinese healers with whom they are most familiar, and they may avoid Western services in the future as a result.

However, an important caveat must be added here. In Chinese culture, personalized relationships with respected individuals of authority are simultaneously formal and hierarchical, contradictory as this may seem to mainstream Americans, who tend to equate personal relationships with informality and equality. Thus, Chinese will expect service providers to maintain both professional authority and formal demeanor even while exchanging personalized information to establish rapport.

Personal Rapport Is a Prerequisite for Disclosing Private Matters to the Clinician   Chinese are typically reluctant to discuss private family matters with people outside of the family, especially matters that are considered highly negative, shameful, or stigmatizing, as is the case with some of the symptoms of dementia. Clinicians and service providers frequently find that Chinese families will not be forthcoming about such matters until some kind of personal rapport has been established with the service provider. Nor will family members necessarily be honest about their growing inability to care for a demented elder and their desire for outside help, both of which are also a potential source of shame and stigma, if they do not personally know and trust the service provider.

How Does One Build Rapport?   Service providers must understand that it may take several sessions with clients before enough rapport is established to facilitate full client disclosure. Rather than maintaining the impersonal mask of Western professionalism, service providers should allow time at the beginning of an evaluation for engaging in social chit-chat with the patient and the patient's family, in which both sides exchange information about their backgrounds, interests, and hobbies. If a Chinese client discovers that the service provider has similar interests or hobbies or has had similar personal experiences—positive or negative—this will greatly enhance rapport and allow the client and his or her family to trust and relate more easily to the service provider. This will, in turn, lead to more complete and honest disclosure of information vital to the clinical process. A practitioner might set the tone for this social chit-chat by asking patients and their families where they come from, how long they have been in the United States, and what kind of food they enjoy eating. The Chinese saying "People regard food as the most important aspect of life" illustrates the relevance of this topic for Chinese Americans, especially those who are recently arrived immigrants.

Communication Styles That Enhance Interactions

1   Respect should be shown to patients, clients, and family members by addressing them by their last names. Particular respect should be shown to elderly people. The cultural importance of showing respect according to age is reflected in the Chinese language itself by the use of differentiated terms of address. A Chinese man, a Mr. Wong, for example, would prefer to be addressed as *Wong sin-san* (in Cantonese) or *Wang xiansheng* (in Mandarin) if he is a relatively young man. However, if he is elderly he would prefer to be addressed as *Wong bark-bark* (in Cantonese) or *Wang gong-gong* (in Mandarin). Non-Chinese-speaking practitioners can approximate such verbal indicators of respect by using deferential intonations and polite language in English.

Elders, especially ones who are less well educated and from rural areas, often view themselves as wiser than younger people. Therefore, recommended treatments and services may not be accepted during an initial session, especially with a younger service provider, depending on how an elder or members of his or her family weigh the prestige and authority of the practitioner against that of the elder concerned. Practitioners should show much respect even when an elder is demented. The demented individual may still be able to sense what might be construed as disrespect and become angry or agitated. Family members present at an evaluation will also want proper respect to be shown to their elder, whether the elder him- or herself is able to understand what is going on.

2   Assure clients of confidentiality. Despite cultural reluctance to discuss private matters outside of the family and the potential stigma regarding dementia, more and more Chinese are willing to approach service providers for help, especially if confidentiality is assured and personal trust established. The practitioner should emphasize that knowing certain information is very important for giving the patient the best, most helpful care and that this information will be made available only to other practitioners who will also want to give the patient the best care possible.

3   It is best to avoid constant direct eye contact while interacting with patients and family members. At best, this will be considered very rude. At worst, this may be interpreted as a challenge or confrontation of some kind (Lee, 1982, p. 548). The clinician should make brief, repeated eye contact while conversing with Chinese individuals, alternated with periods of looking away (at the patient's chart, e.g.).

4   Be aware of cultural taboos. It is crucial to understand that strong taboos exist in Chinese culture about discussing certain topics. These topics include sex, illness, accidents, hospitals, police stations, family problems, and death and dying (Lee, 1982, p. 537). From the Chinese perspective, discussion of these topics can bring bad luck. In fact, seeking a medical evaluation around the Chinese New Year can be unlucky, in and of itself. More traditional Chinese people do not wish to begin a new year in such an inauspicious manner, for this might bring them an entire year of misfortune. Clearly, working with demented elders and their families will require discussing some taboo topics, but they should be approached with the utmost care. A practitioner might, for example, preface a question about one of these topics by emphasizing, as in the case of assuring confidentiality, that finding out about these things that people should, of course, not normally discuss is necessary in order for him or her to give the patient or client the best, most accurate, and most helpful care and that, therefore, the client must excuse the asking of such a sensitive question and make an exception in discussing it.

5 Try to persuade family members that improvements are, in fact, possible in coping with a demented elder if they learn how to manage difficult behaviors. Persuading family members of this is especially important if they are fatalistic about the situation in which they find themselves.

6 Make sure family members understand any recommendations being made. A good way to do this is to ask the patient or family member to repeat at the end of the session, in his or her own words, these recommendations to the clinician, or the translator (Haffner, 1992, pp. 258–259). To accommodate poor ability in English or forestall translation problems, use simple and direct language. Keep in mind that Chinese who do not really understand what they have been told may say they do out of politeness or embarrassment. Service providers should also take the initiative with families who are unfamiliar with the organization and structure of Western services by making appointments for them and guiding them step by step through the process, if possible.

Western Interventions Can Be Adapted to Match the Needs of Chinese Patients and Families

Throughout this chapter, it has been emphasized that there are cultural values, concepts, social structures, and ways of interacting and communicating with other people that are widely shared among the Chinese. Chinese-speaking immigrants will confront frailty and illness in a demented family member and seek help in coping with this very human predicament in ways that are natural for them and culturally assumed, like people from any cultural background. To provide genuinely valuable help to demented Chinese-speaking elders and their families, Western service providers must come to understand, respect, and work, at least in part, within the framework of cultural values very different from their own. The vignettes and practical suggestions included in this chapter are examples of how this can be done. Practitioners are encouraged, as well, to learn enough about Chinese culture and social structure to devise their own solutions to individualized situations as they come up.

Avoid Cultural Stereotyping

The most common danger for service providers who are working with individuals from a different cultural background, and who know something in general about that particular culture, is the tendency to engage in cultural stereotyping, simplifying and misinterpreting culture as something frozen into immutable "traditions," which then apply mechanically, equally, and predictably to all individuals from a particular background. The truth is that individuals can vary in unexpected ways, even within the same kin network, as two of the chapter vignettes illustrated. Cultural traditions are, in reality, changing all the time, and have always done so.

Professionals working with Chinese-speaking families must integrate knowledge of what is, in general, culturally shared among the Chinese with the heterogeneity that nonetheless exists among families and individuals, here and in Chinese-speaking countries. They can accomplish this, ironically, by doing what is most familiar to them, acting as good clinicians, and using case-specific models. All good clinicians work from generalized bodies of knowledge, whether these bodies of knowledge refer to human physiology, to the social services available, or, in this case, to Chinese cultural values and social structures. The difficult, challenging task is, as always, to apply this knowledge to individual patients and clients, discovering what is and what is not true and what the implications of this are in each particular case. Chinese-speaking patients and their families will be more satisfied with services provided to them, and more likely to return for additional services, if a Western practitioner can accomplish this task.

REFERENCES

Anderson, R., & Newman, J. F. (1975). Societal and individual determinants of medical care utilization in the United States. *Milbank Memorial Fund Quarterly, 51*(1), 95–124.

Brownlee, A. T. (1978). *Community, culture, and care: A cross-cultural guide for health workers*. St. Louis: C. V. Mosby.

Farquhar, J. (1994). *Knowing practice: The clinical encounter of Chinese medicine*. Boulder, CO: Westview Press.

Gould-Martin, K., & Ngin, C. (1981). Chinese Americans. In A. Harwood (Ed.), *Ethnicity and medical care* (pp. 130–171). Cambridge, MA: Harvard University Press.

Green, J. W. (1982). *Cultural awareness in the human services*. Englewood Cliffs, NJ: Prentice-Hall.

Haffner, L. (1992). Translation is not enough—interpreting in a medical setting. *The Western Journal of Medicine, 157*(3), 255–259.

Kleinman, A. (1980). *Patients and healers in the context of culture: An exploration of the borderland between anthropology, medicine and psychiatry*. Berkeley: University of California Press.

Kleinman, A. (1986a). Concepts and a model for the comparison of medical systems as cultural systems. In C. Currer & M. Stacey (Eds.), *Concepts of health, illness and disease* (pp. 27–50). New York: Berg.

Kleinman, A. (1986b). *Social origins of distress and disease: Depression, neurasthenia, and pain in modern China*. New Haven, CT: Yale University Press.

Lee, E. (1982). A social systems approach to assessment and treatment for Chinese American families. In M. McGoldrick, J. K. Pearce, & J. Giordano (Eds.), *Ethnicity and family therapy* (pp. 527–551). New York: Guilford Press.

Lieberman, M. A., & Fisher, L. (1994). Alzheimer's disease: The impact of family characteristics on spouses, offsprings and inlaws. *Family Process*, 305–325.

Nee, V. G., & Nee, B. B. (1973). *Longtime Californ': A documentary study of an American Chinatown*. New York: Pantheon Books.

Phillips, M. R. (1993). Strategies used by Chinese families coping with schizophrenia. In D. Davis & S. Harrell (Eds.), *Chinese families in the post-Mao era* (pp. 277–306). Berkeley: University of California Press.

Valle, R. (1981). Natural support systems, minority groups and the late life dementias: Implications for service delivery, research and policy. In N. Miller & G. D. Cohen (Eds.), *Clinical aspects of Alzheimer's disease and senile dementia* (pp. 287–299). New York: Raven Press.

Valle, R. (1989). Outreach to ethnic minorities with Alzheimer's disease: The challenge to the community. *Health Matrix VI* (1, Winter 1988–89), 13–27.

Yang, M. M. (1994). *Gifts, favors, and banquets: The art of social relationships in China*. Ithaca, NY: Cornell University Press.

Chapter 9

Techniques of Working with Japanese American Families

Phyllis M. Tempo
Ann Saito

Families of elderly Japanese Americans may benefit from culturally sensitive approaches by health care professionals, given the likelihood that dementia increases with age and acculturation. Larson (1993) reported that the prevalence of risk factors for vascular dementia in this population is high and therefore raised concerns as the number of older Japanese Americans increase (see Chapter 2). This chapter describes the needs and culturally based behaviors of this population, identified by each generation, historical experiences, cultural beliefs and practices, and degree of acculturation, while taking into account individual differences. Several case studies are presented. One case describes how the stigma attached to the behavioral aspects of dementia may be perceived by a Japanese American family and their ethnic community, as a result of a lack of education about and understanding of the illness. This chapter also explains how Japanese American family structure departs from its traditional definition in the acculturation process and addresses how service providers can assess family members' degree of cultural identification so that appropriate and culturally sensitive approaches may be applied. As there has been limited research in this specialized field of study, the goal of this chapter is to sensitize practitioners to the major cultural issues, needs, and empirical observations of this population so that education, training, and services can be effectively modified.

HISTORICAL AND CULTURAL BACKGROUND

Historically significant events experienced by the pioneering Japanese immigrants and their succeeding generations have influenced the acculturation of Japanese Americans. Henkin (1985) explained that naming each generation in the United States is unique to Japanese Americans, thus distinguishing them from other immigrant groups in the United States. Naming emphasizes a generation's degree of attachment to either a traditional or a new value. Furthermore, a Japanese descendant's cultural and individual identification can be determined by that person's proximity to traditional Japanese values and social norms (Henkin, 1985). The generations described in this chapter include the following: *Issei*, the first-generation Japanese immigrant; *Nisei*, the American-born second generation; and *Sansei*, the third generation. Owing to the limitations of this chapter, the *Yonsei* and *Gosei*, the fourth and fifth generations, respectively, are not elaborated on. There are also the *Kibei*, who have returned to the United States after living in Japan, and the "new Issei," the Japanese who have immigrated since 1954, including the *kai-sha*, the relocated Japanese businessmen (Kitano, 1981).

Issei: The First Generation

The pioneering Issei immigration of young males, mostly from the southern prefectures of Yamaguchi and Hiroshima, occurred between 1890 and 1924. This group established a legacy of tolerance and perseverance despite numerous adversities. Marital arrangements by means of "picture brides" created the first Japanese American families (Kitano, 1981). Immigration was halted because of the 1924 Immigration Exclusion Act, which denied Japanese people admission into the United States because they were ineligible for citizenship and which limited all immigration to the United States (Herman, 1974). Ichioka (1988) explained that this act symbolized the Issei's inability to stop exclusion, despite all their efforts to adapt and assimilate; therefore, they assumed their traditional values of moral obligation and duty to support their Nisei children, and hoped for a brighter future through Nisei life experiences and accomplishments. This act was not repealed until 1952, and limited immigration ensued for Japanese and other Asian immigrants (Herman, 1974). Other major legal actions that targeted the Japanese in America include the 1906 segregation of Japanese school children by the San Francisco School Board; the 1908 Gentleman's Agreement, which limited immigration of Japanese laborers; and the 1913 (California) Alien Land Law, which was the first anti-Japanese land law, limiting land leases to 3 years. Then on February 19, 1942, President Roosevelt signed Executive Order No. 9066, which authorized the evacuation and internment of people of Japanese ancestry (Herman, 1974).

Traditional Values of the Issei Generation   Kitano (1981) described the Issei as having brought with them certain values and world views reflecting

"Meiji Japan," such as *gaman*, or emotional self-restraint, and *enryo*, or deferential behavior, especially to those in authority. In addition to language difficulties, some Meiji Japan–era values that differ from American values include (a) encouraging collectivity versus preference for individuality; (b) duty and obligation versus will and freedom; and (c) hierarchical orders and dependency versus relying on self, egalitarianism, and independence (Kitano, 1981). Similarly, Henkin (1985) described certain traditional cultural values stemming from Confucian, Buddhist, and Shintoist teachings that have helped to enhance the resiliency and adaptability of Japanese Americans, such as the importance of inner discipline, which encourages individuals to conceal frustrations and disappointments, to suppress individual concerns to those of the group, to acknowledge filial piety (*oyakoko*) and moral obligations to others (*giri*) as having priority over personal desires, to persevere in a task despite displeasure and the probability of defeat or failure, and to have a strong sense of family honor and esteem. As a result of these strongly held values, most Issei have raised families in their ethnic community to maintain their Japanese identity and confine their problem solving to their families.

Nisei: The Second Generation

The Nisei generation were raised under the rubric of the Meiji Japan–era cultural values instilled by their Issei parents. They were simultaneously encouraged to be more American than the Americans, owing to World War II and relocation (Henkin, 1985). Nisei were compelled to prove their loyalty despite their status as American citizens; more than 3,000 men from Hawaii and about 1,500 men from the mainland volunteered to demonstrate their loyalty by serving in the 442nd Regimental Combat Team and the 100th Infantry Battalion. After fighting successfully in seven major military campaigns, these men received 18,143 individual decorations for valor, the most highly decorated units in U.S. history (Presidio Army Museum, 1981). It was not until almost 50 years after the incarceration and loss of their civil rights that Japanese Americans received an apology from the U.S. government (Fong, 1992).

Impact of World War II on the Nisei Family and Community   The internment of individuals of Japanese ancestry caused both Issei and Nisei to rely on their traditional cultural practices of patience, docility, and industry as defenses against racial hostilities (Henkin, 1985). Nisei also inherited the Issei defense mechanism, *shi-ka-ta-ga-nai*, meaning "it can't be helped," which provided inner strength to prevail during this traumatic period (Kitano, 1981). Kitano (1981) described the internment experience as a destruction of the West Coast "ghettos" and family life, because government control took over, which resulted in prison camp norms replacing family norms. Many Nisei spent their adolescent years incarcerated while their older brothers fought in the U.S. Army in Europe or their siblings were relocated to other parts of the country. In addition, the relocation experience disrupted the Japanese community, as Issei and Nisei residents were separated and sent to internment camps in several states. Fong (1992) explained how the government did not trust the Issei as much as the Nisei, and therefore chose to deal with only the Nisei. This process undermined the structures of family and community stability even more (Furuto et al., 1992).

Although the massive internment occurred on the mainland United States, there were also 1,875 people of Japanese ancestry from Hawaii interned in prison camps on the mainland, 981 of whom had been rounded up by federal agents immediately after the bombing of Pearl Harbor (Herman, 1974). Despite the fact that the majority of Hawaiian Nisei were spared, the Martial Law Administration of the territory ordered the closing of Japanese-language schools and the dismantling of the Japanese cultural network, a linkage to Japan. A strong emphasis was placed on Americanization among the Japanese in Hawaii throughout the duration of World War II. Included in this effort was the adoption of unregistered Christian first names. Postwar generations were given official Western first names and traditional Japanese middle names. Some individuals were named after American war heroes (McDermott, Tseng, & Maretzki, 1980).

Both mainland and Hawaiian Nisei share similarities in their efforts to be recognized and accepted as legitimate Americans and to be treated with respect and dignity with full civil rights. They share a conflicted state of existence because they were raised under Issei traditions. According to Kim (1990), despite their not entirely accepting traditional values in their accelerated efforts to assimilate, Nisei have been influenced by their Issei parents, who believe in the Buddhist teachings of "filial devotion and loving indulgence between old and young" (p. 351). The Nisei have incorporated such Issei traditional values in their lives by including their Issei parents in family activities and feeling a strong sense of responsibility for them; they have pursued higher education and economic prosperity as means of not only honoring their parents, but also sustaining their family dignity and pride. In contrast, Osako (1976; as cited in S. Sue & Morishima, 1982) found that although Nisei felt the need to make sacrifices in order to support their parents, the majority felt that a higher priority was providing for their own children's education. This type of closeness within the family where couples frequently give financial assistance to their parents creates problems involving individual desires versus family obligations (S. Sue & Morishima, 1982). Additional research (Leonetti [1983], as cited in Uba, 1994) has found that although there are some older Nisei who expect to live and be taken care of by their family, many retired Nisei generally do not want to live with their adult children. This contradicts one of the sacred traditional values, which Kitano (1990) described as a form of reciprocity, as young parents are expected to raise their children, who then will take care of them when they become older, which is closely tied to family roles and filial piety.

Sansei: The Third Generation

Takaki (1993) described the Sansei generation as recognized for its political action stemming from their investigation of their Issei grandparents' and Nisei parents' past World War II internment experiences. They demanded redress and reparations. In 1988, Congress passed a bill that provided a token financial compensation and provided an official apology for denial of civil rights to the survivors of the internment camps. Although it has been about a century since their grandparents arrived as immigrants to this country and faced a continuous series of anti-Japanese sentiments, this generation has not been free from current acts of racism and discrimination. They have endured widespread Japan-bashing in the 1980s and 1990s, including acts of insensitivity and even physical violence ending in death. Chan (1991; as cited in Fong, 1992) explained that such was the case of Vincent Chin, a Chinese American. He was assumed to be a Japanese American and was killed by two unemployed Caucasian American men who justified their killing on the basis of their frustration that sales of Japanese cars were hurting the sales of American cars (Fong, 1992).

According to Henkin (1985), Sansei, as well as the succeeding generations, are under enormous pressure to make it in the United States, or to overachieve, because they have frequently been raised in their families by assimilation-oriented Nisei who aspire to goals of worldly achievements and material successes and desire their children to be "model modern Americans." The Sansei are therefore caught in a double bind, because unless they are what other Americans may consider conspicuously successful, they may be perceived as failures by their Nisei parents. At the same time, Nisei parents declare that they are encouraging their Sansei children to be flexible in personal and professional choices and goals. Although the Sansei have acculturated to the point of being American in their thoughts, feelings, behavior, dress, and speech, they cannot replace their physical features, which mark their identity with their vulnerability to discrimination. According to Kitano (1981), despite their individual differences, their physical identity is important in shaping their ethnic identity.

Kibei

Daniels (1988) defined Kibei as Nisei who have been sent to Japan to obtain a Japanese education and cultural experience. These individuals differ from other Nisei by their fluency in the Japanese language. The accurate number of Kibei in the United States is unknown, although Nisei males were more likely to have been sent to Japan than were females. It is estimated that there would have been about 11,000 Kibei during World War II. Many anecdotal reports have proved that many Kibei eventually felt uncomfortable in both cultures. The dilemma as to why only some Nisei children were sent to Japan still exists.

New Immigrants

Takaki (1989) reported that there are few newly immigrated Issei; they constituted only 3% of the Asian immigrants between 1965 and 1984. The Kai-Sha, or Japanese businessmen, are part of the new immigrants. They and their families bring special problems related to their temporary stay in the United States, including cultural differences, coping with loneliness and alienation, and establishing meaningful relationships (Kitano, 1981). Their temporary residence status with their families raises questions about how this particular group's needs can be met with our Western health care system and treatment approaches.

Impact of Dementia on Family Cohesiveness

Yamamoto and Iga (1974; as cited in Baker, 1990) reported that the Japanese American family remains closely knit, including the Yonsei, who are considered acculturated. The family values focus on social interactions, interdependency, hierarchical relationships, and empathy (*omoiyan*). This contrasts with Caucasian American culture, which emphasizes democracy and individuality. However, according to Baker (1990), the Issei and Nisei generations view mental illness, such as dementia, as a stigma. If this stigma is known in the community, the family members will be considered undesirable and impaired. Thus, the stigma of mental illness causes the family to be reluctant to seek treatment. A patient may be sick for a very long time before being brought in for help. Therefore, Issei are reluctant to use mental health services. The Issei's emphasis is on self-improvement, tension reduction, relief of psychosomatic symptoms, insomnia, and depression. As a result, the acculturated Nisei and Sansei are in a practical position to advocate on behalf of their older family members with community resources (Baker, 1990).

CASE VIGNETTES

To illustrate some of the important considerations in working with Japanese American families with dementia, the following cases are presented. They are based on actual cases known by authors, although the names have been changed to preserve confidentiality. The fourth case of Mr. Haneda is expanded to illustrate in more detail the process of accepting mental health services, to illustrate points about the stigma of dementia, and to discuss culturally sensitive techniques in treatment.

The Case of Mrs. Ito

Mrs. Ito is an 80-year-old Issei woman with dementia who lived most of her life in Japan. The family lived and worked on a farm. Her husband was not the eldest son and consequently did not share in the inheritance. The farm could not support such a large extended family, and her sons chose to emigrate to the United States where they first worked as field laborers. Over a period of time, they were able to save a little money to purchase a small parcel of farm land. Eventually, each son married an Issei woman. Each of their wives worked on the farm. A short while after Mrs. Ito's husband died, she was called to the United States to live and be taken care of by her sons.

Although she and her sons had not seen one another for several years, it was assumed that Mrs. Ito would be cared for by her family. In addition to all of the changes that life in the United States would present, Mrs. Ito began to show signs of dementia. She had difficulty remembering where she was, the names of people she knew, and the day of the week. Her speech was disassociated and rambling. The family's biggest complaint was that she spent most of the day sleeping and most of the night keeping them awake. They brought her to the senior center hoping that she might enjoy being with other elderly Japanese like herself and also with the hope that she might exhaust herself so everyone could get a good night's sleep.

Initially, Mrs. Ito was delighted to be with such "kind and happy" people. She entered into every activity that was presented and laughed at her efforts. As her dementia worsened and her speech became more fragmented, Mrs. Ito was not able to follow the group activities and would fall asleep.

Mrs. Ito's son's acceptance of responsibility for his mother's care and happiness even after many years of separation is an example of *oyakoko*, filial piety, duty, and obligation to one's parents. It is important to recognize that the family may have authority over the elderly Issei's decisions that must be respected (Benedict, 1946). Mrs. Ito's oldest son was the only person in the family who had contact with the staff of the senior center. All their inquiries were referred to him; he brought his mother to the center and paid all her fees.

The Case of Mrs. Naito

Mrs. Naito is a 75-year-old Issei woman with dementia who had been widowed for several years. She lived alone in her home. Her three children lived in adjacent cities. The family made frequent visits to check on their mother. Mrs. Naito always reassured them that she was well, and they should not worry.

Mrs. Naito's responses to her children's inquiries is an example of the Japanese phrase *meiwaku o kekenai yoni,* meaning "not to put a burden on another person," emphasizing the value of being responsible for yourself (Ishi-zuka,1978). It can be very difficult even for family members to determine if there is a problem and if help is needed.

It became apparent that Mrs. Naito needed help when a relative found her wandering in town, unable to recognize familiar surroundings. Mrs. Naito was still able to remember a familiar face and some names but could not recall what she had done the day before. Initially, she stayed with her son with the understanding that repair work needed to be done on her home. During this time, the family observed unusual behaviors and soon came to realize that their mother could no longer live by herself. She could still perform simple activities such as sweeping, ironing, and washing dishes but could not prepare a meal. Mrs. Naito needed assistance with bathing and began to repeat herself in conversations.

Several family meetings were held to discuss problem-solving strategies. All of her children worked, and no one was available on a continuous basis. One daughter had a flexible working schedule that allowed her to take her mother to a senior day care center and, with the help of her husband and children, look after her during the week. Over the weekend, Mrs. Naito visited either her son or youngest daughter, which gave the oldest daughter's family a brief respite.

The pattern of having the elder parent move from one family to another is observed in other Japanese American families. This type of shared responsibility is one solution to providing care for older persons with dementia. In this case, all members of the family were included at a family meeting in the discussion of what to do with their mother. Each person had a role to play even if it was simply tacit recognition and acceptance of what was occurring.

The Case of Mrs. Tanaka

Mrs. Tanaka is an elderly Issei woman with dementia residing in a nursing home. She was initially contacted by a staff person from the Japanese American Community Senior Center. When approached, she appeared very withdrawn and continued staring at the floor. There was no response even after an attempt to communicate with her was made by kneeling on the floor so Mrs. Tanaka could see who was speaking to her.

A conversation with Mrs. Tanaka's caregiver revealed that there was no one in the nursing home who could speak Japanese or even anyone who was Asian. She spent most of her days alone in her room sitting on the edge of the bed, staring at the floor. Center staff learned that Mrs. Tanaka's daughter visited regularly to assist with bathing her mother. A card was left for her daughter, requesting contact with the senior center. Before leaving, staff members told Mrs. Tanaka that they would be seeing her again and left the Japanese magazines they had brought.

Mrs. Tanaka's daughter called the senior center within a week and was given an appointment. During this meeting, it was revealed that Mrs. Tanaka's family could not care for her in their home and were unaware of the options available in the community. As a result, the family decided to place her in a nursing home that was affordable to the family and located near a bus stop, which was convenient for Mrs. Tanaka's daughter.

Mrs. Tanaka's daughter said she would have to talk with her older brother before her mother could attend the senior day care program and also asked permission to attend with her mother. She was welcomed as a volunteer in the program. Arrangements were made for a taxi to transport Mrs. Tanaka, accompanied by her daughter.

In this family, the staff observed the deference given to the eldest brother, although it was the sister who served as the liaison between the family and the senior center. In his role as head of the family, the older brother is dominant.

> With the assistance of her daughter, Mrs. Tanaka attended the day care program. Initially, she remained uncommunicative and continued to look down at the floor. As time passed, she was observed to be actively listening to others talking and looked up to see who was talking. Although she did not recognize any of the Issei women participants, she showed interest in their conversations. It became apparent that Mrs. Tanaka enjoyed the Japanese-style food served at lunch, as she ate heartily. Eventually, Mrs. Tanaka increased her participation in the program, engaging in simple activities such as passing a ball to others and scribbling with a pen. Although she was unable to recognize faces or names, she seemed comfortable to be in a safe place with familiar food, language, and gentle loving care. She continued to participate in the program until she broke her hip.
>
> The staff at the senior center helped Mrs. Tanaka's family locate another nursing home in the community that cared for other elderly Japanese Americans. The Japanese-speaking caregivers at that facility provided care in a culturally sensitive manner. Mrs. Tanaka's daughter reported that her mother has been singing again and seems happy at that facility. Although Mrs. Tanaka is unable to remember the names of people who care for her, she appears alert and continues to enjoy her meal of specially prepared Japanese food. Mrs. Tanaka's daughter continues to volunteer at the senior center in appreciation for the services provided to her mother.

The elderly Issei rely extensively on family members to provide them with love, attention, and a sense of well-being. The Japanese phrase *toshiyori wo daijini*, which means to treat elders with kindness and respect, best describes Mrs. Tanaka's experiences with culturally sensitive services (Ishizuka, 1978).

The Case of Mr. Haneda

> Mr. Haneda, who calls himself Jim, a nickname for James, a Christian name he gave himself, is an elderly, retired Nisei. He was born and raised in Hawaii and has been living in California. He served in the 100th Battalion during World War II. He has been receiving treatment for his medical problems since he returned from the war, laden with medals of honor. He identifies himself with pride as having been a prominent volunteer and generous contributor in the Japanese American community.
>
> He and his Nisei California-born wife are widowed from their first spouses, both of whom died of cancer in their middle age. He was raised Buddhist, but joined a Christian church with his second wife. His mother committed suicide when he was 8 years old, and soon afterwards his father returned to Japan with one of the older sons. He describes his father as a severe alcoholic. He was raised by his two older brothers in Hawaii. The three of them refused to go to Japan because they did not know the Japanese language and were not eager to adapt to a foreign country. He never saw his father again.

While Mr. Haneda and his second wife's first husband fought in the war, she and her Issei parents spent the war in Heart Mountain Internment Camp in Wyoming. While she was held at the Pomona Assembly Center in Southern California, before arriving at Heart Mountain, she gave birth to the first of five children. When she was reunited with her first husband after the war, they returned to California. They lived in a barn that her in-laws found, as housing was scarce. Because of his extensive wounds, Mr. Haneda spent several years after the war in military and veteran's hospitals for medical treatment before marrying.

Over the years, Mrs. Haneda noticed significant changes in her husband's behavior, particularly increasing memory loss and impulsive, aggressive behaviors. More recently, he demonstrated delusions, believing that someone was after him. They eventually shared these specific changes with his primary care physician, with whom they had a long-standing relationship. After a series of tests, he was diagnosed with dementia of the Alzheimer's type in addition to his other medical problems. However, Mrs. Haneda did not fully understand the diagnosis, and Mr. Haneda thought his condition could be fixed. The couple never mentioned his problems outside of the family for fear of being stigmatized by the community, loss of face, and shame on the family.

According to McGoldrick, Pearce, and Giordano (1982), shame and loss of face are concepts that involve the public exposure of a person's actions and the withdrawal of the confidence and support of the community, family, or society. Because interdependence is highly valued and relied on, the fear of losing face means that the individual will be left to survive alone, without help from others. Therefore, fear of losing face becomes a strong motivation to conform to the family's and society's expectations (McGoldrick et al., 1982).

Mr. Haneda eventually withdrew from his volunteer responsibilities entirely, while his wife maintained the appearance of his dominant role in the family. In this way, she attempted to maintain a sense of family stability and save face in front of others. He always held a traditional, dominant role with his stepchildren, despite their distant relationship, and his irrational behaviors did not endear him to them.

In Japanese family tradition, the role of the father is being the head of the household. His role is free from blame and demands unquestioned respect from his children. The mother is expected to be both supportive to her husband and deferent to him. She avoids confrontations with her husband and displays self-control in front of others (S. Sue & Morishima, 1982). According to Kitano (1990), family roles are formalized in a hierarchy based on male dominance, and this consequently could pose a problem among elderly Japanese American men who have lived with the expectation of being in their dominant position and now find this is not their current reality. In addition, DeVos (1978; as cited in S. Sue & Morishima, 1982) explained that one of the problems of role structure in Japanese American families is that a father may avoid self-disclosure, personal feelings, and expressions of affection; this could result in emotional distance between father and children.

> As Mr. and Mrs. Haneda's relationship deteriorated with the increasing problems related to his forgetfulness and aggressive behaviors, they became desperate and began to talk about divorce. He became more distant from his stepchildren. The only source of social support for him was his wife.

Despite the probable risk of *haji* (shame), they decided to follow through with the advice of their primary care physician as a gesture of *amae* (a Japanese term that describes dependency, to depend and presume on another individual's benevolence; McGoldrick et al., 1982). According to Kitano (1990), amae may be displayed in elderly clients, which encourages and acknowledges a dependency relationship with an authority figure (e.g., professional staff). This dependent behavior may mean they are seeking more personalized assistance because a businesslike, bureaucratic approach is too stressful. As a result, Mr. and Mrs. Haneda's brief attempts at couples and individual counseling sessions were unsatisfactory because they were unable to reveal their reasons for dissatisfaction. In true Japanese tradition, *gaman* (emotional self-restraint) is highly regarded and problems would be exposed subtly and indirectly. In this manner, they were submerging whatever aggression they had felt so as not to offend the counselor and restrained their emotions in general (Henkin, 1985).

Mrs. Haneda consulted with her children, siblings, and Nisei female friends when her husband's irrational behavior became obvious in public. McDermott et al. (1984; as cited in Uba, 1994) described Japanese American families as placing greater importance on discussing family matters than do Caucasian American families. Mrs. Haneda's family and friends perceived Mr. Haneda's aggressive behavior and forgetfulness as deliberate and shameful, and agreed he should be separated from the family. Mr. Haneda's behavior did not conform to that of traditional Japanese Americans, who have been taught that "behaving well" is complying with social expectations based on one's social role rather than behaving according to one's feelings (Uba, 1994). Mr. Haneda's behavior stepped into the realm of *haji*, shame, and along with it came a responsibility to prevent loss of face of his family and community, but because of his dementia he was not capable of dealing with it.

> When Mr. Haneda needed to withdraw from his volunteer activities, he was referred to a day respite program for adults with dementia by a nurse practitioner he trusted. This allowed him to maintain his self-esteem and a sense of identity and dignity while living in the community. He also used an inpatient respite program at a hospital and was given tasks to increase his self-esteem. In addition, Mr. Haneda attended a Japanese American community center's Senior Nutrition Program, which serves Japanese-style food and has cultural activities. Mrs. Haneda participated in a day respite program's Caregiver's Support Group.

Kitano (1990) showed that a positive outcome of this type of group reliance is possible owing to the development of facilities and programs specifically designed for the needs of the elderly Japanese American within their ethnic community.

According to Henkin (1985), the importance of family as a cultural value means recognizing the importance of the group or community in a Japanese American individual's life. An additional cultural value is the importance of nonverbal and nonstraightforward styles of communication for an individual. The confrontational style of intense eye contact, liberal physical gestures, and direct questions about intimate matters is considered offensive and intrusive by Japanese American clients, especially during the initial contact by Western clinicians. In addition, several insights are important in dealing with Japanese American clients: educating clients about the counseling process, allowing time for clients to evaluate and make a decision about proceeding, respecting clients' need to ask questions about the counselor and the process, being patient, and identifying the counselor's role clearly in a nonthreatening and approachable manner. It is very important to ensure confidentiality, as the Japanese American community is small and closely knit, and because seeking counseling is a cultural stigma, it is wise to inquire about clients' family and community relationships (Henkin, 1985).

> After establishing a trusting relationship with the day respite coordinator, Mrs. Haneda shared some concerns about her husband's irrational behavior, and a referral was made to the mental health clinic for a psychiatric evaluation and case management. Several contacts were made to establish rapport and trust with the couple, especially for Mr. Haneda, who could familiarize himself only with faces, not names. Mr. Haneda was interviewed alone by a Japanese American counselor, then by a staff psychiatrist. Some self-disclosure and sharing commonalities of background were made to establish trust. Mr. Haneda remarked at one point that he felt hopeful. Further sharing of information, including facts about dementia and description of operations and services at the clinic, were provided. Mrs. Haneda was included in those discussions. Assurances about confidentiality were given during their assessment. Each of them was given the opportunity to ask questions and take their time in making decisions, so that they could consult with family. Eventually they decided to accept services at the mental health clinic, and neuropsychological testing was performed to evaluate the extent of Mr. Haneda's cognitive abilities. Psychoeducational counseling and case management services were initiated at the clinic. Evaluation and treatment were started by his new psychiatrist.
>
> Soon afterward, Mrs. Haneda stated she would not leave her husband. Once she understood that his aggressive behavior was not deliberate, she wanted to be supportive and enlisted her children's help. Together, they decided to transfer his medical treatment to the same site as the mental health clinic, as they believed it would be more convenient. The mental health clinic psychiatrist encouraged the couple to discuss their plans to transfer to another physician with Mr. Haneda's current primary care physician. They hesitated for some time. They eventually explained to their current physician that their reason to transfer was not due to

dissatisfaction. The physician then suggested that Mr. Haneda explore the relationship with his new physician by making an appointment before making an official transfer. Mr. Haneda followed through with the help of his wife and the mental health clinic staff. He and his wife discovered they were comfortable with the new physician, and transferred Mr. Haneda's case.

Although the entire process took a few months, the couple made a commitment to services based on trust of the health care professionals and family involvement in decision making.

CONCLUSION

The Japanese American family has been undergoing a dynamic state of change throughout its history in the United States. Traditional Meiji-era Japanese values were anchored heavily within the Issei, despite their lifelong history of adversity. Although these cultural values have been diluted because of acculturation, each succeeding generation has inherited some traditional values, including family cohesiveness. With the increasing number of elderly Japanese Americans with dementia, their families will need to draw on their internal and external resources to deal effectively with the unique caregiving problems associated with this illness. In addition, Murase (1992) explained that there have been changing economic circumstances and lifestyles among Japanese Americans that increase the difficulty in caring for older individuals at home. Families increasingly rely on formal services for assistance, such as day care, mental health services, nursing homes, in-home supportive services, and other resources. As a result, there will be a continued need for practitioners to provide culturally sensitive approaches in treatment, as well as to ensure appropriate access to services. Exploring the historical background, cultural values, and unique conflicts of Japanese Americans is necessary to understand the complexity of behavior (D. W. Sue & Sue, 1990). Therefore, it is hoped that further research and culturally sensitive practice with elderly Japanese Americans with dementia and their families will provide increased understanding and effectiveness in treatment.

REFERENCES

Baker, F. M. (1990). Ethnic minority elders: Differential diagnosis, medication, treatment, and outcomes. In M. S. Harper (Ed.), *Minority aging: Essential curricula content for selected health and allied health professions* (DHHS Publication No. HRS P-DV-90-4, pp.560–561). Washington, DC: U.S. Government Printing Office.

Benedict, R. (1946). *The chrysanthemum and the sword: Patterns of Japanese culture.* Cambridge, MA: Houghton Mifflin Company. Boston: Riverside Press.

Daniels, R. (1988). *Asian America: Chinese and Japanese in the United States since 1850.* Seattle: University of Washington Press.

Fong, R. (1992). A history of Asian Americans. In S. Furuto, R. Biswas, D. Chung, K. Murase, & F. Ross-Sheriff (Eds.), *Social work practice with Asian Americans* (pp. 15, 16, 20–22). Newbury Park, CA: Sage.

Furuto, S., Biswas, R., Chung, D., Murase, K., & Ross-Sheriff, F. (Eds.). (1992). *Social work practice with Asian Americans.* (pp. 15–16,20–22,116–117). Newbury Park, CA: Sage.

Henkin, W. A. (1985). Toward counseling the Japanese in America: A cross-cultural primer. *Journal of Counseling and Development 63,* 500–502.

Herman, M. (1974). *The Japanese in America 1843-1973* (pp. 1–52). Dobbs Ferry, NY: Oceana.

Ichioka, Y. (1988). *The Issei.* New York: Free Press.

Ishizuka, K. (1978). The elder Japanese. In *A cross-cultural study of minority elders in San Diego* (pp. 21, 47). San Diego, CA: Campanile Press.

Kim, P. (1990). Asian American families and the elderly. In M.S. Harper (Ed.), *Minority aging: Essential curricula content for selected health and allied health professions* (DHHS Publication No. HRS P-DV-90-4, p. 351). Washington, DC: U.S. Government Printing Office.

Kitano, H. (1981). Counseling and psychotherapy with Japanese Americans. In A. Marsella & P. Pedersen (Eds.), *Cross-cultural counseling and psychotherapy* (pp. 228–242). Elmsford, NY: Pergamon Press.

Kitano, H. (1990). Values, beliefs, and practices of the Asian American elderly: Implications for geriatric education. In M. S. Harper (Ed.), *Minority aging: Essential curricula content for selected health and allied health professions* (DHHS Publication No. HRS P-DV-90-4, pp. 344–346). Washington, DC: U.S. Government Printing Office.

Larson, E. B. (1993). Illnesses causing dementia in the very elderly. *The New England Journal of Medicine, 328*(3), 204.

McDermott, J., Tseng, W., & Maretzki, T. (Eds.). (1981). *People and cultures of Hawaii, a psychocultural profile.* Honolulu: University Press of Hawaii.

McGoldrick, M., Pearce, J., & Giordano, J. (Eds.). (1982). *Ethnicity and family therapy.* New York: Guilford Press.

Murase, K. (1992). Models of service delivery in Asian American communities. In S. Furuto, R. Biswas, D. Chung, K. Murase, & F. Ross-Sheriff (Eds.), *Social work practice with Asian Americans* (pp.116–117). Newbury Park, CA: Sage.

Presidio Army Museum. (1981). *Go for broke: An exhibit honoring the Japanese American 100th Infantry Battalion and the 442nd Regimental Combat Team—"most decorated unit of World War II . . ."* (GPO 790–507). Washington, DC: U.S. Government Printing Office.

Sue, D. W., & Sue, D. (1990). *Counseling the culturally different: Theory and practice.* New York: Wiley.

Sue, S., & Morishima, J. (1982). *The mental health of Asian Americans.* San Francisco: Jossey-Bass.

Takaki, R. (1993) *A different mirror: A history of multicultural America.* Boston: Little, Brown.

Uba, L. (1994). *Asian Americans: Personality patterns, identity, and mental health.* New York: Guilford Press.

Chapter 10

Filipino American Families and Caregiving

Melen R. McBride
Heide Parreno

This chapter discusses cultural values and practices of Filipino Americans associated with caregiving for their elders. Some patterns of help-seeking by the family and of shared caregiving are discussed as major elements of many Filipino American families' holistic approach to the complex process of caring for an aging family member. Some practical suggestions are outlined, and illustrative vignettes are included to highlight certain concepts. They are useful in increasing cultural awareness and will contribute to skill building of health providers who interact with Filipino American clients or patients. The demographic and historical perspective is included in the discussion as background information on the Filipino population in the United States.

FILIPINO DEMOGRAPHY

The Filipino American community is a culturally eclectic group. Their ancestral heritage has been influenced by many cultures. From precolonial times to the present, parts of the Malayan, Chinese, Euro-Spanish, American, Muslim, and Judeo-Christian traditions have found their way into the Filipino culture as it is known today. Its multiculturalism has also been influenced by geographic boundaries defined by 7,200 islands, of which only 1,000 are livable. Thus, the art of blending and infusing cultural traits and values has become a dynamic feature of the Filipino personality.

On the basis of the 1990 U.S. Census, Filipino Americans now rank as the second largest foreign-born population, an increase of 82% over a 10-year period (U.S. Bureau of the Census, 1991). In 1980, the group ranked seventh. Currently, Filipino immigrants constitute 82% of this subgroup (Guillermo, 1993). Among the Asian Pacific Islander American (APIA) population aged 65 and older, Filipino elders are the third largest group, following the Chinese and Japanese, which rank first and second, respectively (McBride, Marioka-Douglas, & Yeo, 1996; U.S. Bureau of the Census, 1991).

In California, where more than 50% of the Filipino Americans live, those who are 65 years and older are the second largest group among the over-65 APIA population (California State Census Data Center, 1990). Not included in this count are elders who came to the United States after enactment of the 1990 U.S. Immigration Act, Section 260, which granted immediate citizenship to an estimated 175,000 eligible Filipino World War II veterans who resided in the Philippines. It is estimated that close to 3,000 of these veterans are now living in the United States. This is a subgroup of Filipino elders 62 years and older who are without a stable support network in the United States, are at risk for health crises, and are ineligible for the usual veterans benefits (Chin, 1993; Federal Council on Aging, 1994; McBride, 1993). It is projected that the flow of aging Filipino immigrants could continue into the next century.

The economic profile of Filipinos in the United States shows a per capita income of $13,616. This is below the national average of $13,806 and the average for Asian Americans ($13,806). Thirty percent of Filipino households have three or more members in the workforce, and 75% of the households participate in the labor force (U.S. Bureau of the Census, 1993). How do Filipino American families manage the caregiving needs of their elders? These elders constitute 22.9% of APIAs age 65 and older, yet a 1992 data tabulation by the Planning Section of the State Department of Health Services shows that fewer than 1% of long-term care residents in California were Filipinos. Where might the Filipino elders be? It can be assumed that many families are involved in precariously balancing family responsibilities, employment, and caregiving of frail elders.

At least 66% of Filipino households speak a non-English language, 35.6% do not speak English very well, and 13 % are linguistically isolated (U.S. Bureau of the Census, 1993). Truly monolingual elders may be difficult to find among Filipino elders, yet the preference to communicate in a Filipino language is strong. There are an estimated 80 or more languages in the Philippines. However, eight major distinct languages are spoken (Lamzon, 1978). These languages—Tagalog, Cebuano, Ilocano, Illongo, Bikolano, Waray, Kapampangan, and Pangasinanes—are well represented in the Filipino American community (Bautista, 1993; Peterson, 1978; Valencia-go, 1989). For many Filipino immigrants, English-speaking skills are much more developed than comprehension skill. However, verbal skills are strongly influenced by the indigenous language they speak.

IMMIGRATION HISTORY

The year 1763 marked the arrival of the first Filipino immigrants in the United States. They were the first Asian immigrants, settling in Louisiana to escape forced labor and enslavement in Spanish ships involved in the Spanish-Mexican galleon trade (1565–1815), carrying cargos from the Philippines. These "Manilamen" and their descendants, the Filipino cajuns, introduced wine making from coconut (*tuba*) and initiated the shrimp sun-drying process to export the product. From 1763 to 1906, mariners, adventurers, and domestic helpers arrived in the southeastern part of Louisiana. Some moved on to California, and others went to Hawaii, Washington, and Alaska, seeking employment in the whaling or fishing industry (Espina, 1974; Tompar-Tiu & Sustento-Seneriches, 1995).

The second period (1906–1934) of Filipino immigration consisted of three subgroups. Calling themselves *sakadas*, these rural poorly educated laborers were recruited to replace Japanese labor on Hawaiian plantations, intended to return home, and had little inclination to be a part of American society. Those who stayed and remained single are referred to as *manongs* (older brothers), or "old-timers" in the Filipino community. The *pensionadas*, a group of Filipino scholars with limited government subsidies, returned home after completing their education while the unsuccessful ones stayed behind. Later immigrants, the *pinoys*, came to seek economic prosperity and join their families. Many worked in the farmlands of San Joaquin valley, Sacramento, and Salinas in California; the Alaskan canneries; and the service industries as domestics, busboys, and janitors. Considered an economic and social threat, the pinoys experienced discrimination and violence that eventually led to changes in the immigration laws and expansion of the antimiscegenation laws in California and other states to include Filipinos (Tompar-Tiu & Sustento-Seneriches, 1995; Yeo & Hikoyeda, 1992). Many remained unmarried, relegated to low social status and low-paying jobs. Some of the Filipino elders today may have been part of this group or might have been children at that time.

The third period (1935–1965) of Filipino immigration included more women and families. It consisted of World War II veterans, military staff and their families, students, and professionals and their families. Although this period began the "brain drain" in the Philippines, their contribution to the American society was significant despite the economic exploitation and racism they experienced (Tompar-Tiu & Sustento-Seneriches, 1995; Yeo & Hikoyeda, 1992).

From 1965 to the present, more diversity occurred in the Filipino American community. In this fourth period of immigration, this highly educated, predominantly female group were professionals; participants in the 1965 Family Reunification Program, especially the elders; aging World War II veterans; refugees of the Marcos regime; and short-stay visitors (students, businesspeople, and tourists). The Filipinos with short-term visas developed into a labor pool for low-paying jobs or unpopular employment such as long-term care facilities, the home care industry, and other establishments with undesirable working conditions. Most Filipinos who are now caregivers to elders in their families may have came to the United States during the third- and fourth-period Filipino immigration or are children of earlier immigrants. Some immigrants of the later periods have grown old, expecting to be cared for in the community by their children or other members of the extended family. Such expectations come from the traditional Filipino values of filial responsibility and respect for elders.

FILIPINO FAMILY SYSTEM AND VALUES

The Filipino family has been described as a most able social service system in which respect and love for parents are taught and expected of Filipino children (National Media Production Center, 1974). Traditional Filipino American families pass this value on to the new generation. In Philippine society, it is acceptable for several generations of families to share one household. Thus, caring for aging family members is integrated over time into the family dynamics. Putting the family welfare before the self, loyalty, and interdependence are traits deeply imbedded in the Filipino culture (Almirol, 1982; Medina, 1991). Family is the major source of emotional, moral, and economic support.

A traditional family consists of the nuclear family, the bilateral (father's and mother's side) extended family, and kin (cousins, in-laws, godparents, townmates, or friends) who keep close emotional, moral, spiritual, and economic ties with the family (Medina, 1991). It is an open system, absorbing new members not only by marriage but also through kinship, compassionate friendships, or feelings of indebtedness. Shared responsibilities, recognition of kin relations beyond the nuclear family, and maintenance of expressive and emotional relations are considered essential elements of the extended family (Castillo, Weisblat, & Villareal, 1968).

Studies of Filipino indigenous personality theory describe an emphasis on shared identity interacting as co-equals, or *kapwa* (Enriquez, 1990), as the core value or foundation of Filipino values. These values—interacting with others on an equal basis, sensitivity to and regard for others, respect and concern, helping out, understanding and making up for others' limitations, and rapport and acceptance—stress the importance of sensitivity and close attention to other people and to interrelationships. They may have evolved out of the survival needs of Filipino ancestral tribes, living in an agricultural archipelago of 7,200 islands where natural calamities are common occurrences and only 1,000 islands can sustain human life (Enriquez, 1990; Tompar-Tiu & Sustento-Seneriches, 1995). Later, other historical events and sociopolitical conditions, including integration into new cultures (e.g., American culture) may have contributed to strengthening and reshaping these values in the Filipino culture. In a way, it is advantageous to Filipino elders to preserve these values to ensure a caregiving system free of bureaucratic elements.

Levels of Interaction

To collect qualitative information in the Filipino community, social psychologists have identified eight interrelated levels of relationships used in the Filipino community for everyday interaction (Enriquez, 1979; Pe-Pua, 1990; Santiago, 1982). Five levels are considered to fall into the external or "outsider" category (*Ibang-Tao*), and three levels are considered to fall into the internal or "one-of-us" category (*Hindi ibang-Tao*). These modes of interaction range from civility (*Pakikitungo*, Level 1) to oneness, full trust (*Pakikiisa*, Level 8). At Level 2 (*Pakikisalamuha*), the person may chose to interact with someone or mix with company, whereas joining or participating (*Pakikilahok*, Level 3) incorporates some form of commitment from the respondent. Conforming (*Pakikibagay*, Level 4) and adjusting (*Pakikisama*, Level 5) are zones of interaction in which some behavioral or attitudinal change may be anticipated. When relationships reach the points of mutual trust (*Pakikipagpalagayang-loob*, Level 6) and active involvement (*Pakikisangkot*, Level 7), the chances of major breakthroughs are very strong. Few interactions reach Level 8, although striving for oneness and full trust (*Pakikiisa*) has its merits. Health care providers may find these points of social interaction helpful in encouraging collaboration from family members when planning care for a Filipino elder.

Respect for Elders

Language and nonverbal behaviors are used by the Filipino family to teach and show respect. Early on, children are taught to be respectful to persons older than they even when the age difference is small (Blust & Scheidt, 1988; Ishisaka & Tagaki, 1982). Family members are accorded special titles of respect and reverence. These titles include *Lolo* (grandfather); *Lola* (grandmother); *Tatay, Tatang,* and *Amang* (father); *Nanay, Nanang,* and *Inang* (mother); *Kuya* and *Manong* (older brother); *Ate* and *Manang* (older sister); *Tio* and *Tito* (uncle); *Tia* and *Tita* (aunt); *Pinsang-Buo* (first cousin); *Pinsan* (cousin); *Manong* and *Mang* (man older than you, often without biological ties); and *Manang* and *Aling* (woman older than you, often without biological ties). To show respect, the first name follows the title when addressing the person (e.g., Lola Maria, Kuya Ben, etc.). For verbal communication, respectful and polite responses to elders or strangers must include the word *po* for emphasis. For example, "Thank you, grandfather" translates to *Salamat po, Lolo* (Lamzon, 1978; Wolff, 1988).

A nonverbal greeting of respect and affection expressed by younger family members toward their elder has several critical maneuvers. The younger person bends slightly forward while reaching for the hand of the elder, who may be standing, sitting, or reclining. She or he takes the elder's hand, which should be positioned palm down, brings the back of the elder's hand forward to touch her or his forehead, accompanied by a verbal request that must be spoken gently:

"Mano po, Lolo?" (conceptual translation, "May I greet you with respect, please?") Thus, the oldest family members are the most respected persons in the household (Eggan, 1968; Medina, 1991), and Filipino American parents continue to impart this value to their children. Competing expectations and highly individualistic social norms in American society tend to lessen the impact of this tradition in younger Filipino Americans. Some tensions in intergenerational or multicultural households may be associated with these changes. However, filial piety remains strong in Filipino American families (Superio, 1993), and Filipino researchers assert that caring for the elder as a family obligation is still well rooted in the mores of Philippine society (Enriquez, 1992; Medina, 1991).

CAREGIVING IN FILIPINO FAMILIES

There is little information for Filipino American elders on disability rates associated with aging and major chronic health problems, including dementia (McBride et al, 1996). However, cardiovascular disease is the number-one cause of death in the population (Liu & Yu, 1985; Nora & McBride, 1995). Strokes, Alzheimer's disease, and multi-infarct dementia may be taking their toll on the Filipino elders and their families, but culturally appropriate interventions have yet to be designed to assist family caregivers. The multilinguality of Filipino elders who are predominantly immigrants has important implications in the differential diagnosis of cognitive impairments. Health beliefs systems of the elder and the family may significantly influence the caregiving approach and willingness to access resources (Bautista, 1993; Orque, 1983).

Because caring for elders is a strong Filipino value, the tendency for Filipino American families to accept caregiving responsibility by keeping elders at home may create stressful and difficult situations. Conversely, when the family is able to act on its value system, a sense of harmony, satisfaction, and inner peace are the potential rewards of family caregivers.

In a pilot study, McBride and Parreno (1992) reviewed three cases of frail elders and interviewed their caregivers ($N = 10$) to describe their caregiving roles and responsibilities. Positive strategies used by the families to ease the caregiving burden were also identified. All participants had college educations; 80% were professionals and 20% were in home-based industry. Four primary caregivers, aged 28–48 years, were asked how the primary caregiver role evolved. Decisions were made by consensus (50%), self-assignment (25%), and default (25%). Other family members ($n = 6$) considered themselves to be secondary caregivers, and the following tasks were their responsibilities: assessing family resources, linking family to community resources, providing caregiving information, teaching home care skills, and providing psychosocial support to family members.

The primary caregivers' major responsibilities were physical care, health maintenance, financial management, leisure and recreation, spiritual care, transportation, and supply inventory. Secondary caregivers provided backup for these responsibilities to provide respite care. Debriefings, family meetings, music sessions, family events, pastoral visits, and telephone conferences and networking were some strategies used to share caregiving functions. Seven caregivers lived within a 15-to 75-mile radius of the elder's home, a factor that enabled the families to share caregiving roles and offer emotional support to each other. Limited short-term home care services were received by the elders. These resources were carefully screened by family caregivers before services were accessed.

With the increasing demands and contemporary pressures on many Filipino American families, their help-seeking patterns are being noticed and described more and more in anecdotal accounts by service providers and leaders in the Filipino community. At the Stanford Geriatric Education Center, Melen McBride has summarized these oral reports into modes of help-seeking patterns with indigenous descriptive labels: *kayahin na natin* (rely on ourselves), *maghanap ng paraan* (search for a strategy), *tingnan natin* (let's see how it goes), *magbisitahan* (visit family), *magkuha ng bantay* (get a trusted companion), and *iuwi na* (take elder home). These modes of help-seeking also appear to be adapted for other issues, such as childrearing and parenting.

The rely-on-ourselves pattern may involve a conscious decision to alter the household's priorities. A family member, often a woman, may reduce or leave employment to be the primary caregiver. Responsibilities for family priorities are redistributed, and young family members are also expected to rearrange their priorities, thus reluctantly attending to important tasks. The case of a socially active, 24-year-old native-born daughter illustrates this point. As a member of the household, she was asked to be the companion to a frail 83-year-old family friend. She was expected to take this role three times a week, while going to graduate school, juggling two part-time jobs, and maintaining her outside interests. Preparations to incorporate the elder into the family household were also in progress.

In the search-for-a-strategy pattern, caregiving resources outside the family may be considered. The family might exercise much caution in accessing services, partly to limit the flow of information into the community about a family member with dementia. Fear of stigma and concerns about inherited illnesses could act as barriers to full utilization of services (Anderson, 1983; Tompar-Tiu & Sustento-Seneriches, 1995). When services are used, delaying conclusions about the effectiveness of services falls into the let's-see-how-it-goes pattern. For these patterns, the availability of a culturally compatible provider is critical to utilization, particularly when the elder has had minimal social contact outside the family system before the impairment.

The remaining help-seeking patterns—visiting family, get a trusted companion, and take elder home—require linkage with the extended family network in the United States and the Philippines. Long stays with families living in the

United States might be arranged for a variety of reasons, such as respite care, redistribution of the financial burden, closure on unfinished family matters, returning past indebtedness, and so forth. For the elder with undiagnosed dementia, instability in the environment may lead to more problems. Providing a companion who is often brought over from the Philippines may have a more positive outcome. Yet this option would not be available to many Filipino families. Taking the elder back to the Philippines has its advantages and disadvantages. For traditional families, the presence of an elder, even one who is frail, may be a source of comfort and validation of the family's identity and cultural values. How and when the decision is made and eventually implemented could keep families occupied with numerous trans-Pacific arrangements. Families who cut close ties in the Philippines would not be able to take advantage of this option. For many Filipino Americans, dealing with complex caregiving issues may be their first experience with a family crisis in the United States.

In some instances, the Filipino community takes on caregiving responsibilities, as the extended family, for elders who do not have biological ties in the United States For example, in the San Francisco Bay area, a group formed to assist newly naturalized World War II Filipino veterans who were frail and at risk of elder abuse because of their social and living conditions (Chin, 1993; McBride, 1993). Basic needs were assessed, and formal and informal resources were mobilized. For the few elders who opted to return to the Philippines after social service interventions, community support for their decision was generated. The Filipino value of helping out and concern for the other person (Enriquez, 1990), as demonstrated in this situation, is also known as *bayanihan*.

As traditional families become acculturated, and generations of Filipino Americans adopt more American values, filial piety and respect for aging parents may be expressed in new ways. Superio (1993) interviewed four age groups of Filipino Americans to ascertain their beliefs about filial responsibility and compared these beliefs across age groups. Ninety percent of the participants believed that the duty to care for aging parents should be taught to the children. When the issue of caring for elders in the children's home was raised, 57% of the young native-born, 54% of the young foreign-born, and 50% of the older foreign-born participants believed that children should care for them in their homes. Seventy-four percent of the middle-aged foreign-born participants preferred their children "to give support" and "to make other arrangements," but decidedly "not a nursing home." It may be worthwhile to note that at the time of the study, this middle-aged group may actually have been involved in caregiving. In the gerontology literature, they are often referred to as the "sandwich generation."

It appears that Filipino Americans still hold strong beliefs that children should care for their aging parents. Thus, supporting family caregivers and preparing for gradual shifts in future caregiving practices should be incorporated into cross-cultural caregiving programs.

SOME SUGGESTIONS IN WORKING WITH FILIPINO AMERICAN FAMILIES

Because of the diversity among Filipino Americans, the following strategies may not work with every Filipino family. Awareness of the extent to which acculturation has reshaped values and beliefs should be considered in modifying these approaches for the best possible culturally sensitive care of a Filipino elder with dementia.

Family and Cultural Assessment

1 Identify beliefs about health and aging that the family is using to explain the cause and prognosis of the elder's memory impairment or disability. Family stories provide important information and allow time for building rapport.

2 Ascertain how the family makes decisions, who makes major decisions, and who the "expert consultants" in the family are. These experts, the family's internal resource, may be health professionals.

3 Encourage the decision makers, family experts, and caregivers to describe help-seeking options they may be considering.

4 Create an extended-family genogram that represents the various caregiving roles and resources for the elder. These may include individuals who live outside the United States.

5 Identify aspects of the immigration history of the family, the caregiver, and the elder that may be useful in the treatment and management of dementia.

Communication and Trust Building

1 Whenever possible, a bilingual bicultural health care provider should make the first and subsequent follow-up contacts until the plan of care has been agreed on. This person can then be designated as the "culture expert" who can be called on for consultation for as long as service is provided.

2 Create a pool of "culture experts" by providing appropriate staff education for those who express interest and are active in the Filipino community. Keep in mind that not every Filipino is an expert in her or his culture.

3 Develop a list of words (Filipino and English) that are used often by the caregiver, family, and elder to talk about dementia and other issues. Then incorporate them into the service provider's vocabulary when interacting with the elder and the family.

4 Be prepared to answer personal questions, such as Are you married? and Do you have children? Although they may have no bearing on the provider's agenda for the visit or interview, building personal relationships (superficial as they may be) enables most Filipino families to translate the interaction into

human terms. These "ice breakers" may move you sooner to the higher levels of interactions described earlier in this chapter.

Issues Related to Advance Directives or Guardianship

An advance directive is a person's written declaration of treatment preferences and of a designated decision maker in the event of serious incapacitating or terminal illness that renders the person unable to make decisions for her- or himself.

    1   Traditional elders usually prefer to pass on family responsibility to their firstborn. Gender is less of an issue than birth order.

    2   Determine what an advance directive means to the elder and the family. Currently, this concept is not a household word in many Filipino American families. Some may feel superstitious about it, and others may harbor guilt feelings from unexpressed or unexplored moral and ethical conflicts. Many Filipino immigrants were raised in Catholic teachings. Often, learning took place in an authoritative environment.

VIGNETTES AND CONCLUSION

The following vignettes highlight some points discussed in this chapter. These actual cases were altered for confidentiality without sacrificing major content.

All Children Are Responsible

Mr. H., an 84-year-old widower, was admitted to a skilled nursing facility for short-term rehabilitation after a mild stroke. He was considered cognitively intact, although the staff noted occasional memory deficit. Family members were asked about signing an advance directive. Mr. H.'s three daughters had discussed this issue with him at different times before his illness. However, he had not expressed his preference at that time. The family indicated they would again discuss the issue with their father before the social worker's interview. After several sessions with the social worker, Mr. H. felt ready to complete the document. He listed the names of his three daughters in birth order as legally responsible for his welfare while at the facility.

Although the family was not consulted by Mr. H., the siblings accepted the arrangement. Mr. H. felt confident that his daughters, who were all professionals, would be able to handle issues that might come up. The daughters clarified with the staff that in an emergency, they should contact family members according to birth order.

A Family Health Team

Mr. and Mrs. T., an aging couple, immigrated to the United States to join their adult daughter who was their firstborn child. They left behind a son and his family, and an unmarried son and daughter who were also scheduled to immigrate to the United States in a few months. When they were reunited, they decided to live together and share resources. The oldest daughter, who continued to live on her own, facilitated the adjustment period. Because of her previous work experience as a public health nurse, she was able to guide the family to access health and community resources. Visits with extended family members residing in the East served to rekindle kinships from the past. Years later, when the father died, the household had stabilized. All the siblings who lived in the United States remained single. When Mrs. T. had her first stroke, the oldest daughter (the public health nurse) negotiated with Mrs. T.'s physician to treat the episode in the home. In 3 days, Mrs. T. pulled out of the crisis with slight hemiplegia, apraxia, and mild dementia. A home rehabilitation program was instituted with the assistance of a home care agency. The son learned ambulation techniques, and the other daughter took over personal care training. Treatment continued to be arranged through the oldest daughter. Full physical recovery was not expected, but the poststroke residuals were managed by the family. Mrs. T. feels she is receiving the best care any mother could get from her children.

These vignettes underscore the importance of cross-cultural awareness and communication. Creating a culturally competent health care system has many challenges. The first step is to become aware of one's cultural values to understand how they might facilitate or hinder constructive patient–provider interactions.

In this chapter, some aspects of the Filipino culture, beliefs, practices, and family life were discussed as they relate to caregiving for frail elders in Filipino American families. Variations or diversity in the extended family system were presented, and areas for research on Filipino family caregiving were identified.

REFERENCES

Almirol, E. (1982). Rights and obligations in Filipino-American families. *Journal of Comparative Studies, 13*(3), 291–305.

Anderson, J. (1983). Health and illness in the Pilipino immigrants. *Western Journal of Medicine,* 139(6), 811–819.

Bautista, M. (1993). *Social service utilization between noninstitutionalized frail Pilipino and White elders.* Unpublished master's thesis, San Francisco State University, San Francisco, CA.

Blust, E., & Scheidt, R. (1988). Perceptions of filial responsibility by elderly Filipino widows and their primary caregivers. *International Journal on Aging and Human Development,* 26(2), 91–106.

California State Census Data Center. (1990). [Summary Tape File 2, Table PB5, 1990 Census]. Stanford, CA: Stanford Geriatric Education Center.

Castillo, G., Weisblat, A., & Villareal, F. (1968). The concepts of nuclear and extended family: An exploration of empirical referents. *International Journal of Comparative Sociology, 9*(1), 1–4.

Chin, S. (1993, December 20). Filipino veterans poor in land they faught for. *San Francisco Examiner,* p. A-5.

Eggan, F. (1968). Philippine social structure. In G. Guthrie (Ed.), *Six perspectives in the Philippines* (pp. 1–48). Manila, Philippines: Bookmark.

Enriquez, V. (1979). Towards cross-cultural knowledge through cross-indigenous methods and perspective. *Philippine Journal of Psychology, 12,* 9–15.

Enriquez, V. (1990). *Hellside in paradise: The Honolulu gangs* (Report for the Community Affairs Committee, Center for Philippine Studies). Honolulu: University of Hawaii.

Enriquez, V. (1992). From colonial to liberation psychology: The Philippine experience. Quezon City, Philippines: University of the Philippine Press.

Espina, M. (1974). Filipinos in New Orleans. *The Proceedings of the Louisiana Academy of Sciences, 37,* 117–121.

Federal Council on Aging. (1994). *Annual report to the President.* Washington, DC: Author.

Guillermo, T. (1993). Health care needs and service delivery for Asian and Pacific Islander Americans: Health Policy. In *LEAP, The State of Asian Pacific America: Policy Issues to the Year 2020* (pp. 61–78). Los Angeles: Asian Pacific Public Policy Institute and Asian American Studies Center, University of California.

Ishisaka, H., & Tagaki, C. (1982). Social work with Asian and Pacific Americans. In J. Green (Ed.), *Cultural awareness in the human services* (pp. 122–156). Englewood Cliffs, NJ: Prentice Hall.

Lamzon, T. (1978). *Handbook of Philippine language groups.* Quezon City, Philippines: Manila University Press.

Liu, W,. & Yu, E. (1985). Asian Pacific American elderly: Mortality differentials, health status, and use of services. *Journal of Applied Gerontology, 4*(1), 35–64.

McBride, M., Marioka-Douglas, N., & Yeo, G. (1996). Aging and health: Asian/Pacific Island American elders (Working Paper Series No. 3, 2nd ed.). Stanford, CA: Stanford Geriatric Education Center.

McBride, M. (1993, March). *Health status of recently naturalized Filipino WWII veterans.* Paper presented at the annual conference of the American Society on Aging, Chicago.

McBride, M., & Parreno, H. (1992). Generativity and caregiving: Functions at midlife of women in Filipino families. *The Gerontologist, 33,* 268.

Medina, B. (1991). *The Filipino family.* Diliman, Quezon City: University of the Philippines Press.

National Media Production Center. (1974). The Filipino family: Most able social welfare agency. *New Philippines, 23.*

Nora, R., & McBride, M. (1993, June). The health needs of Filipino Americans. Presented at the Asian Pacific Islander American Health Summit, San Francisco, CA.

Orque, M. (1983). Nursing care of Filipino American patients. In M. Orque et al. (Eds.), *Ethnic nursing care: A multicultural approach* (pp. 149–181). St. Louis, MO: C.V. Mosby.

Pe-Pua, R. (1990). Pagtatanung-tanong: A method for cross cultural research. In V. Enriquez (Ed.), *Indigenous psychology: A book of readings* (pp. 213–249). Quezon City, Philippines: Philippine Psychology Research and Training House.

Peterson, R. (1978). *The elder Pilipino* (Research Monograph, Center for Aging, San Diego State University). San Diego, CA: Campanille Press.

Santiago, C. (1982). Pakapa-kapa: Paglilinaw ng isang konsepto sa nayon (Pakapa-kapa as a method for clarifying an indigenous concept in the barrio). In R. Pe-Pua (Ed.), *Filipino psychology: Theory, method and application* (pp. 161–170). Quezon City, Philippines: Philippine Psychology Research and Training House.

Superio, E. (1993). *Beliefs held by Pilipinos regarding filial responsibility*. Unpublished master's Thesis, San Jose State University.

Tompar-Tiu, A., & Sustento-Seneriches, J. (1995). *Depression and other mental health issues: The Filipino American experience*. San Francisco: Jossey-Bass.

U.S. Bureau of the Census. (1991). *Subject report: Asian and Pacific Islander persons by groups for the United States, 1990*. Washington, DC: U.S. Government Printing Office.

U.S. Bureau of the Census. (1993). *We the American Asians*. Washington, DC: U.S. Department of Commerce, Economics and Statistics Administration.

Valencia-Go, G. (1989). *Integrative aging in widowed immigrant Filipinos: A grounded theory study*. Unpublished doctoral dissertation, Adelphi University. (University Microfilms No. 8923910)

Wolff, J. (1988). *Pilipino phrasebook*. Oakland, CA: Lonely Planet.

Yeo, G., & Hikoyeda, N. (1992). Cohort analysis as a clinical and educational tool in ethnogeriatrics: Historical profiles of Chinese, Filipino, Mexican, and African American elders (Stanford Geriatric Education Center Working Paper Series No. 12). Palo Alto, CA: Stanford University.

Chapter 11

Service Delivery Issues and Recommendations for Working with Mexican American Family Caregivers

Dolores Gallagher-Thompson
Melissa Talamantes
Rosa Ramirez
Irene Valverde

BACKGROUND AND INTRODUCTION

The Hispanic population over 65 currently represents 5% of all Hispanic Americans. According to 1990 Census data, 49% of this diverse group are of Mexican heritage, 15% are of Cuban heritage, and 12% are of Puerto Rican background, with the remaining 25% reflecting other Hispanic origins, such as Guatemalan, El Salvadorean, and Chilean. The 80-and-older population of Hispanic elders is expected to increase dramatically from 3% (219,000) in 1990 to 14% (4.5 million) (U.S. Bureau of the Census, 1993). Past and future immigration patterns have contributed to the continued growth increases. The U.S. Bureau of the Census has further predicted (1993) that if the recent mortality and immigration trends continue, the elderly Hispanic population will grow 3.9% per year from 1990 to 2050. This growth increase surpasses the annual rate increase of 2.3% for the total Hispanic population.

The parent support ratio is defined as the number of persons age 80 years and older per 100 persons age 50–64 years. In Hispanic families, the parent support ratio is expected to increase–from 11 in 1990 to 36 in 2050 (U.S. Bureau of the Census, 1993). These statistical projections present several challenges for current and future family caregivers and health and human service providers, as rates of dementia also increase with age (Evans et al., 1989) and therefore result in larger numbers of frail elders (of all ethnicities) needing an array of long-term care services (U.S. Congress, 1990).

Researchers and practitioners have both investigated and reported on the vast differences among the many varied Hispanic communities in this country (Braus, 1993). At this time, it is clear that the heterogeneity of cultural attitudes within the realm of family caregiving is great. Although there are differences among Hispanic caregivers, there are also commonalities. These commonalities include, in general, (a) limited knowledge about dementia, (b) lack of knowledge and access to resources for care support, (c) limited trained bilingual or bicultural providers, (d) limited culturally appropriate educational materials, and (e) increased levels of burden and stress (Valle, 1989).

For the purposes of this chapter, the authors focus on these issues as they relate to Mexican American family caregivers of loved ones afflicted with Alzheimer's or a related dementia. This is because of the greater size of this group relative to other Hispanic subgroups and the greater amount (comparatively speaking) of research that has been conducted with them. The reader will receive an overview of cultural issues unique to the changing Mexican American family structure, along with strategies for conducting outreach and for building cultural competency. Also included is a discussion of some successfully used interventions for distressed caregivers and, finally, a listing of several national resources for caregiver information and support.

MEXICAN AMERICAN FAMILIES

Familial support is common and occurs frequently in the Mexican American community. In a three-generation study conducted in San Antonio, Texas (Markides, Boldt, & Ray, 1986), older Mexican Americans maintained strong helping networks with their children. The older generation relied on their children, primarily daughters, for help when sick and for minor medical problems. However, in this study, mutual reciprocity was also noted between older Mexican Americans and their adult children. In a separate study on sibling relationships among elderly Mexican Americans, functional reciprocity in terms of exchanges of goods and services was very common, especially among the over-80-years-old cohort (Talamantes, 1987). Similarly, Sotomayor and Randolph (1988) reported that reciprocal relationships are maintained for instrumental support (at least) when elderly relatives are sick and frail. The types of instrumental exchanges reported included babysitting for grandchildren, allowing family to move into their homes, and the provision of religious guidance to grandchildren. The literature reveals that high levels of intergenerational interactions exist. How much of these interactions occur as a result of living arrangements, socioeconomic factors, culture, and role expectations or other factors is unknown at present.

Acculturation may play a significant role in how caregiving roles and responsibilities are assumed and dealt with. The acculturation continuum encompasses, at one end, the retention of traditional values and beliefs from one's culture of origin, through the midpoint of a person being both bilingual and bicultural (whereby individuals can easily shift from traditional practices to adopting beliefs, values, and practices of the majority society), and, at the other end, more fully adopting the values and beliefs of the host society (Valle, 1989).

The extent of acculturation seems to vary greatly both within persons and across situations. For example, when caring for a family member with osteo-arthritis, a family caregiver may use the Western system of care (e.g., go to a family practice physician) and a more traditional healer (*sobador*, or massage therapist) simultaneously. Or a caregiver may try Western medicine to help with a family member's memory problems, such as using medications such as Hy-dergine or Cognex, while at the same time using herbal remedies. In contrast, at other times that same family may use only Western medicine or only folk remedies, depending on the disorder.

Because of the heterogeneity of family systems, which are often complex and ever changing, it is critical to view acculturation as only one aspect of how the caregiving role is carried out (Lockery, 1991). There are many other internal and external forces that may influence how a family system cares for a demented relative. For example, controversy continues to exist regarding whether the Mexican American familial elder support system prevails or whether it has eroded as a result of industrialization and urbanization (Gratton & Wilson, 1988). Also, changes in family values can lead to changes in the role and status of elderly persons within their family systems (Maldonado, 1979).

In the Mexican American family, there is typically a primary caregiver who provides the hands-on day-to-day personal care. In a study of Mexican American and Puerto Rican elderly persons, these elders were more likely to say when identifying help received from others that they received help from their daughters (Sotomayor & Randolph, 1988). Sotomayor (1992) has suggested that family continues to play a key role in caring for elderly family members, that intergener-ational ties remain strong, and that the notion of filial responsibility continues to exist in family caregiving interactions. Nevertheless, it is anticipated that care-giving in Mexican American communities will change as a result of more women working and dealing with the demands of caring for their children. Carnoy, Daley, and Ojeda (1993) reported that Mexican American women are more likely to have less education and, therefore, to earn less income than their White counterparts. In addition, Mexican American women are more likely to marry and have children early in life, which may have a negative effect on their educational attainment (Carnoy et al., 1993). As the numbers of older Latinos increase, it has been predicted that these family caregivers will undergo increased family strain, which will negatively affect their availability to provide informal care (Wallace & Lew-Ting, 1992).

CULTURAL OVERVIEW FOR WORKING WITH MEXICAN AMERICAN FAMILIES

Culture is the vehicle that transports words, acts, gestures, events, and even illness symptoms into a particular ethnic group's assumptions about and inter-pretation of the world, other people, goals and the meaning of life, what is right or wrong, how to behave socially, and how others should behave in all of life's situations (Green, 1982). Culture is then the formulation of ideas that are ultimately true, real, and "natural" for a group or an individual. No human being can exist without culture and the orientations to self and others that it provides and sustains.

Sensitivity to cultural expectations is crucial when working with individuals from varied ethnic and cultural backgrounds. Health care professionals who understand how various ethnic groups interpret symptoms of chronic debilitating illnesses such as dementia will be able to provide services that are acceptable and accessible, resulting in better utilization of all that is available.

It is critical for providers to receive education and training to be culturally competent not only when working with Mexican American caregivers and elders, but also with individuals from other ethnic groups. Ethnic competence has been described by Green and Leigh (1989) as the ability to assist clients in ways which are acceptable and useful to them in that they are consistent with the clients' cultural background and expectations.

A culturally competent framework should include the ability to use appropriate symbolic language, be interactional, and behave in ways that are consistent with the value and belief systems of the group (Valle, 1986). For example, a provider's recognition of Mexican American elderly persons' and family caregivers' preferred written and spoken language is essential for the development of rapport and useful educational materials and outreach methods. Cultural symbols unique to Mexican American elders and their families may be connected to familial celebrations or tied to religious ceremonies or other traditional celebrations. Valle suggested that understanding the natural helper social network, including family members, peers, and community groups, is essential for understanding interactional patterns among families. A Mexican American elder with dementia may have an extensive familial network that may include a daughter who is the primary caregiver, another daughter who is the service broker and care coordinator, and a son who is only peripherally involved in the actual hands-on care but who plays a key role in decision making about care.

Understanding these group norms, values, and beliefs is essential for the provision of culturally competent services and care. Recognition of where individual families are on the acculturation continuum will also help to facilitate the degree of intervention or willingness of the caregiver to accept help. Other factors such as filial responsibility, extent of kin and nonkin interactions, type and degree of dementia, intergenerational stress, and socioeconomic differences will also play an important role in the caregiver's willingness to accept an intervention. In addition, understanding the caregiver's knowledge base about dementia and role expectations for providing care will also affect how services are developed and delivered (Pousada, 1995).

Achieving ethnic competence cannot occur by means of a 1-day training on working with Mexican American families; rather, providers must learn over time through in-depth interaction with the particular community and family. Green

(1982) suggested a method for teaching cultural competence. This method recommends that providers do the following: (a) Ask general questions with relevance to the particular group, (b) listen carefully for unique words and phrases when answers are provided, and (c) record the words used by caregivers to describe how they provide personal care and how they link to community services.

Achieving cultural competence is not an easy task. All human beings are faced with overcoming personal biases and stereotypes about various groups. To more effectively conduct outreach efforts to Mexican American caregivers who may be isolated and suffering from depression, stress, and high levels of burden, a strategic plan developed by providers must incorporate an agency's commitment to hire and recruit bilingual and bicultural staff and board or advisory council members. It is also necessary to develop culturally appropriate educational materials that address all levels of education, to partner and collaborate with existing agencies who currently serve the community, and to train other staff on cultural competency in serving this population (Aranda, 1990).

BARRIERS TO ACCESSING SERVICES

Although Alzheimer's disease and other types of dementia have become well-known disorders of elderly persons, intensive efforts toward outreach, education, and public awareness are still a priority in the Hispanic community, which has received little specific attention in this regard. A number of issues come into play in determining a typical response from this population. Limited education (an average of 5 years) may serve as a barrier, exposing families to nonsuccessful experiences when attempting to infiltrate the system. Simply not having the knowledge to ask the right questions, not having enough information or experience, or not knowing the difference between a government agency and a nonprofit agency serve as barriers to securing services or benefits. Lack of assertiveness often means that Mexican American families do not get the services they deserve and need. This is commonly coupled with an embarrassment about their situation. Traditional concepts of respect prohibit families from sharing the dementia experience so as to not further shame the family member. Many deeply religious Mexican American families may accept the situation as the will of God and may also believe that only God can change the circumstances, thus making it difficult for health care providers to be of assistance or provide assistance.

Because families, especially families with loved ones in the early stages of dementia, often do not have sufficient information about the nature of Alzheimer's disease, it can be viewed as a normal part of aging, and diagnosis and treatment may not be sought (Henderson, 1990). Other barriers can include beliefs about diseases in general. According to Mexican American cultural traditions, health is viewed as a result of balance. It is a combination of faith, nutrition, and how one lived his or her life that may bring on an illness. In the dementia–Alzheimer's denial process, families may deny the process of memory impairment because the person always ate well and was a very religious person. For an individual who has had a history of improper behavior or who led a bad life (known as *la vida mala*), such a condition would, in a sense, be justified as a punishment from God for past sins. Hispanic families, therefore, accept the good and the bad that come from God, believing if He willed it, He also has the power to change it. With this in mind, Hispanic families then feel this is their cross to bear.

Another common health myth is a belief that a person can become ill when given a certain look by another, known as *el mal de ojo* or *el ojo* (the evil eye). To be cured of el ojo, one must visit *el curandero* (the folk healer), who can heal the individual by cleansing the person of this wrongdoing. There also is the belief that the memory impairment is caused by *nervios* (nerves), a temporary state that can be cured by the curandero. Yet another belief is that the brain "dries up," leading again to behaviors *como un niño* (childlike). All of these beliefs may be present simultaneously. It is critical for health care providers to ask about the specific beliefs that a particular Mexican American family may have about aging, in order to develop an appropriate treatment plan.

Regarding the caregiving role, it is the accepted custom that women are the preferred caregivers of the family. Outside of the immediate family, the Mexican American culture has strict ideas about behaviors with strangers of the opposite sex and believes it is more effective for female caregivers to work with females and male caregivers to work with males. Culturally, Latino men have conformed to strong, traditional male roles. It is culturally accepted for men not to participate in the hands-on caregiving of a loved one, but to participate in other areas, such as financial management for the care of the impaired family member.

OUTREACH STRATEGIES TO ENGAGE MEXICAN AMERICAN FAMILIES IN DEMENTIA CARE SERVICES

This section highlights key factors in successful outreach and marketing of dementia services to Latino families. The lessons presented here are primarily those learned from the El Portal: Latino Alzheimer's Project, a national demonstration effort under the federal Health Resources and Services Administration. This project was realized through a collaboration of 17 public and private agencies and organizations with leadership from the Los Angeles County Chapter of the Alzheimer's Association in California.

The goal of the project was to implement the first dementia-specific outreach and service effort targeting Latinos (primarily Mexican Americans) who live in the east and southeast areas of Los Angeles County. This county is home to 9 million persons, of which 40% are Hispanic, representing 42% of California's total Hispanic and Latino population age 60 years and older.

Hispanics have historically confronted multiple barriers that have affected their access to health and social services in general. These include language differences, limited income, lack of adequate health insurance, lack of knowledge about formal and informal support networks about dementia, and lack of culturally appropriate services. The project was intended to develop a model of service delivery to this multichallenged population.

The El Portal project consists of a toll-free Spanish-language helpline, two community-based care advocates (who act as service brokers), the development of culturally and linguistically appropriate respite and day care services, and support groups. All project personnel are bilingual and bicultural and receive ongoing training on dementia through the Alzheimer's Association. Outreach efforts have resulted in more than 540 calls to the Spanish-language helpline in a 20-month period. Nearly 90% of all callers are Hispanics caring for someone with a dementia or with dementia symptoms. Outreach strategies have included the use of Spanish- and English-language media, development of a project brochure, and presentations to community groups. The lessons learned from using these strategies include a sensitivity to the level of information on dementia available to this community, language needs, and the need to integrate culturally relevant themes in the marketing of specialized dementia services.

In a market research survey conducted by the Gallup Organization on behalf of the Alzheimer's Association (1993) in 1992, findings indicated widespread knowledge of Alzheimer's disease. In sharp contrast, the most common response on a community survey conducted by the Roybal Institute of Gerontology of the California State University at Los Angeles, in the project's catchment area (a largely Mexican American community), was "what's that?" This finding exemplifies the information–knowledge gap created by effective mainstream English-language public awareness campaigns on Alzheimer's disease and the lack of those promoting awareness among Latino and other ethnic groups. The foundation of any outreach and marketing plan to this population must be the appreciation of and sensitivity to these differences. Having an impact on this information gap involves both the development of language-appropriate materials and a methodology for promoting access to the information.

Language preferences will vary among members of the same family. Latino families may have members with varying levels of English-language proficiency living in the same household. Although some members will be bilingual, they may have strong preferences for either Spanish or English. There is often a member of the family who acts as an intercultural liaison by translating, accessing, and often engaging the family in available services. These liaisons are important targets for outreach efforts.

The implications of these lessons are that outreach materials using Alzheimer's disease or any associated terminology developed by providers such as *caregivers, respite*, and *adult day care* will be unfamiliar at best and irrelevant at worst. Materials developed must be available in both languages to meet this community's range of language preferences. Translations and adaptations of existing material must be carefully developed, as the following example illustrates.

When the term *respite care* is literally translated into Spanish, *cuidado de respiro*, the literal definition is "care for breathing." This can be interpreted by the community as a new treatment for asthma or other respiratory disorders. Similarly, the term caregivers has no direct or real translation in Spanish. Interestingly, it is also not found in popular English-language dictionaries.

Many of the terms used in aging and dementia are words created by the evolution of gerontology. This terminology is most familiar to providers, who often must apply labels to a client's care and activities. It is common for flyers to announce Alzheimer's support groups or caregiver support groups. Unless persons have been told that they are indeed caregivers, very few would self-identify with this term. Thus, families who could benefit from services may not respond to outreach efforts with this emphasis.

The cultural relevancy of the services being marketed is another important factor to consider. Marketing involves touching people's daily life experiences. Literature and program information must be relevant to the daily life experiences of Mexican American caregiving families. Some of these realities for a significant number of this population include low literacy levels, poverty, chronic health problems, language preferences, a strong sense of duty, responsibility, and spirituality. These factors will affect how information is received.

The marketing of dementia day care and respite services tends to emphasize the benefits to the caregiver. Among Mexican Americans, the focus on the caregiver rather than the patient would prove insensitive and may be insulting. Engaging in services to benefit yourself as a caregiver suggests that you are unwilling to accept or incapable of accepting your role and responsibility. Family members may be outraged as they perceive the caregiver as being selfish. The sense of *obligacion* (obligation and reciprocity), particularly to aging parents, is very strong. Accepting respite would be admitting that caring for an elder is a burden, another term frequently used in dementia-care literature.

In marketing dementia day care and respite services, the benefits to the patient should be stressed. It is much more culturally acceptable to use day care services if they are perceived as having concrete therapeutic benefits for the patient. These may be presented as physical exercise to improve cardiovascular functioning, a well-balanced meal to supply essential nutrients, cognitive stimulation to help maintain levels of functioning, and social–recreational activities to improve depressive symptoms. These factors were considered in the creation of the El Portal project brochure, which has been a key marketing tool.

The brochure was developed by a bilingual, bicultural, and biliterate task group composed of providers and caregivers. Their major task was to agree on content. The brochure cover reads *El Portal* and depicts an ivy-laced arch, symbolizing access to service. The arch is a common architectural motif in many Latin American countries and thus provides a sense of familiarity. The cover also contains key words *memory problems, information, access*, and *assistance*. Given the low levels of information and knowledge in this population, the term Alzheimer's disease was not used on the cover but was explained inside the brochure. The photograph selected for the cover depicts a granddaughter with her *abuelita* (grandmother). This intergenerational bond captures the strength of the Hispanic *familia* (family) and also conveys a message of hope. It communicates the fact that this agency respects the multigenerational family that it hopes to serve. In addition, information sheets in both Spanish and English are included in the brochure to describe specific services offered by El Portal. Also provided are hours of operation, specific service area covered, and the toll-free helpline number. Feedback from the community has indicated that this brochure has been a very successful marketing tool, resulting in very heavy use of the full range of El Portal's services by Hispanic families.

Other methods of outreach include use of community linkpersons (Valle, 1989) and extensive networking with members of the local community who actually serve the minority group that one is trying to reach. These individuals tend to be trusted by elderly minorities, and so a recommendation from them to participate in a particular program or service will generally not be discounted (Gallagher-Thompson et al., 1994). A related key point that is made repeatedly regarding outreach to minority elders in general, and Hispanic families in particular, is the need to actually be able to provide necessary services that are subsequently requested. In other words, the health care provider must deliver the goods or the resulting disappointment in the system and fear of being exploited will prevent future successful outreach efforts and further add to resistance to health care (see Arean & Gallagher-Thompson, in press, for review of this and related issues). Successful outreach efforts, however, resulting in high service utilization are both possible and likely when care has been taken to involve the community in the project from the outset and to provide services that are both appropriate and culturally relevant (Aranda, 1990).

INTERVENTION PROGRAMS FOR HISPANIC CAREGIVERS

Despite the difficulty in accessing this population, several programs have been reported in the literature that hold promise for alleviating some of the stress and burden associated with long-term caregiving. Henderson, Gutierrez-Mayka, Garcia, and Boyd (1993) described a program that successfully developed Spanish-language support groups for Hispanic caregivers. They emphasized making the program user-friendly, in that it was developed with full support from the community and filled a very pressing need. Also, services were offered in a flexible manner (in terms of number of meetings, location of the meetings, and the agenda to be followed), and practical problems that provided barriers to caregivers' attendance were dealt with (such as transportation difficulties). An evaluation of that program indicated that it was viewed very positively by the community and is likely to be continued, as long as appropriate bilingual and bicultural staff are available. Furthermore, Henderson and Gutierrez-Mayka (1992) provided some interesting observations on the content talked about in these support groups and how that content may differ from that of "typical" support groups that are conducted in English and that tend to be homogeneous in terms of ethnicity or culture. They noted that certain ethnocultural themes (such as the stigma associated with any illness that is perceived as mental) predominate, along with much discussion about how traditional sex roles determine caregiving functions. They also pointed out the importance of recognizing generational effects (e.g., middle-aged daughters or daughters-in-law are more likely to seek out and use a support group on a regular basis than are their older parents or siblings). These and other factors that are culturally specific need to be taken into account when designing any formal program for Hispanic caregivers.

A novel program has been developed by the Salinas Valley branch of the Monterey County chapter of the Alzheimer's Association in California. This program, called the Support Group on Wheels, has been very popular in this rural agricultural area in which small towns are the rule rather than the exception and where transportation difficulties may be significant. The concept involved renting a van to pick up support group participants and then having the group drive together to the central meeting place. This approach significantly reduces the amount of frustration involved in scheduling a day and time for the group to meet and significantly increases regular attendance. The social support and interaction that occur while driving to the site (which may be as much as 45 minutes away from where many of the participants actually live) also stimulate further positive gains from the overall experience. Although no formal evaluation has been done of this program, it has been enthusiastically supported by its participants, who strongly support its continuation. In addition, new referrals to that chapter of the Alzheimer's Association have been generated by the positive word of mouth that this program has generated.

An additional program, developed originally for caregivers in general and then modified with substantial community input to meet the specific needs of Mexican American caregivers of dementia victims, involves the use of a psychoeducational approach to reduce caregiver distress. This program is based on principles of social learning theory and combines both an emphasis on skill-building and support encouragement from other participants. It is structured as a class or workshop in coping with frustration and is held for a total of 8 consecutive weeks (2 hours each time) with an average of 8 participants. This number may be increased by the presence of other family members besides the primary caregiver, who attend to obtain information and to learn some of the basic skills for dealing with the frustrations of caregiving. A series of skills are taught, including simple methods of relaxation and learning to be assertive with close family members. Classes are conducted in Spanish by fully bilingual and bicultural leaders, and preliminary evaluation results have indicated that this approach has been extremely well received by the caregivers and their other family members. Manuals have actually been developed (for both the English- and Spanish-language versions of the class), and they are available from Dolores Gallagher-Thompson (Gallagher-Thompson, Arguello, Johnson, Moorehead, &

Polich, 1992; Gallagher-Thompson, Rose, et al., 1992). Both leaders' and participants' versions have been developed to enhance the perception of this intervention program as a class and to encourage "homework" and practice of the skills between class meetings. Although many of the Hispanic caregivers who participated in this program had little formal education, they have benefitted from the class's action-oriented style. Most have expressed considerable improvement in handling their negative emotions (e.g., anger and frustrations about caregiving) and have been very grateful for the opportunity to participate. Again, word of mouth has resulted in increased demand for this program, which is planned to continue in the future throughout northern California.

CONCLUSION

Although these are only a few examples of successful intervention programs that have been developed and implemented for Hispanic caregivers, the future is bright, with the promise of more to come. New interventions need to be developed that are maximally responsive to the needs of specific communities and that offer long-term support that is consistent with the changing needs of caregivers over time.

Other helpful suggestions when working with Mexican American families are the following:

- Never begin a conversation with specific issues; exchange pleasantries first.
- The older Hispanic person will most likely not express dissatisfaction with an individual or agency or ask questions. Invite the individual to ask questions several times throughout the conversation. Ask if anything you are doing or saying makes him or her uncomfortable.
- Any type of aggressive care planning will not be effective, even if the Hispanic elderly person seems to be agreeing with you. It is preferable to approach slowly.
- If you must inquire into their personal finances or situation, first ask for permission.
- When requesting demographic information or information on ethnicity from persons of Mexican descent, ask how they like to be referred to: Mexican, Mejicano, Chicano, Latino, Hispanic, Hispano, or Mexican American?
- When making a home visit, you may be offered a refreshment. Be receptive. You are allowing the person an opportunity to do something in return, as well as establishing trust. There may also be certain customs or rules of etiquette to follow when leaving the home. You may be asked to see the flower garden, family pictures, or mementos. By taking the time to do this (rather than rushing off in a hurry) you will understand the person and family network better.
- Be knowledgeable of folk remedies or prescription medicines from Mexico that families may use. Ask about the use of such remedies, and discuss other care options in addition to, not in lieu of, home remedies.

REFERENCES

Alzheimer's Association. (1993, February 18). *Program memo: Summary of Gallup market research, Phase I.* (Available from Alzheimer's Association National Offices, Chicago, IL)

Aranda, M. P. (1990). Culture-friendly services for Latino elders. *Generations, 14,* 55–57.

Arean, P., & Gallagher-Thompson, D. (in press). Issues and recommendations for the recruitment and retention of older minorities into clinical research. *Journal of Consulting and Clinical Psychology.*

Braus, B. (1993). What does "Hispanic" mean? *American Demographics, June,* 46–58.

Carnoy, M., Daley, H. M., & Ojeda, R. H. (1993). The changing economic position of Latinos in the U.S. labor market since 1939. In R. Morales & F. Bonilla (Eds.), *Latinos in a changing U.S. economy: Comparative perspectives on growing inequality* (Vol. 7, pp. 28–54). Beverly Hills, CA: Sage.

Evans, D. A., Fundenstein, H., Albert, M. S., Schert, P., Cook, N. R., Chown, M. J., Herbert, L. E., Hennekens, C. H., & Taylor, J. O. (1989). Prevalence of Alzheimer's disease in a community population of older persons higher than previously reported. *Journal of the American Medical Association, 262,* 2551–2556.

Gallagher-Thompson, D., Arguello, D., Johnson, C., Moorehead, R. S., & Polich, T. M. (1992). *Como controlar la frustracion: Una clase para cuidantes* (Controlling your frustration: A class for caregivers; class leader and class participant manuals). Palo Alto, CA: Department of Veterans Affairs Medical Center.

Gallagher-Thompson, D., Moorehead, R. S., Polich, T. M., Arguello, D., Johnson, C., Rodriguez, V., & Meyer, M. (1994). A comparison of outreach strategies for Hispanic caregivers of Alzheimer's victims. *Clinical Gerontologist, 15,* 57–63.

Gallagher-Thompson, D., Rose, J., Florsheim, M., Jacome, P., DelMaestro, S., Peters, L., Gantz, F., Arguello, D., Johnson, C., Moorehead, R. S., Polich, T. M., Chesney, M., & Thompson, L. W. (1992). *Controlling your frustration: A class for caregivers* (class leader and class participant manuals). Palo Alto, CA: Department of Veterans Affairs Medical Center.

Gratton, B., & Wilson, V. (1988). Family support systems and the minority elderly: A cautionary analysis. *Journal of Gerontological Social Work, 13,* 81–93.

Green, J. W. (1982). *Cultural awareness in the human services.* Englewood Cliffs, NJ: Prentice Hall.

Green, J. W., & Leigh, J. E. (1989). Teaching ethnographic methods to social service workers. *Practicing Anthropology, 11,* 8–10.

Henderson, J. N. (1990). Alzheimer's disease in a cultural context. In J. Sokolovsky (Ed.), *The cultural context of aging: Worldwide perspectives* (pp. 315–330). New York: Bergin & Gravey.

Henderson, J. N., & Gutierrez-Mayka, M. (1992). Ethnocultural themes in caregiving to Alzheimer's disease patients in Hispanic families. *Clinical Gerontologist, 11*(3/4), 59–74.

Henderson, J. N., Gutierrez-Mayka, M., Garcia, J., & Boyd, S. (1993). A model for Alzheimer's disease support group development in African-American and Hispanic populations. *The Gerontologist, 33,* 409–414.

Lockery, S. (1991). Family and social supports: Caregiving among racial and ethnic minority elders. *Generations*, *15*, 58–62.

Maldonado, D. (1979). Aging in the Chicano context. In E.E. Geilfund & A. J. Kutzik (Eds.), *Ethnicity and aging: Theory, research and policy* (pp. 175–183). New York: Sprague.

Markides, K. S., Boldt, J. S., & Ray, L. (1986). Sources of helping and intergenerational solidarity: A three-generations study of Mexican-Americans. *Journal of Gerontology*, *40*, 390–392.

Pousada, L. (1995). Hispanic-American elders: Implications for health care providers. *Clinics in Geriatric Medicine*, *11*(1), 39–52.

Sotomayor, M. (1992). Social support networks. In *Hispanic aging research reports: Part I and Part II* (pp. 94–105). Bethesda, MD: National Institutes of Health, National Institute on Aging.

Sotomayor, M., & Randolph, S. (1988). A preliminary review of caregiving issues among Hispanic elderly. In M. Sotomayor & H. Curiel (Eds.), *Hispanic elderly: A cultural signature* (pp. 137–160). Edinburgh, TX: Pan American University Press.

Talamantes, M. A. (1987). *An exploratory study of the nature of sibling relationships among Mexican American adults.* Unpublished master's thesis, Baylor University.

U.S. Bureau of the Census. (1993). Economic and Statistics Administration, Department of Commerce. *Racial and Ethnic Diversity of America's Population*, *11*(3), 1–8.

U.S. Congress, Office of Technology Assessment. (1990). *Confused minds, burdened families: Finding help for people with Alzheimer's & other dementias* (OTA-BA-403). Washington, DC: Author.

Valle, R. (1986). Cross-cultural competence in minority communities: A curriculum implementation strategy. In M. R. Miranda & H. L. Kitano (Eds.), *Mental health research and practice in minority communities: Development of culturally sensitive training programs* (DHHS Publication No. (ADM)89-1569, pp. 29–49). Washington, DC: U.S. Government Printing Office.

Valle, R. (1989). Cultural and ethnic issues in Alzheimer's disease family research. In E. Light & B. D. Lebowitz (Eds.), *Alzheimer's disease treatment and family stress: Directions for research.* Washington, DC: National Institute of Mental Health.

Wallace, S. P., & Lew-Ting, C. Y. (1992). Getting by at home-community-based long-term care of Latino elders. *Western Journal of Medicine*, *157*, 337–334.

APPENDIX: RESOURCE INFORMATION

Following is a selected listing of current national resources about aging, dementia, or Hispanic aging issues (in alphabetical order).

Alzheimer's Association, Inc. (National Office)
919 North Michigan Avenue, Suite 1000
Chicago, Illinois 60611-1676
(312) 335-8700

The Alzheimer's Association is the national voluntary health agency dedicated to research into the prevention, cure, and treatment of Alzheimer's disease and related disorders and to providing support and assistance to afflicted patients and their families. This organization develops and distributes multilingual materials on Alzheimer's disease on a variety of topics for both families and providers, including considerable written information in Spanish, along with a Spanish-language videotape depicting caregiving issues and resolutions. They have also established numerous local chapters in communities across the country, including several that offer Spanish-language support groups. Contact the national office for a listing of chapters and support groups and to be placed on their mailing list to receive their quarterly *Newsletter* and other vital communications.

Alzheimer's Disease Education and Referral Center (ADEAR), a Service of the National Institute on Aging
P.O. Box 8250
Silver Spring, Maryland 20907-8250
(800) 438-4380

The National Institute on Aging established the Alzheimer's Disease Education and Referral Center in response to a growing need for information on Alzheimer's disease, its impact on the family and health professional, and research into the possible causes and cures. The center was specifically authorized by Congress to collect and distribute information about Alzheimer's disease for health professionals, patients, their families, and the general public. It welcomes inquiries and serves as a clearinghouse for extensive, current information about all aspects of the disease, along with caregiving issues, policy concerns, and so forth.

Alzheimer's and Long Term Care Resource Center
280 Broadway, Room 213
New York, New York 10007

This group has produced the *Family Guide: Coping with Alzheimer's Disease at Home*, which is available both in English and in Spanish (*Cuidando con Carino: Una Guia para la Familia Sobre el Manejo en el Hogar del Hogar del Paciente de Alzheimer*). This is a series of audiotapes and accompanying written information that is extremely practical and that has been well received by families.

National Aging Dissemination Center
1225 I Street, NW, Suite 725
Washington, DC 20005
(202) 898-2578

The center produced a *Compendium of Products on Minority Aging Issues* with support from the Administration on Aging and U.S. Department of Health and Human Services.

National Association for Hispanic Elderly (Asociacion Nacional Pro Personas Mayores)
3325 Wilshire Boulevard, Suite 800
Los Angeles, California 90010
(213) 487-1922

The National Association for Hispanic Elderly produces a comprehensive series of health awareness materials, called ''A Nuestra Salud,'' on topics such as diabetes, depression, high blood pressure, and senility. These materials are available in both English and Spanish. This group also manages outreach campaigns, conducts social science research, develops media publications, and provides employment opportunities for low-income Hispanic elderly persons nationwide.

National Coalition of Hispanic Health & Human Services Organizations
1501 16th Street, NW
Washington, DC 20036
(202) 387-5000

Members include health care organizations and individual professionals in Hispanic health and human services organizations. This group's mission is to improve the quality of life and services provided to Hispanic families, aged and disabled. They publish (quarterly) the *COSSMHO Reporter*.

National Council of La Raza
1111 19th Street, NW
Washington, DC 20036
(202) 785-1670

The National Council of La Raza conducts research and policy analysis on Hispanics, networks with organizations serving Hispanics, and provides technical assistance to community organizations.

National Council on Aging (NCOA) Family Caregivers Program
409 3rd Street, SW
Washington, DC 20024
(202) 479-1200

The National Council on Aging is a private, nonprofit national organization concerned about the quality of life of older persons. Its focus is broad, encompassing such areas as health care, income, housing, employment, and community services. It sponsors a Family Caregivers Program that supports families caring for dependent older adults, disseminates information, and advocates for public policy that supports family caregiving.

National Hispanic Council on Aging
2713 Ontario Road, NW
Washington, DC 20009
(202) 265-1288

This group has resource materials on the needs of aging Latinos in all parts of the United States. It provides an opportunity for Hispanic elderly persons to use the resources of an organized effort to promote and facilitate the process of self-help and mutual help to find solutions to their problems. It publishes a quarterly newsletter called *Noticias* (in English), detailing activities of local chapters as well as national news of broad interest.

National Institute on Aging (NIA), U.S. Department of Health and Human Services

9000 Rockville Pike
Building 31, Room 5C27
Bethesda, MD 20892
(410) 396-1752, Information Officer

This office distributes consumer materials free of charge. Some information has been translated into Spanish and other languages such as Mandarin Chinese. Topics are nutrition, cancer, diabetes, hypertension, dental care, Alzheimer's disease, menopause, osteoporosis, aging and alcohol abuse, minorities and how they grow old, and so forth. Professional materials on Alzheimer's disease are also available. Publication list provided on request.

National Institute on Aging Information Center

P.O. Box 8057
Gaithersburg, MD 20898
(800) 222-2225

This agency produces Spanish-language "Age Pages" available free of charge. These currently include *Digestive Do's and Don'ts* (1988), *Heat, Cold, and Being Old* (1988), *Nutrition: a Lifelong Concern* (1988), *Skin Care* (1988), *Accidents and the Elderly* (1986), and *Who's Who in Health Care* (1988). Health publications available free of charge. Publication list provided on request.

National Institute of Mental Health, Information Resources and Inquiries, Office of Scientific Information

5500 Fishers Lane
Parklawn Building, Room 7C-02
Rockville, MD 20857
(301) 443-4513

This agency distributes consumer publications on aging, depression, Alzheimer's disease, mental health services, schizophrenia, anxiety disorder, panic disorder, obsessive compulsive disorder, biofeedback, and suicide. A variety of Spanish materials are available, dealing with such topics as mental health in general, mental health services, stress, schizophrenia, AIDS, depression, and panic disorder. Others are being developed to focus more specifically on depression and Alzheimer's disease in the Hispanic community.

Chapter 12

Cultural Dynamics of Dementia in a Cuban and Puerto Rican Population in the United States

J. Neil Henderson

The comprehensive nature of health among any age group is best understood from a biocultural perspective. Biological perspectives of health alone are extremely powerful in specifying the pathophysiology of disease. Yet, there is another critical aspect of the physical disruptions of disease. The subjective, personal experience and meaning of the disease symptoms are the illness aspects. Illness ultimately involves belief systems that define, create, or eliminate cognitive categories related to sickness episodes (Cassell, 1976; Helman, 1994). Together, disease and illness can provide a much more comprehensive explanatory model for sickness and serve as a parallel construct to the biological and cultural components of sickness (McElroy, 1990).

Ethnicity and dementia symptoms serve as conjoint phenomena that can be dissected from their interwoven natural state into multiple components in order to understand their interactive dynamics. Ethnicity is a cultural construct of great variety and elasticity, not a biological phenomenon. "Dementia" is a disease taxon, but is actually a classificatory construct used to refer to brain diseases due to neuronal loss (cf. Gubrium, 1986; Herskovits, 1995). Yet, even dementia is difficult to diagnose, and criteria for diagnosis are not universally agreed on. Moreover, some elders considered to be clearly demented do not show the classic lesions in the brain at autopsy, and some elders considered to be essentially cognitively normal show lesions of the types and numbers that cross the threshold for "caseness" (cf. Drachman, 1983; Khachaturian, 1985). It can be seen from these examples that even the biological reality of changed anatomy and physiology cannot escape the influence of humanly crafted constructs based on prevailing beliefs of a given health technology era.

In this chapter, the illness aspects of dementing disease are highlighted in order to explicate some of the salient cultural features of dementia in the context of Latin families. Some of the features include organization of the caregiving tasks in light of culturally based values such as stigma, generational cohorts, intervention sites, lack of salience of the Catholic church, gender, and personalism.

There is still a propensity for some to understand cultural phenomena as a series of unique traits found in "ethnic" groups. More useful is the notion that most societies hold many beliefs and behaviors in common, but that each attaches its own degree of importance to them. For example, women serving as caregivers is a nearly worldwide universal. However, when it occurs in Latin families, the value intensity, or valence, is very high relative to other cultural entities.

PRESENCE OF CULTURAL THEMES

The purpose of this chapter is to demonstrate the presence and specific nature of cultural themes among Hispanic caregivers to dementia patients. In so doing, a greater awareness of sociocultural factors of caregiving can be obtained. Applications of such sociocultural information are multidimensional, including its use to render more effective clinical intervention with Latin caregivers in areas of mental health and coping (Henderson & Gutierrez-Mayka, 1992).

These findings are part of a larger project designed to test the hypothesis that ethnic minority underuse of Alzheimer's disease support groups on a national basis is a function of sociocultural disincentives and not of lack of cases (Henderson, Gutierrez-Mayka, Garcia, & Boyd, 1993). Neither is it due to the presence of fully functioning family groups negating need for intervention (Gutierrez-Mayka & Henderson, 1993; Henderson, 1987, 1990; Henderson & Gutierrez-Mayka, 1992). This project demonstrated that community health interventions like Alzheimer's disease support groups can be successfully developed in Hispanic populations when cultural factors are adequately identified, understood, and meaningfully integrated into the support group intervention plan. As an analog to this culturally syntonic community health intervention, individual clinicians working with ethnoculturally distinct patients can improve their skills and success through specific inquiries into the cultural beliefs and values of their older patients (Henderson, 1994a).

SAMPLE

The Hispanic caregivers comprise an opportunistic sample of 37 caregivers and their patients, all of whom had some form of dementing disease. These caregivers live in Tampa, Florida, and consist mainly of Cuban, Spanish, and Puerto Rican

Hispanics. The caregivers in this sample were identified from senior adult day care centers, the Suncoast Gerontology Center's Memory Disorder Clinic at the University of South Florida, Alzheimer's disease registries, and, most important, by word-of-mouth snowball effect. Data regarding their life experiences as Spanish-speaking community members in their caregiving settings were collected by means of in-home interviews. Data were also collected during ethnic-specific Alzheimer's disease support group meetings. In addition, survey questionnaires were used to record caregiving tasks and frequencies as well as to explicate the Hispanic caregiver helper network configuration.

QUALITATIVE RESEARCH METHODS

The qualitative researcher working with ethnic minority elders is confronted with several sources of cultural variation. For example, the unit of research, whether individuals or groups, needs to be assessed in terms of the acculturation continuum. The extent of involvement among ethnic minorities in the majority culture can be seen as a continuum ranging from minimal involvement or participation to assimilation. Also, intracultural variations within ethnic minority groups should be expected. The in-depth involvement of qualitative research in ethnic minority life will highlight the artificial and nearly arbitrary nature of historical and government-generated rubrics such as ''American Indians.'' The researcher is challenged to understand each participant in the context of the larger elderly American Indian population on a national scale and also finds it mandatory to bring specific detail to the particular ecological and regional grouping out of which the participants' culture grew, the political climate in which this group exists, its status as a subgroup of a larger ''tribal'' community, specific language groups and dialects within the larger groups, and, if relevant, specific lineage and clan organizational structures.

Qualitative research among ethnic minority elders must include sensitivity to detect situational variation in the amount of personal culture revealed to the researcher (Henderson, 1994b). Ethnic minority elders adapt to life in a multicultural society by revealing their ethnic culture in certain situations and concealing it in others. The choice to conceal one's ethnic identity is affected by the penalizing experience of being perceived as different. Moreover, cultural overlap can be observed when the majority group and the minority group have independently used similar behaviors. The trick for the researcher is to determine the variable context from which these superficially similar behaviors derive. Also, cultural overlap can occur when two different cultures borrow from each other to adapt to changing conditions. As a result, they come to share values and behaviors. The sharing, however, does not necessarily mean that the two cultures are interpreting the common behavior or belief in the same way.

Cultural overlap reveals subtle but significant elements that can be crucial in understanding the behavior patterns of ethnic minority elders. For example, older ethnic minority elders who grew up in a pre–Civil Rights era now have adult grandchildren who grew up in a post–Civil Rights era. The difference in cultural eras results in ethnic minority elders who are less likely to seek and use services than their younger relatives even though both reside in the same national context (Maldonado, 1985).

CULTURAL DYNAMICS IN DEMENTIA RESPONSES

The failure to account for ethnic minority culture between health care providers and ethnic minority patients is well recognized and serves as a model for larger scale intercultural difficulties (Henderson & Gutierrez-Mayka, 1992). For example, cohort effects pertain when the clinician and patient are of different generational groups that hold variant beliefs about gender roles. A young Anglo male clinician may suggest that an elderly Hispanic woman tell her husband that she will not prepare meals too high in fat content. Such advice is predicated more on the clinician's relatively recent cohort learning regarding women's generally greater assertiveness and quality of life. However, the elderly Hispanic woman may feel as if she has no right to go against the wishes of her husband in this case. In another instance, the stigma of mental health crises is more apparent for elders than for today's young adults. Mental health was once handled by state institutions, which were perceived as prisons for punishing the weak (Ho, 1987; Levine & Padilla, 1980). When older ethnic minority members have greater adherence to traditional cultural values than do younger cohorts, they avoid the helping services until very serious needs occur or a younger ethnic minority member assists the elder in getting services (Maldonado, 1975.) There may also be a reluctance to maximize the use of community helping resources (Cox & Monk, 1990; Wood & Parham, 1990). Ethnic minority elders are likely to show subjugated role behavior in the presence of clinical authority figures (Haug, 1981).

Although usually unacknowledged, cosmopolitan health care practitioners have likewise learned what is actually a health care belief system. Kuhn (1962) and other historians of science and health care have demonstrated that clinicians perceive their professionally derived knowledge as fact when it is actually part of an evolving belief system. When a professional belief system is acknowledged, the structural dynamics of the clinician–patient encounters are more balanced. No one has the edge on possessing the ultimately correct data set. In an egalitarian atmosphere, the clinician does not condescend to the patient's "magical" folk beliefs, nor does the patient achieve enlightenment by elevation to the lofty pinnacle of "true" clinical fact. Both negotiate acceptable fits for their own health care belief systems to produce more optimal communication, compliance, and treatment outcomes (Good & Good, 1981; Hill, Fortenberry, & Stein, 1990; Katon & Kleinman, 1981: Kleinman, 1980; Pfeifferling, 1981; Stein, 1990).

Valle (1989) noted that when treating ethnic minority elders, clinicians must make a correct assessment of the patient's location along an acculturation continuum, which is a means of marking one's degree of ethnic identification. On the acculturation continuum, the traditional position is characterized by a strong orientation toward cultural origins and homeland. A bicultural position is marked by person's partial allegiance to his or her homeland culture and partial affinity with the current mainstream culture. An assimilated position is closely integrated with the mainstream culture. Of particular note are the bicultural and assimilated positions. These can be mistakenly ignored by clinicians because they do not appear "ethnic enough" to warrant special attention. In reality, such people have not lost their ethnic minority heritage; they have simply added to it a great facility for using the cultural system of the majority population. Consider an example of a person who is a fourth-generation member of a family that emigrated to the United States from Spain and in which the youngest generation (ages 5–9) cannot speak Spanish but does participate with bilingual parents (who feel most comfortable using English) in Spanish holiday traditions, food preparation, religion, gender role behavior, and so on. First names are English, and surnames are European. Their political identification is the United States, yet their Spanish cultural roots are still alive and well.

Service providers recognize that the ethnic minorities who are bicultural or assimilated may value what they remember as the intent, spirit, or benefit of their more traditional family values and lifestyle. In fact, they may search for their "comforting presence in some surrogate form" (Valle, 1989, p. 129). For example, the value placed on personal, individualized interaction modeled by familial and small nonfamilial groupings is not often found in service bureaucracies. When the personal empathy and shared perception are found in support groups such as the ethnic-minority-specific support group for Alzheimer's disease developed by this project, participants make use of the service and refer to the support group as a "little family."

Another major aspect of Valle's (1989) work underscored the importance of understanding intraethnic cultural variation. Valle (p. 131) wrote,

> Culture is not only expressed with considerable variation along a continuum, but also unevenly with indistinct domains of daily living where individuals and groups act out their lives. Behavioral and coping responses will situationally change as social environments change. One person's expression of ethnic culture may vary at home, the work place, and the broader community.

The stress of caregiving and its episodic crises do not cause caregivers to drop "ethnocultural veils" (Valle, 1989). On the contrary, cultural response patterns have often served a positive and protective function in the life of the individuals and families involved (Simic, 1985). Ethnicity, such as when relying on the family in time of need, with its familiar patterns unique to an ethnic minority group, becomes protective and sheltering. The episodic-crisis aspect of caregiving does not lessen the presence of differential, ethnocultural responses to dementia.

COMMUNITY HISTORY AND CULTURAL CONTEXT

Unlike in Miami, Florida, the presence of a large population of Spanish-speaking immigrants in Tampa, Florida, goes back in time 100 years. Consequently, contemporary life for these immigrants is quite heterogeneous culturally. The turn-of-the-century immigrants hailed mainly from Spain, Cuba, and Puerto Rico. In the late 1800s, Cuban tobacco entrepreneurs and a civil engineer from Spain had declined Mobile, Galveston, and Pensacola as sites for extending Cuban-based hand-rolled cigar factories, deciding instead on Tampa. Within several months, the influx of Cubans and other Spanish-speaking people arriving in Tampa to provide labor for the cigar factories had established a significant Latin cultural base. By 1908, enough cigar factories and laborers were present to produce 6.5 million hand-rolled cigars in 1 week, mainly at the hands of Cubans and other Latins (Mormino & Pizzo, 1983).

Today, the descendants of these workers live in Tampa, although the cigar industry exists only in a few small factories and at a minuscule production rate compared with the heyday. Because of its long history of Cuban and Puerto Rican connections, Tampa has served as a magnet for many future immigrants from the islands as political and economic fortunes have shifted over time.

The political exigencies of Cuba from the 1950s to the 1990s represent another migration pressure affecting Tampa. Miami's proximity to Cuba is related to its density of recent Cuban immigrants, whereas Tampa's long-term Latin population and vigorous Latin culture were attractive to others. Miami has its well-known Little Havana area in which the density of people and cultural infrastructure constitutes a home away from home. Tampa has its 100-year-old Ybor City, named after a Cuban revolutionary of the late 1800s who was also a major force in the cigar industry. However, today it is largely a symbolic area of Tampa relative to Latin cultural tradition because many of the original inhabitants and their descendants have moved elsewhere in the city in a more dispersed habitation pattern, even though there are discernable areas of Latin concentration.

In today's Tampa, the Cuban and Puerto Rican citizen experiences a quite heterogeneous Latin community. Some persons are either descendants of well-established, long-term Latin families or, if they are more recent immigrants, can live in a highly interdigitated cultural mix. Nonetheless, there are well-established cultural boundaries demarcating the mainstream culture from the Latin culture. Also, there are strong intraethnic group boundaries related to the Latin history of Tampa and points of home origin, politics, or both.

Tampa's original Latin immigrants transferred an Old World sociocultural organizational device with them. These are the clubs in which membership is tied to places of home origin. These so-called clubs were much more than social-recreational groups. The clubs also operated health care services by purchase of annual membership, which were essentially like HMOs. The club concept included, in at least two cases, large inpatient hospitals that operated into the late

1980s. The recent cost of health care delivery led to the collapse of the Latin clubs' hospitals and clinics. Intra-Latin community variations include a strong sense of allegiance to one's own club and some sense of status competition between clubs. The Latin clubs, particularly their acute care health systems, were notorious among the mainstream American citizens of Tampa for their "care-for-their-own" image.

Many Latins explicitly reported that nursing homes were simply not the way in which Latins responded to their dependent elders. This ethic is so strong that the health service system of their own design did not include long-term care during its entire operational history. The dependent elders were cared for exclusively at home by relatives.

Families of Cubans and Puerto Ricans in Tampa have numerous socioeconomic indicators similar to those of Anglos of the larger community. There is great heterogeneity in acculturation and enormous facility in participation in mainstream American society. Still, cohort effects are quite noticeable within families of multiple generations that began in the early years of this century and now extend to great-grandchildren. For long-term families, the result is a panorama of living history reflecting the dynamics of acculturation. For more recent immigrants, there is a vast array of possible sociocultural niches in which to participate, nearly at one's will. A person may choose to become a part of a cadre of monolingual Spanish speakers and remain embedded in a type of encapsulated home culture brought to another land. A person may also choose to capitalize on the cultural experience of his or her longer term compatriots in Tampa and become as much of the fiber of Tampa's mainstream American culture as possible. Of course, for many, cultural expression is situational and not an either–or proposition.

Understanding a case of dementia in the Latin community of Tampa requires great sensitivity to the aforementioned cultural contexts. There are few "exotic" elements of cases, and at a casual glance, a given case may have the appearance of having no Latin cultural aspects. However, close examination of cases coupled with long-term exposure to them has virtually universally revealed Latin culture-specific case attributes.

CULTURAL ASPECTS OF DEMENTIA AMONG CUBANS AND PUERTO RICANS OF TAMPA

The cultural factors most observable in the Latin cases of dementia are disease-associated social stigma, gender role performance expectations in caregiving, the use of intergenerational brokers for entry into support group participation, the value placed on personalism of professional–client interactions, scant use of the Catholic church as a focal point for assistance with management of the caregiving burden, and symbolic associations with support group meeting site selection.

Social Stigma

Disease-associated social stigma is common when symptoms involve odd behaviors not considered indicative of special capabilities such as spirit contacts for healing purposes. Dementing diseases certainly fit this criterion as the person passes from simple memory impairment to more confused and delusional symptomatology. Moreover, the person is typically ambulatory and looks physically unaffected for much of the disease process. Consequently, the person can be in public places and be involved in group activities ranging from employment to recreational outings when odd behaviors occur. Embarrassment felt by family members constitutes the discomfort resulting from the person's behavior. Unless the person is in the very early stages, he or she may not be acutely aware of his or her socially embarrassing behaviors.

The value valence placed on social appearances is particularly strong in Latin culture. Indicators of social fitness include, at least in concept if not in reality, immaculately clean houses and apparel, grooming, and a socially impeccable community image. Because there is a culturally valued focus on relationships with others (as opposed to things or ideas; Hernandez, 1992), phenomena that bolster socially desirable qualities receive enormous attention. These things garner respect; lack thereof degrades the respect quotient.

In terms of dementia and its symptomatic behaviors, the family is at high risk of losing some degree of self-comfort afforded the family before the elder's disease. For example, the elder's leaving the house and wandering the neighborhood clad only in underwear or even naked can mortify family members. Incontinence can also be supremely embarrassing, particularly if there is an odor in the house. The messes that the person can make by undoing household cleaning and straightening tasks can result in caregivers becoming isolated and not allowing visitors into the home. Moreover, the person may become involuntarily confined to the house even though exercise can be very good for him or her.

Gender Role Performance Expectations

The value valence placed on women as caregivers is very powerful in Latin culture. The concepts of role performance and role strain are seen in operation here. Female caregivers are not always available in the immediate nuclear family. However, as substitutes are considered, families seek the help of nonrelated women before resorting at last to related male caregivers (Henderson & Garcia, 1986).

Acculturative processes are also operative here. The temporal and cultural distance between just one generation is evident between a mother and her adult daughter confronted with a diagnosis of dementia in the husband–father (Henderson, 1990; Henderson & Gutierrez-Mayka, 1992). The mother assumed that of her male and female children (now adults and living in Tampa) and her grandchildren, her daughter and she would be the primary caregivers, even though the daughter was divorced and had grandchildren of her own. However, the daughter would not hear of it. The daughter cited the presence of her brother, whose wife raised his children in their home. In the daughter's estimation, this qualified the brother to be more able to provide care than she. The mother was shocked at her daughter's recalcitrant behavior. The mother was, after all, only applying the cultural rules as she knew them. Likewise, the daughter applied cultural rules as she had come to know them in another place and time.

Intergenerational Brokers for Community Support

Although the word *foreign* is somewhat archaic and has a pejorative connotation, it communicates well the sense of displacement, fear, and longing for one's familiar home culture. For some of the oldest generations of Latin caregivers in Tampa, there remains at times a feeling of being foreign. This is especially true when it comes to accessing community services. For the older generation who had a pre–Civil Rights socialization experience, the ordinary use of community and social services can feel inappropriate or even degrading. Their children, however, are well versed in the nature of social assistance and have acquired a sense that services are due to them (Maldonado, 1985).

The Latin Alzheimer's disease support group provides a window into the elder's experience of reluctance and tentativeness in using a service felt by its organizers to be as user-friendly as anything can get. If the support group was devoid of cultural barriers, the intergenerational broker phenomenon would not be present. However, consider the case of an 81-year-old woman whose husband was severely demented, although still cared for at home (Henderson, 1990; Henderson & Gutierrez-Mayka, 1992). The woman's oldest son accompanied her on her first attendance to the support group. Actually, she had first tried to enlist her stepdaughter to accompany her, but the stepdaughter was unavailable on the meeting nights. Consequently, her son brought her to her first and second meetings. After this, the stepdaughter made arrangements to bring her. At this first meeting, the son spoke for his mother, even answering questions put to his mother by others in the group. Over time, the woman spoke for herself and was brought to the meeting by same-aged caregivers whom she had met at the group. Without knowledge of this intergenerational dynamic, service providers might have mistaken her reticence to participate as something more problematic than a person simply "being her culture."

Personalism of the Professional–Client Interaction

Although it is true of many ethnic groups, personalism is particularly powerful among Latins. It is offensive to be treated like a number, no matter how much time efficiency is a criterion for quality of service. Moreover, a disease that has socially stigmatizing aspects requires that the family be treated all the more sensitively when attempting to intervene. In the development of the Alzheimer's disease support group, almost a year of time was expended in developing rapport with the potential users. Developing rapport was a multifaceted endeavor. It included giving educational seminars at social clubs relevant to the Latin community, at public health clinics, at cultural clubs, and to medical staff. Perhaps more important was the time allowed for the slow development of a roster of cases and visits in homes.

The project staff left their desks as much as possible in order to be a part of the community as opposed to a distant intellectual neighbor. The development of the highly valued Latin personalism coevolved with the home visits and numerous calls for information to the project staff. These calls also included calls to staff's homes on weekends and at nights. Inevitably, the conversations began to carry information beyond the technical details of the course of the disease and community services. Over time, caregivers began to exchange holiday greeting cards and birthday cards. Actual friendships began. Not only was the detached researcher whose involvement stops when data collection stops inappropriate, no one, including staff, wanted it that way. The ethics and definitions of boundaries between researcher and researchee must be adequately addressed when conducting fieldwork with people of Latin culture.

Caregiver Nonreliance on the Catholic Church

In the public eye, Latins and Catholicism are an assumed dyad. Because churches are in part designed to provide solace to those experiencing trying times, it was thought that caregivers would make heavy use of the church. However, this was not the case. The caregivers relied most on family-based assistance.

One explanation of why the Catholic church was not the primary source of assistance may be related to Protestant versus Catholic concepts of church. Maldonado (personal communication, 1989) has captured a distinction between the two churches: A Catholic is more likely to state, ''I attend Mass at . . . ,'' whereas the Protestant is more likely to state that ''I belong to the First Baptist church.'' Of course, the Catholic church is vitally important to the Latin community, but not in terms of caregiver reliance. It would be a mistake to assume that Latin caregivers need no extrafamilial support because of the church's presence.

In a few cases, caregivers wondered out loud if they were being punished for some sin. Although this is a direct connection to the religious domain, fieldworkers never encountered Catholic clergy in caregivers' homes nor did they record conversation about seeking assistance from the church. However, one woman caregiver who was musing about the early stages of dementia reported that she had detected a change in her relationship with her husband that she attributed to some variance of relationship trajectories of unknown origin. She even convinced her husband to seek relationship counseling from their priest. In retrospect, however, she now attributes the relationship changes to early symptoms of dementia that were disturbing to her husband but that he felt he could still conceal from others. Such withholding of early-stage symptoms is common among dementia victims.

Community Symbol Values of Support Group Locations

Tampa's lengthy Latin community history includes several mutual support clubs founded for the maintenance of social, political, and health care needs. The clubs' constituencies were related to points of geopolitical origins of the members. For example, the Centro Espanol club had members mainly from Cuba. However, the Centro Asturiano club had members mainly from Spain, with greatest specificity for the region known as Asturia. Moreover, the Latin community is hierarchically stratified relative to value and prestige of one's home origins. Briefly stated, the highest value associated with home origins was reportedly accorded to those directly from Spain, in a literal way "the real Spanish." Next were those who could trace very recent generations to Spain. Following these people were Cubans without refugee status, Cubans with refugee status, and then Puerto Ricans.

The relationship of these organizations to the location of the support group meeting sites became exceedingly important. In the early stages of the support group implementation process, it was thought that association of the support groups with the health component of the clubs was a natural and very culturally relevant fit. However, only one support group per month was feasible. Out of six possible club sites for meetings, only one could be used. Rotating to each of the sites over time was declined so that a permanent place could be announced without confusion.

The project's liaison with the Latin community was a lifelong member of Centro Espanol Hospital. She was able to quickly arrange for the use of a nicely appointed conference room for the monthly meetings. However, it became clear within a few months that there were others who were not members of Centro Espanol who felt somewhat uncomfortable at not being on their home turf. There may also have been people in the community who would not attend owing to the location that seemed to the project staff to be so perfectly suitable.

The location was changed to a hospital that was not associated with any club but was located in an area of town that had recently grown to have many Cuban and Puerto Rican residents. This was convenient for them, but not so for the residents who belonged to the clubs. The members of the old clubs resided in other parts of town far removed from this hospital, the original locations for the Spanish-speaking populations.

Once again the location was changed to try to find a niche that had the combined features of being located where the majority of the Latin people lived, was easily accessible, and violated no club loyalty boundaries. This move was possible owing to an opportunity provided by a man whose mother had dementia. He had started attending the group at the hospital site where recent population growth included many Spanish-speaking people. This man was the owner and administrator of a small clinic operated in the fashion of an HMO. The clinic had been operated by a Latin father-and-son physician team for more than 40 years. Although they no longer practiced there, the clinic retained its name, location, and orientation to the Latin population. This site became the place in which the correct attributes were present and where the support group found a home.

The above report of the multiple efforts at implementing a culturally relevant intervention in terms of location of support groups shows the need for careful reflection, as the anthropological professionals were well trained in cultural dynamics and had good intentions, yet had an imperfect outcome.

Of course, the explanation for "missing" the best location in the early stages of the project could be due to incompetence on the part of program staff. However, two issues must be examined. First, this program was federally funded and had limited time in which to achieve good results (i.e., large numbers of target population contacts). Second, and perhaps more important, there was a lesson learned regarding preconceived notions of just what, exactly, is "cultural relevance." At first glance, finding the highest degree of linkage to obvious cultural elements or dynamics would seem to serve the purpose of identifying that which is culturally relevant. Yet the highest degree of cultural relevance may have as its prime characteristic the nature of being exquisitely subtle yet highly significant.

Those most obvious aspects of the target group's culture may be nothing more than outsiders' illusions. Also, "obvious culture" may not be deeply rooted enough for purposes of culturally relevant service intervention because to the native it may have the stigma of being co-opted by the dominant society that uses it to homogeneously describe the minority group and may come to be seen as an obvious cultural aspect that is present but superficial (cf. Green, 1995).

Location seemed to require a high degree of cultural relevance. However, not meeting at the culturally obvious clubs suggests that the best place was one that was culturally irrelevant. Yet, this is unsatisfactory because suggesting that there is truly zero cultural context for something like a landmark institution is absurd. However, knowing what is the next deeper cultural stratum requires a degree of ethnographic penetration that cannot be gotten in short order.

Last, the nature of this project was that it was not only a model program field test, it was a research project using qualitative methods. Qualitative methods are sensitive to the unexpected exigencies of human dynamics (Denzin & Lincoln, 1994; Gubrium & Sankar, 1994). There is an assumed value in pursuing avenues of inquiry that unpredictably emerge during the real foment of project implementation. These qualitative research characteristics assisted project staff in reassessing and revamping the program design as needed. "Workability and why" were the gold standards for project implementation. Although this real-life flexibility may not always be possible when using nonqualitative methods, particularly under duress of limited time, the experience demonstrates the value of a flexible approach to the success of programs with diverse cultural populations.

REFERENCES

Cassell, E. (1976). *The healer's art: A new approach to the doctor–patient relationship.* New York: Lippincott.

Cox, C., & Monk, A. (1990). Minority caregivers of dementia victims: A comparison of Black and Hispanic families. *Journal of Applied Gerontology, 9,* 340–354.

Denzin, N. K., & Lincoln, Y. S. (Eds.). (1994). *Handbook of qualitative research.* Thousand Oaks, CA: Sage.

Drachman, D. A. (1983). How normal aging relates to dementia: A critique and classification. In D. Samuel, S. Gershon, S. Algeri, V. E. Grimm, & G. Toffano (Eds.), *Aging of the brain* (pp. 114–125). New York: Raven Press.

Good, B. J., & Good, M.-J. D. (1981). The meaning of symptoms: A cultural hermeneutic model for clinical practice. In L. Eisenberg & A. Kleinman (Eds.), *The relevance of social science for medicine* (pp. 165–196). Boston: Reidel.

Green, J. (1995). *Cultural awareness in the human services* (2nd ed.) Englewood Cliffs, NJ: Prentice-Hall.

Gubrium, J. F. (1986). *Old times and Alzheimer's: The descriptive organization of senility.* Greenwich, CT: JAI Press.

Gubrium, J., & Sankar, A. (Eds.). (1994). *Qualitative methods in aging research.* Thousand Oaks, CA: Sage.

Gutierrez-Mayka, M., & Henderson, J. N. (1993). Social work for non-social workers: An example of unplanned role negotiation in a community health intervention project. *Journal of Gerontological Social Work, 20,* 135–146.

Haug, M. (Ed.). (1981). *Elderly patients and their doctors.* New York: Springer.

Helman, C. G. (1994). *Culture, health and illness.* Oxford, United Kingdom: Butterworth-Heinemann.

Henderson, J. N. (1987). Mental disorders among the elderly: Dementia and its sociocultural correlates. In P. Silverman (Ed.), *The elderly as modern pioneers* (pp. 357–374). Bloomington: Indiana University Press.

Henderson, J. N. (1990). Alzheimer's disease in cultural context. In J. Sokolovsky (Ed.), *The cultural context of aging: Worldwide perspectives* (pp. 315–330). New York: Bergin & Garvey.

Henderson, J. N. (1994a). Caregiving in culturally diverse populations. *Seminars in Speech and Language, 15,* 216–225.

Henderson, J. N. (1994b). Ethnic and racial issues. In J. F. Gubrium & A. Sankar (Eds.), *Qualitative methods in aging research* (pp. 33–50). Thousand Oaks, CA: Sage.

Henderson, J. N., & Garcia, J. (1986, November). *Ethnic primary caregivers to Alzheimer's patients.* Paper presented at the Gerontological Society of America, Chicago.

Henderson, J. N., & Gutierrez-Mayka, M. (1992). Ethnocultural themes in caregiving to Alzheimer's patients in Hispanic families. *Clinical Gerontologist, 11,* 59–74.

Henderson, J. N., Gutierrez-Mayka, M., Garcia, J., & Boyd, S. (1993). A model for Alzheimer's disease support group development in African-American and Hispanic populations. *The Gerontologist, 33,* 409–414.

Hernandez, G. G. (1992). The family and its aged members: The Cuban experience. *Clinical Gerontologist, 11*, 45–58.

Herskovits, E. (1995). Struggling over subjectivity: Debates about the "self" and Alzheimer's disease. *Medical Anthropology Quarterly, 9*, 146–164.

Hill, R. F., Fortenberry, J. D., & Stein, H. F. (1990). Culture in clinical medicine. *Southern Medical Journal, 83*, 1071–1080.

Ho, M. K. (1987). *Family therapy with ethnic minorities.* Newbury Park, CA: Sage.

Katon, W., & Kleinman, A. (1981). Doctor-patient negotiation and other social science strategies in patient care. In L. Eisenberg & A. Kleinman (Eds.), *The relevance of social science for medicine* (pp. 253–279). Boston: Reidel.

Khachaturian, Z. S. (1985). Diagnosis of Alzheimer's disease. *Archives of Neurology, 42*, 1097–1104.

Kleinman, A. (1980). *Patients and healers in the context of culture.* Berkeley: University of California Press.

Kuhn, T. S. (1962). *The structure of scientific revolutions.* Chicago: University of Chicago Press.

Levine, E. S., & Padilla, A. M. (1980). *Crossing cultures in therapy: Pluralistic counseling for the Hispanic.* Monterey, CA: Brooks/Cole.

Maldonado, D. (1975). The Chicano elderly. *Social Work, 20*, 213–216.

Maldonado, D. (1985). The Hispanic elderly: A socio-historical framework for public policy. *Journal of Applied Gerontology, 4*, 18–27.

McElroy, A. (1990). Biocultural models in studies of human health and adaptations. *Medical Anthropology Quarterly, 4*, 243–265.

Mormino, G. R., & Pizzo, A. P. (1983). *Tampa: The treasure city.* Tulsa, OK: Continental Heritage.

Pfiefferling, J.-H. (1981). A cultural prescription for medicocentrism. In L. Eisenberg & A. Kleinman (Eds.), *The relevance of social science for medicine* (pp. 197–222). Boston: Reidel.

Simic, A. (1985). Ethnicity as a resource for the aged. *Journal of Applied Gerontology, 4*, 65–71.

Stein, H. F. (1990). *American medicine as culture.* Boulder, CO: Westview Press.

Valle, R. (1989). Cultural and ethnic issues in Alzheimer's disease research. In E. Light & B.D. Lebowitz (Eds.). *Alzheimer's disease treatment and family stress: Directions for research* (pp. 122–154). Rockville, MD: National Institute of Mental Health.

Wood, J. B., & Parham, I. A. (1990). Coping with perceived burden: Ethnic and cultural issues in Alzheimer's family caregiving. *Journal of Applied Gerontology, 9*, 325–339.

Chapter 13

African American Families: Management of Demented Elders

Irene Daniels Lewis
Marie S. Chavis Ausberry

Caring for frail elders in today's society is a growing concern of many individuals. This chapter describes the sociocultural context of African American families who are caring for demented elders and some of the traditional supportive groups used by them. Throughout the chapter, the role of spirituality as a supportive entity is discussed. The authors conclude with some useful strategies that health care professionals may use for more effective decision making when African American families are managing demented elders.

At least 11 studies of African American family caregivers of patients with dementia have been reported, and an excellent review article by Gonzales, Gitlin, and Lyons (1995) comparing those research efforts is available. In summary, the results indicate the following:

1   Some studies found no differences in burden between Anglo and African American caregivers of dementia patients (Morycz, Malloy, Bozich, & Martz, 1987; Wood & Parham, 1990), whereas others found that African American caregivers report less burden (Hinrichsen & Ramirez, 1992; Lawton, Rajagopal, Brody, & Kleban, 1992). Lawton et al. (1992) also found more favorable scores among African American caregivers on indices of caregiving ideology, caregiving as an intrusion, and caregiving satisfaction. Mui (1992) found African American daughter caregivers reported less role strain, although the caregiving role demand for them was greater than among the Anglo daughters. Other findings

related to burden among African American caregivers were that caregivers in larger households showed less burden (Wood & Parham, 1990) and impairments in instrumental activities of daily living and memory and behavior problems were less stressful, due in part to greater confidence in being able to handle the problems than their Anglo counterparts (Haley, Coleton, Isobe, & West, 1992).

2   African American caregivers were less likely to seek information about dementia and more likely to use cognitive coping strategies such as reframing the situation and determination to survive; they were also more likely to use prayer than the Anglo caregivers (Segall & Wykle, 1988–1989; Wood & Parham, 1990; Wykle & Segall, 1991).

3   African American caregivers reported less depression and gastrointestinal symptoms, but more respiratory and neurological symptoms and greater number of illnesses and poorer self-rated health than Anglo caregivers (Haley et al., 1995; Lawton et al., 1992).

4   African American caregivers were found to be knowledgeable about formal services but used them infrequently, relying more on informal support services. The greater the impairment of the dementia patient, the more likely the caregivers were to use services (Cox & Monk, 1990). Haley and colleagues (in press) found no difference between African American and Anglo caregivers on their reliance on extended family members for informal support services.

The rest of the information shared in this chapter is based primarily on studies conducted by the authors. One author has 5 years of experience with demented African Americans and their caregivers; the other has completed a study of poststroke survivors (some in the early stages of dementia) and their caregivers.

SOCIOCULTURAL CONTEXT

According to Shimkin and Uchendu (1978), Sudarkasa (1988), and others who have studied Black family organization, the concept of consanguinity better describes how African American families operate than does the concept of conjugality. The first refers to kinship that is biologically based and rooted in blood ties, and the latter embodies ties through marital lines (between spouses). In Mother Africa, families consisted of clans with a male as head of household (Sudarkasa, 1988). Typically, widows normally married someone in their deceased husbands' lineage, a brother, for example. Family was along bloodlines, not in-laws, as through marriage (Smith, 1973). Nieces, nephews, and cousins were viewed as strong blood relatives, and these relationships were more solid than those along spousal lines.

Family was the only support institution viable for African Americans during slavery (Franklin, 1988). Frequently, marriage was consummated merely from suggestions by owners. In the antebellum period, many freedmen overcame tremendous barriers to make their family institution legal. For African Americans, the strong sense of family tradition remained intact and was (is) highly valued. Family helped members of this group overcome the slave system, years of legal segregation, "Jim Crow," organized poverty, and a hostile environment.

Findings from the authors' work with African American families are consistent with reports by Jawanza Kunjufu (1994) about the makeup of local church congregations, that is, that they are predominantly female and consist of groups of blood relatives: siblings, aunts, uncles, children, cousins, nephews, nieces, parents, grandparents, grandchildren, great-grandparents, great-grandchildren, and great aunts and uncles. In many respects, the church congregation is reflective of five or more sets of extended blood ties (families) or clans (Lewis, 1995).

This group is a natural support group that can and does respond to the many needs of African American frail elders. The "church family" is the arena in which some African Americans expect to get help with the management of elders with dementia. It is included in this cultural context because the church is the formal institution in which lie the cultural and philosophical roots of Africans in the United States (Nobles, Goddard, Cavil, & George, 1987).

Belief in the absence of any separation of the spiritual world and daily life practices of individuals is formally called the ontological principle of consubstantiation, according to Nobles et al. (1987). This principle is the basis for all African and African American religious and social practices (e.g., belief in ancestral spirits, elaborate funeral rites, respect for elders, etc.; Nobles et al., 1987, p. 84).

Today, in most African American church families, young parishioners are expected to care for elders with mental and physical needs.

CHANGING DEMOGRAPHY AND LABELS

African Americans constitute the largest single ethnic subgroup, making up 8% (2.5 million) of the people age 65 years and over in the United States. By the year 2050, the percentage of elderly African Americans will rise to 10 (U.S. Bureau of the Census, 1993a), and the numbers of the frailest elders, those 80 years and older, are projected to increase most rapidly. This trend is significant because the population 80 years and older has the highest rate of dementia. In 1990, 62% of this group were female and 38% were male (U.S. Bureau of the Census, 1993a).

Of the 50 states, New York has the largest number of African Americans, and California has the second largest number. The majority (55%) of the 30 million African Americans of all ages are, however, concentrated in the southern region of the United States (U.S. Bureau of the Census, 1993b).

A salient fact to keep in mind as one interacts with African American elders is "labeling." Members of the current cohort of elders have lived through several different labels for its group members. In the 1920s, they may have been called *Negras* or *niggers*; from the 1930s until the 1940s, they may have been called *colored*; in the 1950s, *Negro* was fashionable; and being "Black and proud" was the appropriate label during the Civil Rights movement of the 1960s. Later,

Afro-American came into vogue. Today in the 1990s, the label is *African Amer-ican*; many elders, however, still prefer Negro. If listening is practiced during the first encounter with an elder, one will usually learn from the conversation how to address a person. When in doubt, use the title "Mr." or "Mrs." and the person's surname.

DEMENTIA AND SUPPORT GROUPS

In 1992, the National Advisory Panel on Alzheimer's Disease reported that multiple infarcts (silent small strokes) or transient ischemic accidents (or "brain attacks") is the etiology of most dementia in African Americans. Typically these transient ischemic accidents go unnoticed until one day the family becomes aware that the elder is acting a little strange, is more forgetful than usual, or gets lost in familiar areas. At this point, dementia is acknowledged but usually not ac-cepted as long as the elder can function. In some instances, a much more dramatic onset is experienced, such as a sudden paralysis of one side of the elder's body and an inability to speak. During rehabilitation, changes in the elder's functional performance surface and are noted as the onset of dementia.

Nonreligious Structures

Included in the social support network of African Americans are both nonreli-gious institutions and religious ones. Frequently, persons in the nonreligious support groups tend to follow bloodlines. Individuals may be distant cousins, nieces, nephews, or other blood relatives. In the Deep South, before African Americans attended and graduated from colleges and universities, they became members of the (Black) Prince Hall (freedmen) Masons. Their wives or daughters were eligible to become members of the Order of Eastern Stars. These two nonreligious secret orders provided a privileged and highly respected social support group for mature African Americans. Members looked out for each others' health and well-being.

   Blacks fortunate enough to attend college frequently joined one of the sup-portive Greek letter sororities and fraternities (Alpha Kappa Alpha, Delta Sigma Theta, Sigma Gamma Rho, or Zeta Phi Beta for women; for men, Omega Psi Phi, Alpha Phi Alpha, Kappa Alpha Psi, or Phi Beta Sigma). Similar to the Masons and Eastern Stars, these fraternities and sororities help care for elders with dementia. They may help keep elders involved after their health has failed. Members make telephone calls, friendly visits, send cards and flowers, bring food, and provide transportation and other forms of instrumental support. At the national level, some fraternities, sororities, masons, or stars have 24-hour institutions for their elder members. Others are planning or developing similar facilities.

Religious Structures

The church family is instrumental in helping families manage elders with varied forms of dementia. For example, a state university was funded to implement a "train-the-trainer" approach to increase the knowledge and skills of local African American ministers in the care of families with demented elders (Copeland & Pollard, 1989). The authors know church families who have provided consistent and continued emotional and instrumental support to families as part of their responsibilities and duty. For example,

> Gwen is a 70-year-old daughter who cared for her demented, bedridden, poststroke 100-year-old mother in her home. She wanted to attend a family reunion in Arkansas in July, but decided she could not because she had no reliable person to care for her mother. Helping Gwen with the day-to-day chores of caregiving was a feeble elderly widow from the church. The pastor, Reverend J., found out about Gwen's desire and her subsequent decision not to go. He intervened. Reverend J. prayed with and counseled Gwen about the situation. Then he told Gwen about a local respite program for which she qualified, arranged an appointment, took her to the agency, helped her obtain the respite services, and promised to visit Gwen's mother in the facility while she was away. Gwen attended the family reunion; her mother was placed and properly cared for. Reverend J. visited. There were no problems.

This example demonstrates one effective decision-making process that was successful for everybody. In the next section, other useful strategies are discussed.

STRATEGIES FOR WORKING WITH AFRICAN AMERICAN FAMILIES

Concepts of Aging and Dementia

There is a growing body of literature that describes aging as a survival process rather than as an adaptive process. Linda Burton (1992) wrote that survival better characterizes ethnic group members' movement into old age. Consistent with this perspective, the authors have found the following descriptions of aging used by African American families: "overcoming life's hurdles," "this too, will pass," "there's a brighter day coming," and "surviving the day-to-day struggles isn't easy." In many respects, movement into old age is like experiencing a transition, not a crisis (Gibson, 1986). Also, many African Americans are accustomed to a world with multiple helpers, with uncertainty and constant change, and with limited resources. Such experiences tend to help prepare both caregivers and demented elders to cope with the difficulties inherent in the process of managing a chronic, long-term condition.

Gaines (1989) reported that dementia from a southern, Black context is often perceived differently. One cultural belief is that if an individual can function, his or her sense of self-worth is maintained because role performance is valued more than intellectual abilities. Another cultural belief is that thinking too much can drive a person crazy. Families tend to focus on affective functioning rather than on cognitive functioning (Gaines, 1989). This difference in emphasis logically leads to some altered expectations. One such altered expectation may be less risk of psychological trauma and even depression as one's cognitive abilities become limited (Gaines, 1989). The authors have observed that some African American elders with some degree of dementia maintain a sense of value because they are able to perform or function in some family role.

Communication Patterns

In the process of studying and working with African American families, the authors have found that three communication patterns are used. Interactions occurred as equals, from a position of power, or from a lesser position (Bowser et al., 1993). In times of conflicting goals, the interaction reflected a position of power, one of using an on-top divider approach. If management outcomes were being realized, then interaction was as equals, using a side-by-side connecting approach. However, if one of the authors was feeling less than equal, the tendency was to interact from a lesser position, using an on-the-bottom approach. A discussion of the importance of these communication patterns is provided in Chapter 18, and Figure 1 in that chapter describes in more detail this method of understanding communications.

Respect, Cultural Competence, and Other Techniques

Respect is key in working with African American families. It helps to be knowledgeable about and responsive to African American culture in a genuine way. Being sensitive to the collective experiences of the elderly cohort's cultural experiences also helps. Given the multicultural nature of the United States, health care professionals need to strive for cultural competence; merely being culturally sensitive is not enough (Stanford Geriatric Education Center, 1993). Beginning encounters with a brief, friendly conversation sets the stage for more open communications. Contrary to what the reader may have learned, use of selected self-disclosure is useful and is appreciated by African American elders. Explore where they were born and raised, whether they relocated to this area, where they went to school and how far they went, and something about their religious affiliation. If the elder or family practices a religion, explore the level of their involvement and ask about the role their church family plays. If they are members of any nonreligious support group, inquire about their role. Pay attention to communication patterns as described in Chapter 18 (Figure 1, in particular), and note all nonverbal aspects. A mnemonic model the authors found helpful in the continued assessment of, planning for, intervention with, and evaluation of clients is the LEARN model (Berlin & Fowkes, 1983), in which *L* stands for *listen*; *E*, for *explain*; *A*, for *acknowledge*; *R*, for *recommend*; and *N*, for *negotiate*. This model was used to facilitate movement toward the agreed-on outcomes for demented elders. The model was operationalized through the application of the following five-step-process. It works.

1 Listen with an emphasis on understanding to what your client is trying to communicate.

2 Express the client's concerns in a language appropriate to his or her socioeducational–cultural domain.

3 Accept differences between your world and client's.

4 Restate your agreed-on suggestions for interventions clearly and write them down.

5 Never forget the value of a "win–win" outcome.

CONCLUSION

Working with African American families in the management of demented elders is challenging, yet rewarding. Obtaining successful outcomes requires respect, continued assessment, flexibility, knowledge of one's clients' sociocultural and historical context, and professional as well as cultural competence. Our future invites each of us celebrate our diversity.

REFERENCES

Advisory Panel on Alzheimer's Disease. (1992). *Fourth report of the Advisory Panel on Alzheimer's disease* (NIH Publication No. 93-3520). Washington, DC: U.S. Government Printing Office.

Berlin, E., & Fowkes, W. (1983). A teaching framework for cross-cultural health care: Application in family practice. *Western Journal of Medicine, 139,* 934–938.

Bowser, B. P., Auletta, G. S., & Jones, T. (1993). *Confronting diversity issues on campus.* Newbury Park, CA: Sage.

Burton, L. (1992). Families and the aged: Issues of complexity and diversity. *Generations, 17*(3).

Copeland, J., & Pollard, M. C. (1989). *The Black church and the aging network: A helping hand for the elderly. Final report* (AoA Grant 06AM0414). (Available from the U.S. Public Health Service Administration on Aging, Washington, DC)

Cox, C., & Monk, A. (1990). Minority caregivers of dementia victims: a comparison of Black and Hispanic families. *Journal of Applied Gerontology, 9,* 340–354.

Franklin, J. H. (1988). A historical note on Black families. In H.P. McAdoo, *Black families* (2nd ed., pp. 23–26). Newbury Park, CA: Sage.

Gaines, A. D. (1989). Alzheimer's disease in the context of Black (southern) culture. *Health Matrix, 6,* 4.

Gibson, R. C. (1986). Older Black Americans. *Generations, 10*(4), 35–39.

Gonzales, E., Gitlin, L., & Lyons, K. J. (1995). Review of the literature on African American caregivers of individuals with dementia. *Journal of Cultural Diversity, 2*, 40–48.

Haley, W., Coleton, M., Isobe, T., & West, C. (1992, August). *Stress, appraisal, and social support among Black and White caregivers*. Paper presented at the 100th annual meeting of the American Psychological Association, Washington, DC.

Haley, W., West, W., Wadley, V., White, F., Barrett, J., Ford, G., Harrell, L., & Roth, D. (1995). Psychological, social and health impact of caregiving: a comparison of Black and White dementia caregivers and noncaregivers. *Psychology and Aging, 10*(4), 540–552.

Hinrichsen, G., & Ramirez, M. (1992). Black and White dementia caregivers: A comparison of their adaption, adjustment, and service utilization. *Gerontologist, 32*, 375–381.

Kunjufu, J. (1994). *Adam! Where are you?* Chicago: African American Images.

Lawton, M. P., Rajagopal, D., Brody, E., & Kleban, M. (1992). The dynamics of caregiving for a demented elder among Black and White families. *Journal of Gerontology: Social Sciences, 47*, S156–S164.

Lewis, I. D. (1995). *Families redefined in African Americans*. Unpublished manuscript.

Morycz, R., Malloy, J., Bozich, M., & Martz, P. (1987). Racial differences in family burden: Clinical implications for social work. In R. Dobrof (Ed.), *Gerontological social work with families*. New York: Haworth.

Mui, A. (1992). Caregiver strain among Black and White daughter caregivers: A role theory perspective. *Gerontologist, 32*, 203–212.

Nobles, W. W., Goddard, L. L., Cavil, W. E., & George, P. Y. (1987). *African-American families: Issues, insights & directions*. Oakland, CA: Black Family Institute.

Segall, M., & Wykle, M. (1988–1989). The Black family's experience with dementia. *Journal of Applied Social Sciences, 13*, 170–191.

Shimkin, D., & Uchendu, V. (1978). Persistence, borrowing, and adaptive changes in Black kinship systems: Some issues and their significance. In D. Shimkin, E.M. Shimkin, & D.A. Frate (Eds.), *The extended family in Black societies* (pp. 391–406). The Hague: Mouton.

Smith, R. T. (1973). The matrifocal family. In J. Goody (Ed.), *The character of kinship* (pp. 121–144). Cambridge, England: Cambridge University Press.

Stanford Geriatric Education Center. (1993). Objectives for cultural competence. Stanford, CA: Author.

Sudarkasa, N. (1988). Interpreting the African heritage in Afro-American family organization. In H. P. McAdoo, *Black families* (2nd ed., pp. 27–43). Newbury Park, CA: Sage Press.

U.S. Department of Commerce, Bureau of the Census. (1993a). *Profiles of America's elderly* (No. 3, POP/93-1). Washington, DC: U.S. Government Printing Office.

U.S. Department of Commerce, Bureau of the Census. (1993b). *We the American . . . Blacks*. Washington, DC: U.S. Government Printing Office.

Wood, J., & Parham, I. (1990). Coping with perceived burden: Ethnic and cultural issues in Alzheimer's family caregiving. *Journal of Applied Gerontology, 9*, 325–339.

Wykle, M., & Segall, M. (1991). A comparison of Black and White family caregivers' experience with dementia. *Journal of National Black Nurses Association, 5*, 29–41.

Chapter 14

Dementia and American Indian Populations

B. Josea Kramer

CULTURAL DIVERSITY AND HEALTH

The diversity among American Indians cannot be overstated. This population is composed of approximately 500 federally recognized nations, tribes, bands, rancherias, and Alaskan Native villages and an additional 100 nonrecognized tribes in the United States. At first contact with Europeans, an estimated 300 indigenous languages were spoken in North America, and today about 150 languages continue to be used. Just as there is no single American Indian language, there is no single cultural tradition. This variation holds true even in geographically defined culture areas where societies have responded to similar social, technological, political, and economic dynamics. For instance, at first contact with Americans, the Southwest Culture Area included sedentary pueblo agriculturalists living in the oldest continuously inhabited structures in the continental United States; Navajo pastoralists who lived in isolated kin groups, dividing their time between summer and winter grazing ranges; and seminomadic Apache villages based on a hunting-and-gathering economy that exploited seasonal foods across a number of ecological zones.

Tribal, cultural, and regional diversity is evident in health behaviors and incidence of disease. Cancer prevalence is a good example of this diversity. In the Southwest, where cigarette smoking tends to occur at low rates, lower rates of lung cancer have been noted than among the tribes on the northern Plains characterized by heavier smoking patterns. Occurrence of cancer appears to vary both among geographic culture areas and among cultural groups within a region. For instance, American Indian men living in Montana have higher incidence rates for kidney, lung, and prostate cancers than do American Indian men living in the Southwest. Although rates of cervical cancer are elevated in American Indian women in Montana and in New Mexico, the incidence for breast and lung cancer is higher among northern Plains American Indian women than among Southwestern American Indian women (Bleed, Risser, Sperry, Hellhake, & Helgerson, 1992). There is also variation within regions. In Alaska, for example, cancer frequencies vary among the three indigenous populations, the Eskimo, American Indian, and Aleut (Lanier, Bulkow, & Ireland, 1989).

Age-adjusted mortality rates for American Indians served by the Indian Health Service reveal dramatic variation by geographic region (U.S. Department of Health & Human Services, Public Health Service, Indian Health Service, 1993). Whereas the U.S. all-races mortality rate for cerebrovascular disease is 29.7 persons per 100,000, the rate for American Indians varies from a low in the Tucson area of 16.4 persons per 100,000 to a high in the Aberdeen area of 45.2 persons per 100,000. Although mortality from alcoholism is 634% higher among American Indians than among all races, there is astonishing variation across service areas. The mortality rate for U.S. all races is 7.0 persons per 100,000; the Indian Health Service reported mortality as low as 19.5 persons per 100,000 in the Nashville area and as high as 92.6 persons per 100,000 in the Aberdeen area.

This great heterogeneity is further cross-cut by the bifurcation into rural–reservation and urban populations. Unlike the concentrated populations on reservations, urban American Indians are dispersed across the nation and throughout the general population. Although more numerous than the reservation population, urban American Indians are not represented by special governmental institutions. Eligibility for Indian Health Service health care is abrogated after 180 days residence off-reservation (and may be restored if on-reservation residence is reestablished). The Indian Health Service maintains an excellent database on the health of reservation-dwelling American Indians, but there is no comparable database on the health of urban-dwelling American Indians. Thus, little is known about the health of urban American Indians. The social and economic forces that promoted relocation to industrial centers following World War II resulted in extraordinarily heterogeneous American Indian populations in West Coast cities. For instance, a survey of 350 older American Indians in Los Angeles found that the individuals represented 93 tribal affiliations (Kramer, 1992). It would be a mistake to assume that one can easily generalize research results or best-practice models for health and human service delivery systems from the reservation to the urban setting.

DEMENTIA

Dementia among older American Indians appears to occur at low frequencies. Of 60,000 discharges from 41 Indian Health Service hospitals in fiscal year 1993, there were 24 diagnoses of Alzheimer's disease, of which 1 was a primary diagnosis, and 23 diagnoses of vascular dementia, of which 6 were the primary diagnosis (Kaufman, 1994). Combined, these dementias represent only 0.0008% of discharge diagnoses nationally within the Indian Health Service. Also in fiscal year 1993, the Department of Veterans Affairs reported that American Indians with dementia represented 0.001% of the veterans discharged from California Veterans Affairs hospitals (Cooley, 1994).

American Indians represent one population that, given the lower rate of dementia, may shed light on the risk factors for Alzheimer's disease and other dementias (Osuntokun et al., 1992). Cree living in Manitoba, Canada, are the only tribe in which the epidemiology of dementia has been studied. Significant ($p < .001$) differences were found in comparing age-adjusted prevalence of Alzheimer's disease between Cree and non-Indian Canadians over age 65 years (Hendrie et al., 1993). The age-adjusted prevalence of Alzheimer's disease among Cree was 0.5%, whereas the age-adjusted prevalence for the non-Indian sample was 3.5%. In contrast, there was no difference in prevalence of all other dementias, at 4.2% for both populations. A second major difference between the two populations was the relatively younger age of Cree diagnosed with multi-infarct, alcohol-related, and epilepsy-related dementias and the relatively older age of Cree diagnosed with Alzheimer's disease (see Table 1).

The findings in the Cree study require some caution in interpretation. The sample of 192 Cree was relatively small, and only one case of Alzheimer's disease was discovered. Failure to identify even 1 or 2 persons with Alzheimer's disease would affect the study's conclusions. It is not clear that this single study of one isolated Canadian Indian population can be generalized to all native people of North America.

The extremely low prevalence of Alzheimer's disease, both in Indian Health Service databases and in the Canadian study, raises questions about possible barriers to diagnosis and limitations of standard screening and diagnostic criteria. Potential institutional barriers within the Indian Health Service relate to resource allocation. There are only 25 psychiatrists employed by the Indian Health Service throughout the United States, and 11 of these psychiatrists serve a single area in the Southwest (Nelson, McCoy, Stetter, & Vanderwagen, 1992). Cultural barriers to accessing health care include distrust of providers and a perception that non-Indians are both insensitive to American Indian beliefs and behaviors and likely to disrupt family and community life by imposing non-Indian diagnostic criteria or treatment plans (LaFramboise, 1988).

The relevance of the diagnostic criteria in the *Diagnostic and Statistical Manual of Mental Disorders* (4th ed., American Psychiatric Association, 1995)

Table 1 Dementia in Cree and Non-Indian Populations

Age in years	Cree–AD			English–AD			Cree–other dementia			English–other dementia		
	No. cases	No. in cohort	%	No. cases	No. in cohort	%	No. cases	No. in cohort	%	No. cases	No. in cohort	%
65–69	0	66		0	20		1	66	1.5	0	20	
70–74	0	51		0	35		3	51	3.5	0	35	
75–79	0	31		0	54		2	31	6.4	1	54	1.9
80–84	0	27		7	82	8.5	0	27		1	82	1.2
85–89	0	12		7	32	21.8	0	12		1	32	3.1
90–94	0	3		40	14	28.6	0	3		0	14	
95+	1	2	50.0	2	4	50.0	0	2		0	4	

Note. Adapted from Hendrie et al. (1993). AD = Alzheimer's disease.

in relation both to depression (Manson, Shore, & Bloom, 1985) and to dementia (Hendrie et al., 1993) for American Indians has been questioned. At the time of the Hendrie et al. study, the *DSM–III–R* definition of dementia included decline in social and occupational functioning as a criterion. However, Hendrie et al. noted that Cree continued to be extremely active in old age, in contrast to the lifestyles of retired older non-Indians. Hendrie et al. hypothesized that criteria for decline might differ between these two populations. Differences in adaptive and coping skills have been incidentally reported in the literature on American Indian aging. For example, Kunitz and Levy (1991) described an older "dependent" Navajo man whose hands were crippled by arthritis and who was experiencing fainting spells, active tuberculosis, and recurrent prostate problems, but who continued to live in a relatively isolated area, chopped wood, herded sheep, and traveled by horseback. The meaning of activities and occupations over a lifetime has not been thoroughly explored. However, it should be noted that an extreme change in activity is recognized as a symptom of dementia among native peoples of the Amazon who have a large pharmacopoeia to treat such symptoms in older adults as inactivity, speech disorders, confusion, forgetfulness, refusal to eat or drink, gait and balance disorders, and trembling (Shultes, 1993).

Functional decline is a cornerstone of most geriatric assessments. Yet function is tied to culture, not to biology. One definition of American Indian elder status is functional decline in some physical activities (e.g., subsistence activities) with concomitant increase in social activities (e.g., teaching, counseling, grandparenting; Weibel-Orlando, 1989). Differing patterns of organization of work within the household or extended family may allow some elders to "retire" while others remain active. Health-seeking behaviors are also tied to cultural beliefs. Some indigenous cultures treat confusion and forgetfulness in older adults as normal for aging, referring to this life stage as "old timers' disease" or entering a "second childhood"; other cultures treat these symptoms as part of the spiritual preparation for dying (Anonymous, 1994).

CARING FOR ELDERS WITH DEMENTIA

Increasingly, American Indians are living to older ages, and the incidence of dementias can be expected to increase. Although most articles on establishing professional relationships with American Indians are limited to specific tribes or generalizations about reservations, some generalizations are equally valid for urban-dwelling American Indians, such as the appropriate etiquette for establishing a therapeutic relationship that respects openness and trust, mutual consent, and importance of silence and indirect communications (Attenave, 1992). Traditionally, American Indian cultures have valued both autonomy of individuals and interdependence of family and community. American Indian families tend to be more accepting of dependent older relatives than non-Indians (Strong, 1984). Acceptance of the reality of a disabling condition, rather than guilt that the caregiver cannot improve the situation, seems to account for much of the difference. With more than half of the total American Indian population now living in urban areas, health care practitioners can expect to serve increasing numbers of American Indian clients and their families.

REFERENCES

American Psychiatric Association. (1994). *Diagnostic and statistical manual of mental disorders* (4th ed.). Washington, DC: Author.

Anonymous. (1994, April). Forgetfulness among American Indian and Alaskan Native elders. *Agelines.* (Available from Suncoast Gerontology, Tampa, FL).

Attenave, C. (1992). American Indian families and Alaskan Native families: Emigrants in their own homeland. In M. McGoldrick, J. K. Pearce, & J. Giordano (Eds.), *Ethnicity and family therapy.* New York: Guilford Press.

Bleed, D. M., Risser, D. R., Sperry, S., Hellhake, D., & Helgerson, S. D. (1992). Cancer incidence and survival among American Indians registered for Indian Health Service care in Montana, 1982-1987. *Journal of the National Cancer Institute, 84*(19), 1500–1505.

Cooley, S. G. (1994, September). *Ethnicity and dementias in the U.S. Department of Veterans Affairs.* Abstract presented at the Standford University conference on Ethnicity and Dementias, Stanford, CA.

Hendrie, H. C., Hall, K. S., Pillay, N., Rodgers, D., Prince, C., Norton, J., Brittain, H., Nath, A., Blue, A., Kaufert, J., Shelton, P., Postl, B., & Osuntokun, B. (1993). Alzheimer's disease is rare in Cree. *International Psychogeriatrics, 5*(1), 5–13.

Kaufman, S. (1994). [Patient care statistics, Indian Health Service]. Unpublished raw data.

Kramer, B. J. (1992). Health and aging of urban American Indians. *Western Journal of Medicine, 157,* 281–285.

Kunitz, S. J., & Levy, J. E. (1991). *Navajo aging: The transition from family to institutional support.* Tucson: University of Arizona Press.

LaFramboise, T. (1988). American Indian mental health policy. *American Psychologist, 43,* 388–397.

Lanier, A. P., Bulkow, L. R., & Ireland, B. (1989). Cancer in Alaskan Indians, Eskimos, and Aleuts, 1969–1983: Implications for etiology and control. *Public Health Reports 104*(6), 658–64.

Manson, S. M., Shore, J. H., & Bloom, J. D. (1985). The depressive experience in American Indian communities: A challenge for psychiatric theory and diagnosis. In A. Kleinman & B. Good (Eds.), *Culture and depression.* Berkeley: University of California Press.

Nelson, S. H., McCoy, G. F., Stetter, M., & Vanderwagen, W. C. (1992). An overview of mental health services for American Indians and Alaskan Natives in the 1990s. *Hospital and Community Psychiatry, 43*(3), 257–261.

Osuntokun, B. O., Hendrie, H. C., Ogunniyi, A. O., Hall, K. S., Lekwauwa, U. G., Brittain, H. M., Norton, J. A., Oyediran, A. B., Pillay, N., & Rodgers, D. D. (1992). Cross-cultural studies in Alzheimer's disease. *Ethnicity and Disease, 2*(4), 352–257.

Schultes, R. E. (1993). Plants in treating senile dementia in the northwest Amazon. *Journal of Ethnopharmacology, 38,* 129–135.

Strong, C. (1984). Stress and caring for elderly relatives: Interpretations and coping strategies in an American Indian and White sample. *The Gerontologist, 24*(3), 251–256.

U.S. Department of Health and Human Services, Public Health Service, Indian Health Service. (1993). *Regional differences in Indian health.* Washington, DC: U.S. Government Printing Office.

Weibel-Orlando, J. (1989). Elders and elderlies: Well-being in old age. *American Indian Culture and Research Journal, 13*(3&4), 75–84.

Chapter 15

Working with American Indian Elders in the City: Reflections of an American Indian Social Worker

Al Cross

URBANIZATION

Indians have moved to cities and towns across the United States in record numbers over the past 50 years. The urbanizing of American Indians was sparked by two historical events, their participation in World War II in the armed services and as defense workers and their involvement in a program called Relocation that was undertaken by the Bureau of Indian Affairs in the 1950s. This program encouraged and assisted Indian families and individuals in relocating to urban industrial cities across the country in hope of finding a place for the American Indian in the U.S. industrial workforce. The relocation program's impact accounted for a large mass movement of Indians from reservations and rural homesites into cities across the nation. It was second only to the mass movement of Indians under the Indian Removal Act of 1830, when government policy moved all the Indians east of the Mississippi west to Indian Territory.

Today in the 1990s, American Indians living in cities constitute the majority of Indians in the United States. The 1990 Census counted 1.9 million American Indians in the United States. Of that number, about 35% of American Indians (685,000) in the United States were living on Indian lands. Within the population of Indians living in cities, there are now Indian women and men who, for the first time, are living their lives as elders in this new environment, urban settings.

CULTURE

Although the vast majority of American Indians speak English and have attributes and traits of American culture, they also maintain available native languages, practice ceremony and ritual of the particular tribal group, and identify strongly as Indian. As a group of people they differ from the majority of American society in culture and traditions.

Case Example

A memorial for an Indian elder was infused with ceremony and ritual; there were drumming and singers who sang special songs, and there was ritual in differing forms. Following the memorial, the family held a feed (a feast), traditional to their tribe, where they honored special guests and friends of the deceased. The elder, an 83-year-old woman, had suffered an aneurysm while attending a powwow and died following surgery. Her life up until she had the aneurysm had been active. She had lived with a daughter and her family, in which she took the role of the elder, a role that directed and facilitated her being. She was busy teaching her grandchildren Indian ways and traditions. Her role in the community was one of a teacher of Indian traditions. Culture provided her a life full of responsibility and duty.

With the exception perhaps of two Indian elders, most elders the author has met through his role as social worker in the city stayed active and had a role in family and community. This trait seems very much to be a carryover from the traditions of their tribal life. Care for the elders is almost exclusively the responsibility and right of the family.

Acknowledging and understanding the significant role of culture is critical to being able to provide helping services to Indian elders, as most see themselves as Indian and play out their lives in scripts thus written. In addition, it is always important to know something about the specific Indian culture of the person who is being helped. What one does as a Southwest Pueblo Indian for an illness or health concern is far different than what one does as a Nez Perce Indian from Idaho.

WHAT IS KNOWN AND NOT KNOWN ABOUT INDIAN ELDERS IN THE CITY

Perhaps most significant in working with urban Indian elders is that little is known about their lives. In particular, little is known beyond their presence at social functions and when they happen to seek health care or become ill and are hospitalized for care. Other than those instances, the Indian elder is mixed into the mass social setting and highly invisible. At this point, what is not known is vastly larger than what is known about the life of the urban Indian elder. For example, even the most basic question of what constitutes old age in the Indian community remains unanswered. In many Indian cultures, people do not become elders until they reach a period of life where wisdom has been attained. In many tribes, that age is near 70 years.

Unanswered Questions

What has been Indian elders' level of integration into urban society?
What life adjustments have been made in their lives to fit in the urban scene?
How many Indian elders are there in the cities across the nation?
How does one identify an elder?
Does the Indian Health Service provide care for urban Indian elders?
How do Indian elders view growing old or being old in the city?
What part does culture play in their lives?
How do Indian elders cope with illness and sickness or old age?

All these "don't knows" should not be taken as planned or deliberate omissions. What this says is that work needs to be done to find out some of the answers. Get some information on the lives of Indian elders in the city. Try to help, if help is warranted. And stay out of the way if help is not needed.

Chapter 16

Caring for Cognitively Impaired American Indian Elders: Difficult Situations, Few Options

Robert John
Catherine Hagan Hennessy
Lonnie C. Roy
Margot L. Salvini

Research on caregiving to older adults with cognitive impairments has demonstrated the often profound demands and burdens of these helping activities on family caretakers. Caregivers' physical and emotional resources are particularly challenged not strictly by the types and extent of the care recipient's cognitive deficits, but by characteristic problem behaviors that frequently accompany dementia, such as wandering, sleep disturbances, or the need for constant supervision (Quayhagen & Quayhagen, 1988; Rabins, Mace, & Lucas, 1982; Wilder, Teresi, & Bennett, 1983). It is not surprising, therefore, that the literature on family caretaking of dementia-diagnosed individuals has documented chronic fatigue, anger, and depression associated with caregiving activities (Chenoweth & Spencer, 1986; George & Gwyther, 1986; Rabins et al., 1982), as well as comparatively higher levels of stress among caregivers of dementia patients than among caregivers of elders with physical illnesses (Birkel, 1987). Despite these stresses, the large majority of family helpers of elders with dementia provide care at home, often without the assistance of formal services (Caserta, Lund, Wright, & Redburn, 1987; Mace, 1984; Zarit, Todd, & Zarit, 1986).

Although only a handful of studies have examined the prevalence of dementia, including Alzheimer's disease, among U.S. non-Whites—mostly African Americans (de la Monte, Hutchins, & Moore, 1989; Heyman, Fillenbaum, Clark, Prosnitz, & Williams, 1988; Heyman et al., 1991; Schoenberg, Anderson, & Haerer, 1985)—the rise in life expectancy and the rapid growth of minority aging populations (Jackson, 1988) ensure that increasing numbers of minority families will be caring for elders with cognitive impairments. The Recent research on minority caregiving (Hennessy & John, 1995; Lawton, Rajagopal, Brody, & Kleban, 1992; Mintzer, Knapp, Herman, Nietert, & Walters, 1995; Morycz, Malloy, Bozich, & Martz 1987) has suggested that different cultural values in the perceptions of family eldercare may contribute to a higher, or at least a qualitatively different, threshold of burden than among White caregivers. However, despite any cultural variations in caregiver burden that may exist, minority caretakers have been shown to share more similarities than dissimilarities to Whites in the etiology and levels of subjective burden. Indeed, in a study comparing the dynamics of caregiving for a demented elder among Black and White families, Lawton et al. (1992) highlighted parallels between the two groups in the predictors of burden. Thus, despite the well-documented strengths and patterns of assistance among minority families, which frequently include extensive networks of support (Billingsley, 1970; Mindel, Wright, & Starrett, 1986), these caregivers are by no means immune to the stresses and strains of taking care of physically or cognitively impaired elders.

American Indian caregivers have been among the least studied of all ethnic caregivers, despite the rapid growth in the size of the older American Indian population and the comparatively high rates of health impairments among this group. The number of American Indians age 60 and over increased 52% between 1980 and 1990 (John, 1991), and it is further estimated that by the year 2000, the "old-old"—those age 75 and over—will at least double in number from the 42,473 reported in the 1990 census (Manson, 1993; U.S. Department of Commerce, 1991). The proportion of the older native population with self-identified limitations in the ability to perform activities of daily living has also been shown to be high (John, 1995; National Indian Council on Aging, 1981). More recent data from the 1990 Census on the extent of mobility or self-care limitations confirmed the excess prevalence of functional impairments for aged American Indians (U.S. Department of Commerce, 1993). Despite the documented need for long-term care services among American Indian elders, however, modalities of long-term care are generally undeveloped in the current system of services for American Indians (Indian Health Service, 1993; John, 1995; Stuart & Rathbone-McCuan, 1988), and American Indian families, especially in rural and reservation settings, are often the primary, if not sole, providers of long-term care to functionally dependent elders (John, 1988).

The extent to which American Indian caregivers provide assistance to elders with cognitive impairments is largely speculative. Little is currently known about the prevalence of dementia among older American Indians despite anecdotal accounts by clinicians that it is rarely encountered among Native American populations (see, e.g., Gibbons, 1992). Given the state of knowledge, the consequent interest in these populations for epidemiologic studies of dementia, especially Alzheimer's disease (Osuntokun et al., 1992), is well-founded.

In a study of dementia conducted among a Canadian Indian tribe, the Cree of northern Manitoba, Canada, Hendrie et al. (1993) reported a significantly lower prevalence of Alzheimer's disease among this group than among a non-Indian comparison group. Among the 192 Cree participants age 65 and over who were clinically assessed for dementia, the prevalence of all dementias was comparable to the estimate for the comparison group (4.2% for each). The comparative prevalence of Alzheimer's disease, however, was markedly different, with only 0.5% of the Cree (1 participant) meeting the criteria for the condition, in contrast to an estimate of 3.5% for the non-Indian sample. The predominant types of non-Alzheimer's dementias diagnosed in the Cree participants were multi-infarct dementia and alcohol-related dementia. In discussing their findings, the researchers noted that the prevalence of these problems is not unexpected because of the high prevalence of stroke and alcoholism among Canadian Natives.

Although at least one prevalence study of dementia is currently underway with American Indians (Van Winkle, Persson, & Richter, 1994), no statements can currently be made about the frequency of Alzheimer's disease or other cognitive impairments among American Indians beyond the kinds of anecdotal accounts mentioned above. However, on the basis of rates for stroke that approach those of Whites (Indian Health Service, 1994) and the comparatively high prevalence of alcoholism for this group (Indian Health Service, 1994; May, 1994), it is perhaps safe to hypothesize that the occurrence of vascular and alcohol-related dementias is more common among American Indian elders.

The topic of American Indian caregivers providing assistance to elders with cognitive impairments is addressed in a qualitative study (Hennessy & John, 1995) of the experience of burden among family caregivers from five Pueblo tribes in New Mexico. Although the majority of the study participants were caring for elders with physical health problems, a few of the caregivers were providing assistance to elders with a significant degree of "confusion." In describing their views of caretaking and its demands, these primary family caregivers emphasized the lack of social stigma associated with an elderly person with dementia. In particular, caregivers noted that they did not consider the kinds of inappropriate behaviors that can occur with cognitive impairments to be a cause for embarrassment or social unease. They explained that this was because the elder and his or her condition was known to everyone in the rural tribal environment in which they lived and that everyone understood the reason for any unusual behaviors. At any rate, as one daughter caring for her confused father clarified, the respect accorded to elders—whether cognitively intact or not—precluded the kind of infantalization of and anger toward older persons with dementia that she had witnessed among Anglos. As this respondent expressed it,

> Maybe if there were Anglos coming in, because I've seen it in hospitals or other places where I see elderly people in the same situation or almost the same as my Dad's case, and they get after them, they get mad, and they just treat them like little kids. Out here I think we grew up having them to teach us respect for your elders. And I think all the communities, all the Pueblos have the same feelings.

These findings suggest that considerations about socially inappropriate behaviors that can constitute a source of burden for caregivers in the majority population are less salient for these caregivers.

Preliminary findings by Henderson (1994) among the Oklahoma Choctaw suggested that the cultural construction of dementia varies across American Indian tribes in accordance with individually held health beliefs that are part of larger cultural systems. Henderson discovered three general explanations for dementias, including a combination of biomedical and lay models, the belief that dementia is part of normal aging, and the belief that behaviors associated with dementia are a means by which the elder communicates with an afterlife during a period of transition to the next world.

These qualitative studies conducted on American Indian populations provide cultural insight into American Indian perceptions of dementia and caring for a cognitively impaired family member. However, broader substantive questions about the content and nature of caregiving activities to cognitively impaired American Indian elders have not yet been addressed. No study has investigated the range of issues important to bringing knowledge of caregiving among American Indians to the level of the caregiving literature on other populations, particularly Whites. To address this deficit, this chapter describes the caregiving situation of a group of cognitively impaired elders and their primary family caregivers, including the identity and characteristics of the primary caregivers, the types of problems associated with the care needs of these elders (e.g., impairments in the ability to carry out activities of daily living, memory and behavioral difficulties), the types and extent of assistance provided by these family caregivers, the formal services used by the care recipients, and the perceived sources of burden in caring for an elder with cognitive problems.

METHOD AND PROCEDURES

This analysis of the family caregiving situation among cognitively impaired American Indian elders is based on the results of a survey questionnaire administered to 73 Pueblo caregivers in the Indian Health Service's Santa Fe Service Unit. The data on the situation of American Indian primary family caregivers were collected as part of a project to advise the Indian Health Service about long-term care services needed in northern New Mexico. Survey respondents were the primary caregivers of a functionally impaired family member. Selection criteria for inclusion in the study were based on care recipient characteristics, including being age 55 years and older and requiring help with at least one physical activity of daily living or with at least two instrumental activities of daily living. Participants were recruited by local senior services program directors who were familiar with families in the community who were caring for impaired elderly relatives.

During the survey, respondents were asked whether the elder for whom they cared needed help because of physical health problems, problems with loss of memory or judgment, or both types of problems. On the basis of the response to this question, data were analyzed from caregivers who provide help to elders with either memory or judgment problems only or with both memory and physical health problems. This subsample of caregivers who provide care to elders with some level of cognitive impairment contained 26 individuals, or approximately 36% of the original sample.

CHARACTERISTICS OF CARE RECIPIENTS AND CAREGIVERS

Consistent with previous findings of age at greatest risk of experiencing cognitive impairment, the median age of the elders with impaired memory or judgment was 84 years old. About one fourth of the cognitively impaired elders were age 60 to 70 (26.9%), about 15% were 71 to 80, another 15% were 81 to 85, about one third (34.6%) were 86 to 90, and approximately 7% were over 91. Moreover, unlike the entire sample, most of the elders with loss of memory or judgment were male (65.4%). Three fourths (75.3%) of the elders lived with their caregivers.

The vast majority of the primary family caregivers to cognitively impaired elders were female (84.6%). About one fourth of the caregivers (23.1%) were the elders' wives, a large plurality were the elders' daughters (42.3%), and the remaining caregivers (33.6%) were sons, daughters-in-law, or other family members. The median age of the caregivers was 55 years. About 15% of the caregivers were between the ages of 22 and 39, about one fourth (26.9%) were between 40 and 49, about 15% were between 50 and 59, 19% were between 60 and 69, and nearly one fourth (23.1%) were 70 years of age or older. More than half (52.0%) of the caregivers were married, 16% were widowed, 4% were divorced or separated, and more than one quarter (28%) had never been married.

The mean educational level of the caregivers was 10.8 years. The mean household size of the caregivers was 5.8 individuals, and the mean number of children in the household was 1.5. Only about 12% of the caregivers were employed full-time, 3.8% were employed part-time, 23% were retired or homemakers, and approximately 35% were unemployed. The median household income for caregivers was within the range of $851 to $1,250 per month.

LONG-TERM CARE NEEDS

These findings establish that cognitively impaired care recipients need a very high level of assistance. Table 1 summarizes the level of help needed by cognitively impaired elders with routine activities of daily living. This level of need explains why a large majority (72%) of caregivers indicated that the elder for whom they provided care was very dependent on them. Moreover, another 24% of the caregivers indicated that the elder was somewhat dependent, and only 4% of the caregivers (1 case) said that the elder was not at all dependent on

Table 1   Level of Assistance Needed by Cognitively Impaired Elders with Instrumental and Physical Activities of Daily Living

Activity	No help needed		Some help needed		Cannot perform activity	
	N	%	N	%	N	%
Instrumental activity						
Shopping	1	3.8	1	3.8	24	92.3
Use telephone	2	7.7	5	19.2	19	73.1
Transportation	—	—	3	11.5	23	88.5
Meal preparation	—	—	2	7.7	24	92.3
Taking medication	1	3.8	9	34.6	16	61.5
Housework	—	—	3	11.5	23	88.5
Managing money[a]	—	—	3	12.0	22	88.0
Dealing with agencies	—	—	—	—	26	100.0
Physical activity						
Bathing	4	15.4	14	53.8	8	30.8
Toileting	8	30.8	15	57.7	3	11.5
Dressing	3	11.5	19	73.1	4	15.4
Transferring	9	34.6	11	42.3	6	23.1
Eating	18	69.2	7	26.9	1	3.8

Note. Dashes indicate no responses in this category.
[a]*N*s vary because of missing data for this item.

them. The caregivers reported, on average, that the elders could be left alone for only about 4 hours (4.25 hours) at a time. In addition, caregivers reported that they provided an average of more than 8 hours (8.6) of care per day to the elder.

Instrumental Activities of Daily Living

Exceptionally few cognitively impaired elders were able to perform any one of the instrumental activities of daily living without assistance. In fact, using the telephone, taking medication, and going shopping were the only activities that a few elders could accomplish independently. None of the elders with memory loss or loss of judgment could deal with external agencies or arrange services. Moreover, the overwhelming majority of cognitively impaired elders could not go shopping for themselves (92.3%), prepare meals (92.3%), use any type of transportation (88.5%), do household chores (88.5%), or manage money (88.0%). About three fourths (73.1%) of the elders were unable to use the telephone, and nearly two thirds (61.5%) could not take their medication without help.

Physical Activities of Daily Living

As expected, more cognitively impaired elders were able to perform the physical activities of daily living. Bathing and transferring were the activities that pre-

Table 2   Frequency Distribution of Memory, Judgment, and Behavioral Problems Exhibited by Elders

Activity	Never a problem		Occasionally a problem		Always a problem	
	N	%	N	%	N	%
Memory difficulties						
Remembering words	8	30.8	12	46.2	6	23.1
Understanding instructions[a]	4	16.0	13	52.0	8	32.0
Finding way around house	15	57.7	4	15.4	7	26.9
Speaking sentences	18	69.2	7	26.9	1	3.8
Recognizing known people	8	30.8	10	38.5	8	30.8
Behavioral difficulties						
Wanders/gets lost	17	65.4	5	19.2	4	15.4
Restless/agitated[a]	6	24.0	11	44.0	8	32.0
Nervous/worried	2	7.7	15	57.7	9	34.6
Dangerous behaviors	16	61.5	8	30.8	2	7.7
Making it to bathroom	10	38.5	13	50.0	3	11.5

[a]Ns vary because of missing data for this item.

sented the greatest difficulty for cognitively impaired elders. Almost one third of cognitively impaired elders were unable to bathe, and one fourth were not sufficiently ambulatory to transfer from a bed to a chair without assistance. With the exception of eating, the accomplishment of most physical activities of daily living required some help from the caregiver. Almost 9 out of 10 cognitively impaired elders needed some help with dressing, nearly as many needed some help with bathing, and approximately two thirds needed some help using the toilet or transferring from place to place. Almost one third of the elders were unable to eat without assistance, either needing some help with eating (26.9%) or not being able to feed themselves (3.8%).

Memory, Judgment, and Behavioral Problems

Table 2 summarizes the types and frequency of memory and behavioral problems exhibited by the elders in this study. Five types of memory or judgment problems were surveyed. Among the elders who exhibited the greatest deficits in this area, the biggest problems were in understanding instructions (32.0%), recognizing people they know (30.8%), finding their way around the house (26.9%), and remembering words (23.1%). Only one elder had consistent problems speaking sentences. A plurality of elders occasionally experienced difficulties in understanding instructions, remembering words, or recognizing people they knew. Altogether, the inability to understand instructions was the most common form of cognitive impairment that these caregivers confront, at least occasionally affecting 84% of the elders in this sample.

Table 3   Utilization of Health and Social Services by Cognitively Impaired Elders

Service use	Not received		Received	
	N	%	N	%
Health services				
Medical care	11	42.3	15	57.7
Nursing care	17	65.4	9	34.6
Community health representative	18	69.2	8	30.8
Counseling	19	73.1	7	26.9
Physical therapy	23	88.5	3	11.5
CCIC	24	92.3	2	7.7
Social services				
Meal preparation	5	19.2	21	80.8
Senior transportation	13	50.0	13	50.0
Senior companion	18	69.2	8	30.8
Personal care	22	84.6	4	15.4
Social/recreational	24	92.3	2	7.7
Telephone checks	24	92.3	2	7.7
Information & referral	25	96.2	1	3.8
Laundry/diaper	25	96.2	1	3.8
Outreach	25	96.2	1	3.8
Housekeeping assistance	26	100.0	—	—
Senior escort	26	100.0	—	—
Interpreter	26	100.0	—	—

Note. Dashes indicate no responses in this category.

Five types of behavioral difficulties were also surveyed. Approximately one third of cognitively impaired elders exhibit nervous and worried or restless and agitated behavior all of the time. The two least common behavioral problems were wandering or getting lost and engaging in behaviors that are potentially dangerous to themselves or others. Almost two thirds of cognitively impaired elders never engaged in either of these behaviors. However, about one third (30.8%) of the elders exhibited dangerous behaviors occasionally, and 7.7% engaged in dangerous behaviors frequently. Incontinence has been shown to be a special behavioral problem for caregivers from other populations, and almost two thirds of these elders were incontinent, either occasionally (50.0%) or always (11.5%).

Utilization of Services

Table 3 summarizes the responses to 18 items that measured whether the elder received a variety of health and social services at least twice a month. Among the health-related services, more than half (57.7%) of the elders received medical care, about one third received regular nursing care and community health representative visits (34.6% and 30.8% respectively), and about one fourth (26.9%) received counseling services. Only a small percentage received physical therapy (11.5%), and 7.7% received Community Coordinated In-Home Care (CCIC) services (in-home service provided to elders evaluated as eligible for and in need of nursing home placement). Overall, and in relation to the level of impairment, these elders received few medical services on a regular basis.

The receipt of aging social services was also relatively low. The social services received by a majority of cognitively impaired elders were meals programs (80.8%) and senior transportation services (50%). Senior companion services were received regularly much less frequently by approximately one third of these elders. Exceptionally few elders received regular assistance with personal care, social recreational services, regular monitoring, information and referral, laundry and diaper services, or outreach. None of these elders used housekeeping, senior escort, or interpreter services.

Long-Term Care Responsibilities of Caregivers

A number of items measured the intensity of caregiving and the effects that caregiving had on the caregivers' perceived physical and emotional health. More than two thirds of the caregivers viewed the caregiving situation as physically demanding, emotionally demanding, or both. Well more than half (57.7%) of the caregivers reported that caring for the elder was very physically demanding, and another 19.2% reported that it was somewhat demanding. In addition, 42.2% of the caregivers indicated that caregiving was very emotionally demanding, and 38.5% indicated that it was somewhat demanding. When both types of consequences are considered together, fully one third of the caregivers find the caregiving situation very physically and emotionally demanding and another third find the situation somewhat emotionally and physically demanding.

The degree to which caregivers felt that the help they provided to the elder was physically and emotionally demanding was measured by two items with four response categories, ranging from *not demanding at all* to *very demanding*. One-way analysis of variance was used to determine if significant differences in mean scores existed between caregivers to elders with cognitive impairments as compared with caregivers to elders with only physical problems. Results indicated no significant difference in the degree to which either group of caregivers felt that providing care was emotionally demanding. However, significant between-group differences were found in the degree to which the respondents felt that providing care was physically demanding $(F = 7.32, p < .01)$. Caregivers to cognitively impaired elders viewed providing care to a cognitively impaired elder as more physically demanding $(M = 3.3)$ than did those who provided care to a physically impaired elder $(M = 2.6)$.

In fact, the caregiving situation appears to have a broad range of negative consequences for the caregivers of cognitively impaired elders. For example, nearly two thirds (60.0%) of these caregivers reported their self-rated physical

Table 4 Source and Frequency of Caregiver Burden

Burden item	Sometimes		Quite frequently		Nearly always	
	N	%	N	%	N	%
Dependent on caregiver	4	15.4	12	46.2	10	38.5
Caregiver is only one to care for elder	4	15.4	12	46.2	8	30.8
Fear of future	8	30.8	7	26.9	8	30.8
Strained around elder	6	23.1	7	26.9	8	30.8
Pulled between elder & other responsibilities	6	23.1	11	42.3	3	11.5
Asks for more help than needed	7	26.9	10	38.5	3	11.5
Not enough time for self	10	38.5	10	38.5	2	7.7
Not enough money to care for elder	7	26.9	6	23.1	4	15.4
Unable to care for elder much longer	5	19.2	9	34.6	—	—
Uncertain what to do about elder	12	46.2	8	30.8	—	—
Elder negatively affects other relationships	9	34.6	5	19.2	2	7.7
Overall, feel burdened by elder	9	34.6	6	23.1	1	3.8
Not as much privacy as desired	7	26.9	4	15.4	2	7.7
Social life has suffered	14	53.8	4	15.4	2	7.7
Could do more for elder	11	42.3	5	19.2	—	—
Should do more for elder	12	46.2	4	15.4	1	3.8
Wish could leave care to someone else	10	38.5	3	11.5	—	—
Embarrassed by elder's behavior	5	19.2	3	11.5	—	—
Feel angry around elder	9	34.6	2	7.7	1	3.8
Caregiver's health has suffered	8	30.8	3	11.5	—	—
Uncomfortable having friends over	3	11.5	—	—	—	—
Lost control of life because of caregiving	8	30.8	2	7.7	—	—

Note. Response categories of never and rarely are not reported in this table. Dashes indicate no responses in this category.

health as fair or poor, and nearly one fourth (23.1%) reported that their own health interferes with caregiving to a moderate extent. Moreover, half (50.0%) of the caregivers reported that their sleep was interrupted in order to give care to the elder. Of those caregivers who reported sleep interruptions, their sleep was interrupted an average of about six times per week. About one third (30.8%) of the caregivers indicated that it was necessary to reduce their work hours, and 26.9% reported taking time off work to provide care to the elder.

Caregiver Burden

Twenty-two items (see Table 4) measured the degree of perceived caregiver burden among respondents (Hennessy & John, 1995). All items in this scale were measured at the ordinal level. Response categories to each item ranged from *never* to *nearly always*. Overall, these Pueblo caregivers reported substantial levels of perceived burden. Table 4 shows that the vast majority of respondents quite frequently or nearly always (84.7% and 77.0%, respectively) feel that the elder is dependent on them and that the elder seems to expect them to take care of him or her as if the respondents were the only ones on whom the elder could depend. More than half of the respondents quite frequently or nearly always feel afraid of what the future holds for the elder (57.7%), feel strained when they are around the elder (57.7%), feel pulled between caring for the elder and trying to meet other responsibilities for the family or work (53.8%), and feel that the elder asks for more help than needed (50.0%). In addition, more than one third of the respondents reported that quite frequently or nearly always they do not have enough time for themselves (46.2%), feel that they do not have enough money to care for the elder in addition to the rest of their financial responsibilities (38.5%), and feel that they will be unable to care for the elder much longer (34.6%). Approximately one third of the caregivers were uncertain about what to do about the elder (30.8%).

On the remaining measures of perceived caregiver burden, about one quarter of the respondents quite frequently or nearly always feel that the elder currently affects their relationship with other family members or friends in a negative way (26.9%), feel burdened by the elder overall (26.9%), feel that they do not have as much privacy as they would like because of the elder (23.1%), and feel that their social life has suffered because of caregiving (23.1%). A smaller minority of caregivers quite frequently or nearly always feel they could do more for the elder (19.2%), that they should do more for the elder (19.2%), wish that they could just leave the care of the elder to someone else (1.5%), feel embarrassed over the elder's behavior (11.5%), feel angry when around the elder (11.5%), or feel that their health has suffered because of caregiving (11.5%). Finally, only a very small percentage of caregivers frequently feel that they have lost control of their lives since becoming caregivers (7.7%).

One-way analysis of variance was used to determine if significant differences in mean burden scores on the 22-item overall burden scale existed between caregivers who provided care to elders with physical health problems and those who provided care for elders with some level of cognitive impairment. This analysis indicated that caregivers of elders with cognitive impairments exhibited significantly higher levels of burden ($M = 62.5$) than those who provided care to elders with physical problems ($M = 55.0$, $F = 5.77$, $p < .05$). Further analysis revealed that this difference in mean burden scores on the overall scale is accounted for by significant differences in levels of burden on two of the subscale dimensions of caregiver burden identified by factor-analytic procedures. Significant differences in perceptions of burden exist for caregiver efficacy and role strain.

Caregiver efficacy is composed of five burden items: (a) How often do you feel that you will be unable to take care of the elder much longer? (b) How often do you feel you have lost control of your life since you have become a caregiver? (c) How often do you wish you could just leave the care of the elder to someone else? (d) How often do you feel uncertain about what to do about the elder? and

(e) Overall, how often do you feel burdened in caring for the elder? This type of burden reflects the caregiver's feelings of efficacy in providing care to the elder and indicates the degree to which the caregiver experiences serious questions about whether or for how long to continue caregiving to the elder. One-way analysis of variance yielded a significant difference in level of burden between those who cared for elders with some level of cognitive impairment and those who cared for elders with physical problems ($F = 8.61, p < .01$). This analysis indicated that caregivers of cognitively impaired elders exhibited significantly higher levels of this type of burden ($M = 12.5$) than those who provided care to physically impaired elders ($M = 9.6$).

Role strain is composed of four burden items: (a) How often do you feel that the elder asks for more help than he or she needs? (b) How often do you feel that because of the time you spend with the elder you do not have enough time for yourself? (c) How often do you feel strained when you are around the elder? and (d) How often do you feel your health has suffered because of your involvement with the elder? This type of caregiver burden assesses the degree to which the caregiver experiences personal and interpersonal problems as the result of the caregiving role. Significant differences were identified between the two groups of caregivers on this dimension of burden ($F = 5.00, p < .05$). Again, caregivers of cognitively impaired elders exhibited significantly higher levels of role strain ($M = 12.5$) than did caregivers of elders with physical health problems ($M = 10.9$).

CONCLUSION

The state of knowledge of the types and prevalence of dementing illness among American Indian elders and the etiology of these dementias—whether from head trauma, organic biological causes, prolonged alcohol abuse, malnutrition, or stroke—is extremely limited. Certainly, more research needs to be conducted on these issues so that everyone concerned with the well-being of American Indian elders knows more about the problems they can expect to confront in providing assistance.

To this end, this study has investigated the characteristics and needs of a sample of cognitively impaired Indian elders, as well as the degree and types of burden experienced by these elders' primary family caregiver. It is evident from this study that caregivers of elders with cognitive problems endure very physically and emotionally demanding situations. Not only do the majority of caregivers report that their health is only fair or poor, but many also feel that their health has suffered because of caregiving responsibilities. For many, the demanding nature of their caregiver role is further exacerbated by sleep interruptions and work loss. Moreover, the limited availability of health and social services contributes to the demands placed on family caregivers, as is evidenced by the high rate of dependency exhibited by the vast majority of these cognitively impaired elders. When the combination of these factors is considered, there is little wonder that these Pueblo caregivers report substantial levels of perceived burden.

First, significantly more burden is experienced by caregivers of cognitively impaired elders than by caregivers of elders with only physical health problems, and the efficacy of the caregiving role is more dubious for caregivers of elders with cognitive impairments. These caregivers are significantly more likely to exhibit anxiety over losing control of their lives, wish they could leave the care to someone else, feel uncertain about how much longer they can provide care, and feel unsure about what to do about the elder. Clearly, among these caregivers, providing care to elders with cognitive impairments elicits more anxiety over the efficacy and future duration of their caretaking role than does providing care to elders who experience only physical limitations.

Second, feelings of burden concerning competing responsibilities or excessive demands associated with the caregiver role are significantly higher among caregivers of cognitively impaired elders than among the caregivers of physically impaired elders. Feeling strained around the elder and that the elder makes excessive demands, that caring for the elder does not allow them enough time for themselves, and that their own health has suffered because of involvement with the elder are significantly more prevalent among caregivers of cognitively impaired elders. Furthermore, cognitively impaired elders could only be left alone for about 4 hours on average, whereas elders with physical impairments could be left alone an average of about 9 hours at a time. The care needs of elders with cognitive impairments and the limited amount of time that they can be left alone diminishes the amount of time available for self, possibly contributing to the higher levels of role strain.

The finding that caregivers of elders with dementia were significantly more burdened in terms of perceived caregiver efficacy and role strain than were their counterparts who were caring for elders with physical health problems only can be elaborated by qualitative information from a series of focus groups that were also conducted with area caregivers as part of this study (Hennessy & John, 1994). One major source of burden reported by the focus group participants that impinged on their sense of caregiving efficacy was the frequent helplessness they felt in dealing with difficult psychosocial aspects of care. As mentioned above, behavioral difficulties associated with an elder's confusion lack some of the social stigma that typifies the Anglo response to such conditions. However, caregivers reported that they often felt inadequate in dealing with behavioral difficulties such as "stubbornness"—an elder's noncompliance or refusal to cooperate with treatment or caregiving regimens—or with the incessant, repetitive requests of an elder with dementia. Such problems impeded their ability to successfully organize a caregiving routine, which has been shown to be crucial to adapting to the caregiving situation (Albert, 1990; Hennessy & John, 1995).

The caregivers who participated in the focus groups likewise described the role strain and role conflicts that they experienced because of competing demands within the caregiving role and other commitments to work, family, and tribal activities. Many of these caregivers—including those providing help to cognitively impaired and physically impaired elders—had successfully established caregiving routines by enlisting the assistance of other family members. A number of others, however, were frustrated with their inability to communicate the demands of caring for a physically or cognitively impaired elder to other family members or to obtain family assistance with elder care. Few of the caregivers received adequate, much less comprehensive, assistance from formal health or social service providers.

Some observers have suggested that underuse of services is a problem among American Indian elders and have cited a variety of barriers that limit service use. These findings document that service use is limited among this highly dependent and impaired group of elders. However, these elders do appear to make greatest use of the services that are available. For example, among the medical services, service use conforms to the availability of services in the elders' environment. Clinical physical health services are those most available to this population, community-based and in-home health services are more limited, and comprehensive in-home health services are least available. Similarly, social services show the same pattern of use. Meals programs and senior transportation are the most widely available services. There are only a limited number of senior companions, and the remaining social services tend to be relatively unorganized or are not part of the formal service environment because of funding limitations that greatly constrict program development. The pattern of service use documented in this study suggests that if services were available, these elders, with the assistance of their caregivers, would use them.

The obvious consequence of the current health and social service environment is an undue reliance and burden placed on family members of elders who experience some level of cognitive impairment. Unfortunately, the lack of service availability has a direct and unambiguous negative outcome for the primary family caregiver. This research suggests that most caregivers experience some type of negative consequence to their physical health, whether through loss of sleep, belief that their health has suffered, or a general feeling that their health is not good. Moreover, this study suggests that caring for a cognitively impaired elder is also emotionally demanding and results in higher overall levels of perceived burden. More specifically, caregivers of cognitively impaired elders experience more role strain and greater doubts about the efficacy of their ability to provide care. Both of these types of burden have ominous implications for long-term care provided by family members. Role strain is a well-established source of personal and interpersonal difficulties, and higher levels of this type of caregiver burden result in these caregivers' experiencing high levels of personal consequences (health has suffered and not enough time for self) as well as interpersonal difficulties in their relationship with the elder (feeling the elder asks for more help than needed and feeling strained when around the elder).

Feeling higher levels of doubt about the efficacy of the care they provide is even more serious. A number of the items that compose this type of burden imply that the caregiving arrangement is reaching a point where the termination of care could be considered. Continuation of care by someone who feels high levels of doubt about his or her caregiving efficacy has obvious negative consequences for the caregiver. Unfortunately, the current health and social service environment available to rural American Indian elders provides few, if any, alternatives to caregivers who confront extremely difficult situations. In the absence of the full range of supportive services available in urban areas to other populations, American Indian primary family caregivers have no option but to continue care at all costs or place the elder in culturally foreign and lowly regarded off-reservation nursing homes. Without greater assistance and the development of viable comprehensive, community-based, and in-home long-term care options, both the caregiver and the care recipient will suffer unnecessarily, and their quality of life will be compromised.

REFERENCES

Albert, S. M. (1990). The dependent elderly, home health care, and strategies of household adaptation. In J. F. Gubrium & A. Sankar (Eds.), *The home-care experience* (pp. 19–36). Newbury Park, CA: Sage.

Billingsley, A. (1970). Black families and White social sciences. *Journal of Social Issues*, 26, 127–142.

Birkel, R. C. (1987). Toward a social ecology of the home-care household. *Psychology and Aging*, 2, 294–301.

Caserta, M., Lund, D., Wright, S., & Redburn, D. (1987). Caregivers to dementia patients: The utility of community services. *The Gerontologist*, 27(3), 209–213.

Chenoweth, B., & Spencer, B. (1986). Dementia: The experience of family caregivers. *The Gerontologist*, 26(3), 267–272.

de la Monte, S., Hutchins, G. M., & Moore, W. (1989). Racial differences in the etiology of dementia and frequency of Alzheimer's lesions in the brain. *Journal of the National Medical Association*, 1, 644–652.

George, L. K., & Gwyther, L. P. (1986). Caregiver well-being: A multidimensional examination of family caregivers of demented adults. *The Gerontologist*, 26(3), 253–259.

Gibbons, D. (1992, May 21). The amazing immunities of the Navahos. *Medical Tribune*, p. 27.

Henderson, J. N. (1994). *Dementing disease in North American indigenous populations.* Paper presented at the annual meeting of the American Public Health Association, Washington, DC.

Hendrie, H. C., Hall, K. S., Pillay, N., Rodgers, D., Prince, C., Norton, J., Brittain, H. M., Nath, A., Blue, A., Kaufert, J., Shelton, P., Postl, B., & Osuntokun, B. O. (1993). Alzheimer's disease is rare in Cree. *International Psychogeriatrics*, 5, 5–14.

Hennessy, C. H., & John, R. (1994, April). *The experience and perceived service needs of family caregivers of frail elders.* Paper presented at the 7th annual Indian Health Service Research Conference, Tucson, AZ.

Hennessy, C. H., & John, R. (1995). The interpretation of burden among Pueblo Indian caregivers. *Journal of Aging Studies*, *9*, 215–229.

Heyman, A., Fillenbaum, G., Clark, C., Prosnitz, B., & Williams, K. (1988). Differences in prevalence and types of dementia in an elderly biracial population in North Carolina: A preliminary report. *Annals of Neurology*, *24*, 160.

Heyman, A., Fillenbaum, G., Prosnitz, B., Raiford, K., Burchett, B., & Clark, C. (1991). Estimated prevalence of dementia among elderly Black and White community residents. *Archives of Neurology*, *48*, 594–598.

Indian Health Service. (1993). *Consensus statement of the roundtable on long term care for Indian elders*. Rockville, MD: Indian Health Service.

Indian Health Service. (1994). *Trends in Indian health*. Rockville, MD: Indian Health Service.

Jackson, J. S. (1988). Growing old in Black America: Research on aging Black populations. In J. S. Jackson (Ed.), *The Black elderly: Research on physical and psychosocial health*. New York: Springer.

John, R. (1988). The Native American family. In C.H. Mindel, R. Habenstein, & R. Wright (Eds.), *Ethnic families in America* (3rd ed., pp. 325–363). New York: Elsevier.

John, R. (1991). The state of research on American Indian elders' health, income security, and social support networks. In *Minority elders: Longevity, economics, and health* (pp. 38–50). Washington, DC: Gerontological Society of America.

John, R. (1995). *American Indian and Alaska Native elders: An assessment of their current status and provision of services*. Rockville, MD: Indian Health Service.

Lawton, M. P., Rajagopal, D., Brody, E., & Kleban, M. H. (1992). The dynamics of caregiving for a demented elder among Black and White families. *Journal of Gerontology*, *47*, S156–S164.

Mace, N. (1984). *The 36 hour day: A family guide to caring for persons with Alzheimer's disease, related dementing illnesses, and memory loss in later life*. New York: Warner Books.

Manson, S. (1993). Long-term care of older American Indians: Challenges in the development of institutional services. In C.M. Barresi & D.E. Stull (Eds.), *Ethnic elders and long-term care* (pp. 130–143). New York: Springer.

May, P. (1994). The epidemiology of alcohol abuse among American Indians: The mythical and real properties. *American Indian Culture and Research Journal*, *18*, 121–143.

Mindel, C., Wright, R., & Starrett, R. (1986). Informal and formal health and social support systems of the Black and White elderly: A comparative cost approach. *Gerontologist*, *26*, 279–285.

Mintzer, J. E., Knapp, R. S., Herman, K. C., Nietert, P., & Walters, T. H. (1995, May). *Differences in the care-giving experience between Black and White caregivers of demented elderly patients*. Paper presented at the 148th annual meeting of the American Psychiatric Association, Miami.

Morycz, R. K., Malloy, J., Bozich, M., & Martz, P. (1987). Racial differences in family burden: Clinical implications for social work. *Journal of Gerontological Social Work*, *10*, 133–142.

National Indian Council on Aging. (1981). *American Indian elderly: A national profile*. Albuquerque, NM: Author.

Osuntokun, B. O., Hendrie, H. C., Ogunniyi, A. O., Hall, K. S., Lekwauwa, U. G., Brittain, H. M., Norton, J. A., Jr., Oyedrian, A. B., Pillay, N., & Rodgers, D. D. (1992). Cross-cultural studies in Alzheimer's disease. *Ethnicity and Disease*, *2*, 352–357.

Quayhagen, M. P., & Quayhagen, M. (1988). Alzheimer's stress: Coping with the caregiver role. *Gerontologist*, *28*, 391–396.

Rabins, P. V., Mace, N. L., & Lucas, M. J. (1982). The impact of dementia on the family. *Journal of the American Medical Association*, *248*, 333–335.

Schoenberg, B. S., Anderson, D. W., & Haerer, A. F. (1985). Severe dementia prevalence and clinical features in a biracial U.S. population. *Archives of Neurology*, *42*, 740–743.

Stuart, P., & Rathbone-McCuan, E. (1988). Indian elderly in the United States. In E. Rathbone-McCuan & B. Havens (Eds.), *North American elders: United States and Canadian perspectives* (pp. 235–254). Westport, CT: Greenwood Press.

U.S. Department of Commerce. (1991). *The population 50 years and older, by sex, race, and Hispanic origin for the United States, regions and states: 1990*. Washington, DC: U.S. Government Printing Office.

U.S. Department of Commerce. (1993). *1990 census of the population: Social and economic characteristics*. Washington, DC: U.S. Government Printing Office.

Van Winkle, N., Persson, D., & Richter, R. (1994, November). Designing a study of cognitive impairment among Cherokee elders. Paper presented at the 47th annual meeting of the Gerontological Society of America, New Orleans, LA.

Wilder, D. E., Teresi, J. A., & Bennett, R. G. (1983). Family burden and dementia. In R. Mayeux & W. G. Rosen (Eds.), *Advances in neurology: Vol. 38. The dementias* (pp. 239–251). New York: Raven Press.

Zarit, S. H., Todd, P. A., & Zarit, J. M. (1986). Subjective burden of husbands and wives as caregivers: A longitudinal study. *The Gerontologist*, *26*(3), 260–266.

Part 4

Special Issues and Special Populations

Three topics related to subpopulations and specific settings in ethnicity and dementia are the focus of these three chapters. Because multi-infarct dementia is theoretically preventable, it is extremely important to begin to provide special programs for populations whose risk is elevated, such as African American elders.

Nursing homes provide care for large numbers of demented patients. These numbers are predicted to become more ethnically diverse; their staff members are already extremely ethnically diverse. This combination of professional and cultural backgrounds and levels of cognitive status provides the setting for interesting, and sometimes difficult, interactions.

A leading institution in development of geriatric care and training in the United States has been the Department of Veterans Affairs (VA). As the large number of World War II and Korean War veterans from diverse ethnic populations age, the VA geriatric services increasingly need to deal with the issues of cultural diversity.

Chapter 17

Prevention of Multi-Infarct Dementia and Stroke in Ethnically Diverse Populations

Harry Ward
Donald E. Morisky
Desserie Jones

Cardiovascular disease (CVD), coronary heart disease (CHD), and cerebrovascular accident (CVA) are the most prevalent chronic diseases in the United States and the leading causes of premature morbidity and mortality in the country. The principal pathological process of CVD is atherosclerosis with damage to and narrowing of large- and medium-sized arteries, which often leads to CHD and CVA (American Heart Association [AHA], 1994). Of the 7 million Americans annually affected by CVD, more than 500,000 die. CVD costs the United States an estimated \$43 billion a year with direct and indirect costs combined (National Heart, Lung, & Blood Institute [NHLBI], 1990). High levels of serum cholesterol, cigarette smoking, and elevated blood pressure are all risk factors associated with CHD (AHA, 1994). Data on health status and health practices lend support to the estimate that at least 50% of premature mortality (years of potential life lost) is attributable to health behavior (McGinnis & Foege, 1993). CVA is the third leading cause of death in the United States and is the leading cause of neurological disability in elderly people. Particularly disconcerting is the observation that stroke is four times more likely to produce disability than death, leading to more than 300,000 stroke survivors per year (McGinnis & Foege, 1993; NHLBI, 1990; Thom, Epstein, Feldman, Leaverton, & Wolz, 1992).

The authors gratefully acknowledge the expert research and secretarial assistance provided by Lynnette M. Namba and Linda Elliott-Nettles.

Among the consequences of stroke, there is no disability as devastating as the condition of dementia resulting from multiple strokes. Multi-infarct dementia (MID) is defined as a dementia syndrome occurring secondarily to one or more CVAs. To individuals who were highly functional before a stroke, MID can represent a fate worse than death as loss of independence supervenes.

In the earlier sections of this chapter, the scope of the problem of MID is reviewed with special emphasis on risk-factor reduction for stroke and therapeutic intervention in high-risk ethnic minority populations. Because hypertension is the major risk factor for stroke and it afflicts disadvantaged ethnic minority populations in disproportionately high numbers, the role of hypertension as a major risk factor and strategies to improve hypertension care in minorities are discussed in the later sections of the chapter.

EPIDEMIOLOGY OF MID

Of the estimated 3 million survivors of stroke in 1989, about 23% have evidence of MID (Casper, Wing, Strogatz, David, & Tyroler, 1992). The estimated prevalence of MID for those Americans in the 65–74 year age group is 794 persons per 100,000. However, CVA and consequent MID can occur in younger age groups, as especially seen in the hypertensive Black population. Men and women are affected by MID about equally, with overall stroke risk slightly higher in men (Sacco, Boden-Albala, & Lipset, 1995). Stroke incidence is higher and occurs at a younger mean age in Blacks as compared with Whites (Smith & Kiloh, 1981). Blacks are at greater risk for MID than are Whites, and there is early evidence to suggest that Hispanic Whites are at greater risk than Native American and Asian populations (Cooley, 1990; Yeo, Gallagher-Thompson, & Leiberman, 1994). Furthermore, stroke mortality is excessive in Blacks, especially among Blacks in the southeastern United States (the "stroke belt"). In 1980, age-adjusted rates of stroke per 100,000 persons were 12% higher for Blacks than Whites (74.3 persons per 100,000 vs. 66.5 persons per 100,000, respectively; Stamler & Pullman, 1967). These observations support the observation that the highest proportion of dementia cases in Blacks is attributable to MID, in contrast to relatively low numbers caused by Alzheimer's syndrome when compared with Whites with dementia.

MID SYNDROMES

Nearly three quarters of strokes are embolic or thrombotic infarcts, with hemorrhagic stroke accounting for fewer than one quarter of all strokes. However, both infarctive and hemorrhagic strokes can lead to MID. The fundamental requirement predisposing to the MID syndrome is that a sufficient volume of brain tissue destruction occur at the proper location to produce symptoms. In necropsy studies of CVA patients, more than 20–100 ml volume of infarcted brain tissue was associated with dementia, whereas the incidence of CVA in

Table 1   Subtypes of Vascular Dementia

Symptom	Pathologic anatomy
Lacunar state	Small white-matter lesions in basal ganglia, internal capsule, deep hemisphere
Binswanger's disease	Ischemic lesion in hemispheric white matter with sparing u-fibers
Thalamic dementia	Paramedian thalamic and rostral midbrain infarct
Border zone syndrome	Infarcts of cortical and subcortical border zone regions produced by bilateral carotid occlusion or low blood pressure
Angular gyrus syndrome	Infarct of left angular gyrus (inferior parietal lobule)
Microangiopathy	Innumerable small cortical infarcts

Alzheimer's autopsies is low (Tomlinson, Blessed, & Roth,1970). In contradistinction to MID patients, necropsy studies show that fewer than 20% of all demented patients have any evidence of stroke. The most common lesion leading to MID is recurrent lacunar infarcts in hypertensive individuals. These infarcts result in small white-matter lesions in the basal ganglia, internal capsule, and deep cerebral hemispheric regions. They are consequences of occlusions of arterioles by fibrinoid necrosis. It is thought that good hypertension control may be beneficial in preventing this syndrome. Other subtypes of vascular dementia are listed in Table 1. MID syndromes deserving special mention include (a) Capgas syndrome, a delusional state wherein the posthemispheric infarct patient imagines that someone close to him or her (i.e., a spouse) is now being impersonated by a stranger, (b) border zone syndrome, a condition following multiple infarcts of cortical and subcortical border zone regions produced by bilateral carotid occlusion or by hypotension, and (c) Binswanger's disease, which is a progressive dementia syndrome featuring motor deficits, gait impairment, signs of corticospinal tract disease, and diffuse white-matter necrosis and atrophy seen on computerized tomography (CT) scan.

Diagnosis

Neurological signs and symptoms associated with MID include focal signs in 70% of patients, with a lesser incidence of abnormal gait, visual disturbance, aphasia, and emotional incontinence (Hachinski, Lassen, & Marshall, 1974; Marsden & Harrison, 1981). The Hachinski Ischemia Scale has been proposed as a rating scale for the diagnosis of MID (Table 2). It assigns a relative weight of importance to elements of the history and neurological examination. Individuals displaying Hachinski scores approaching 7 are likely to be suffering from MID. Up to 30% of MID patients may display a normal neurologic examination. Cognitive impairment can be debilitating in MID and tends to be milder than that seen in Alzheimer's syndrome. Angular gyrus syndrome affects the ability to read, write, discern right–left orientation, and calculation and is one of the

Table 2   Hachinski Scale

Item	Score
Abrupt onset	2
Stepwise deterioration	1
Fluctuating course	2
Nocturnal confusion	1
Relative preservation of personality	1
Depression	1
Somatic complaints	1
Emotional liability	1
History of hypertension	1
History of stroke	2
Evidence of associated atherosclerosis	1
Focal neurological symptoms	2
Focal neurological signs	2

Note. Scores abore 7 are highly suggestive of multi-infarct dementia.

more severe MID syndromes with respect to loss of cognitive ability (Benson, Cummings, & Tsai, 1982). Electroencephalograms are usually abnormal and reveal focal or generalized showing. Pseudobulbar palsy is not uncommon, with emotional incontinence and primitive release reflexes.

Imaging

Typically in MID, CT of the brain reveals discrete infarcts and diffuse cerebral atrophy. Twenty percent of CT scans demonstrate bilateral regions of infarction (Brant-Zawadzki et al., 1988). However, most patients with MID have multiple small lacunar infarcts. Language impairment in MID correlates with CT analysis of tissue infarction (Wu, Schenkenberg, Wing, & Osborn, 1981). Recently, magnetic resonance imaging (MRI) has been shown to be more sensitive than CT in demonstrating the anatomic lesions of MID (Hershey, Modic, Greenough, & Jaffe, 1987). MRI may still miss up to 20% of the lesions seen in MID. Positive emission tomography has gained utility for marking regions of brain oxygen utilization and extraction for correlation with vascular dementia syndromes. Cerebral blood flow (CBF) studies using xenon washout techniques show a decrease in brain perfusion in MID syndromes. Furthermore, it should be appreciated that unusual causes of cerebrovascular dementia without infarction may occur. Strickland (personal communication, January, 1995) and coworkers reported that CBF is significantly reduced in cocaine abusers with cognitive impairment. Cerebral ischemia and neurological impairment may persist after remote use of cocaine and may be a significant cause of long-term neurologic disability in younger minority populations.

RISK FACTORS FOR MID

Hypertension is the major risk factor for MID, occurring in more than 80% of those so afflicted. Hypertension is present in epidemic proportions in adults in industrialized societies and is associated with a markedly increased risk of developing numerous cardiovascular pathologies. The severity of end-organ damage, both cardiac and renal, especially when coupled with the severe cerebrovascular damage, mandates that more effective public health measures be taken to reduce the incidence of hypertension (Francis, 1991). The continuing debate as to the efficacy of aggressive pharmacological therapy in mild to moderate hypertensive people has led to the search for alternative nonpharmacological management strategies, such as diet modifications, stress management, and exercise. The Joint National Committee of the National Heart, Lung, and Blood Institute (Joint National Committee on Detection, Evaluation, & Treatment of High Blood Pressure [JNCD], 1993) has recommended the use of nonpharmacological approaches to the treatment and management of high blood pressure.

Rates and Risks

Poor people experience CVD death rates twice as high as the less disadvantaged. African Americans, the single largest minority group (estimated at 30 million and representing 12% of the population), suffer nearly 60,000 excess deaths per year as compared with the White population (U.S. Department of Health & Human Services [DHHS], 1985). Black men die from CVAs at almost twice the rate of men in the total population, and their risk of nonfatal CVA is significantly higher. The survival rate after cardiac arrest in Blacks was 0.8% when compared with the 2.6% rate for Whites (DHHS, 1985). Severe hypertension affects four times as many Black men as White men. Rates of smoking, obesity, diabetes (especially its complications), heart disease, and renal failure are all more prevalent among African Americans. Hospital emergency rooms and clinics are a much more frequent source of primary care for Blacks than for Whites, and 20% of Blacks, as compared with Whites, have no usual source of care (Stamler & Pullman, 1967). Access to care may depend on a number of factors, including cultural isolation, reduced public awareness, individual and group attitudes, perception of resource availability, actual resources, socioeconomic status, educational level, and peer behavior (Becker et al., 1993). Because hypertension is usually without significant clinical symptoms, noncompliance with drug therapy and high dropout rates are common among all populations. They are strikingly higher, however, in inner-city populations, where illiteracy, poverty, hopelessness, and a high rate of chemical dependency combine to exacerbate an already serious problem in treating hypertensive patients. These individuals are more likely to be underinsured or uninsured, to be functionally illiterate, to be disinclined to seek health care, and to be less capable of following a prescribed regimen than the populace as a whole. The nature of the therapeutic regimen itself is probably the most important determinant of compliance, and compliance will be improved if a simplified, easy-to-follow approach is implemented (Kelman, 1958).

Solutions to these problems have included changes in population awareness and health behaviors, improved access to care, more appropriate health services, and changes in payment mechanisms. The National Task Force on Black and Minority Health recommended the "building of the capacity of organizations at all levels, including the community level" to address these problems (Morisky, 1986). Addressing this problem requires the dissemination of knowledge and health management in a manner that will ensure coverage of and benefits to the target population. Preventable or controllable diseases and their risk factors should be the primary focus of such a health promotion plan. All aspects of care—access, continuity, and quality—must be included in the planning, and efforts to empower the target population and its leadership must be a part of the overall plan to ensure the program's long-term survival. The majority of African Americans (85%) live in urban areas. Indeed, Los Angeles has the third highest Black population of all U.S. cities. This population is at high risk, but little data exist about successful programs and their sustainability (Steckler & Goodman, 1989).

Risk Factors for Recurrent Strokes

A past history of acute myocardial infarction represents a synergistic increase in risk for MID. Stroke and MID risk increase in proportion to blood pressure levels and are more clearly related to systolic than diastolic pressure. Hypertension control, however, appears to be more important in the prevention of an initial stroke rather than of recurrent stroke. Blood pressure levels greater than 160/95 confer the highest risk for stroke. Isolated systolic hypertension in advancing age increases stroke risk nearly twofold in men and women (Barnett, Mohr, Stein, & Yatsu, 1992). Other known cerebrovascular risk factors exerting their own independent effect on MID risk include transient ischemic attacks (TIA), recurrent CVA, myocardial infarction, atrial fibrillation, congestive heart failure, cigarette smoking, hyperlipidemia, increased plasma fibrinogen, and diabetes mellitus. As mentioned earlier, drug abuse, particularly cocaine use in hypertensive individuals, predisposes one to cerebrovascular ischemia, loss of cognitive ability, and even early onset of renal failure (Strickland, personal communication, January, 1995; Thornhill-Joynes, Ward, Norris. & Barbour, 1995). Reducing elevated blood pressure can lower overall stroke risk at least 30% (Hypertension Detection and Follow-Up Program Cooperative Group, 1982), with consequent reduction in risk for MID. Stroke risk factors—including transient ischemic attacks, previous CVA, myocardial infarction, congestive heart failure, atrial fibrillation, hypertension, diabetes mellitus, hyperlipidemia, cigarette smoking, and increased plasma fibrinogen—are multiplicative rather than cumulative. When effective antihypertensive treatment is combined with a comprehensive approach to reduce risk from comorbid factors such as cigarette smoking, further substantial reduction in stroke and MID should occur. Stroke of cardioembolic origin is responsible for more than 15% of all ischemic strokes. Atrial fibrillation increases stroke risk over five times that of the general population (Flegel, Shipley, & Rose, 1987). The effective use of anticoagulant drugs in atrial fibrillation significantly lowers recurrent stroke risk, whereas arrhythmia control to prevent stroke is more controversial. Other cardiac comorbidities are critical risk factors in recurrent CVA, accounting for 16–42% of all recurrences over 5 years (Sacco, Wolf, Kannel, & McNamara, 1982).

TREATMENT FOR MID SYNDROMES

Therapy for MID can be divided into two phases: (a) measures to prevent stroke recurrence and therapy for its etiology and (b) therapy of secondary behavioral disturbances.

Therapy of Hypertension

The approach to effective management of hypertension in the 1990s has evolved from traditional step care approaches to those advocated by the Joint National Committee on the Treatment of Hypertension (JNCD, 1993). Individualized care may also be used by the physician with attention to the likely pathophysiological mechanisms thought to be operative in the geriatric patient. One should avoid generalizations that classify all patients as salt-resistant or salt-sensitive, as both groups of patients are encountered in the elderly population. Low-dose diuretics, usually in the form of hydrochlorothiazide or chlorthalidone, are effective in normalizing plasma volume in salt-sensitive hypertensive individuals. The Systolic Hypertension in the Elderly Program (SHEP) demonstrated that chlorthalidone alone or in combination with beta blockers was highly effective in reducing stroke and other cardiovascular event risk in patients over 60 years of age with isolated systolic hypertension (SHEP Cooperative Research Group, 1991). The Antihypertensive and Lipid-Lowering Treatment to Prevent Heart Attack Trial (ALLHAT) is a 6-year NHLBI study designed to evaluate the cardioprotective efficacy of several groups of antihypertensive drugs (NHLBI, 1994). This comparison trial among 40,000 patients receiving diuretics, alpha blockers, angiotensin-converting enzyme (ACE) inhibitors, or calcium channel blockers will, one hopes, lend insight into specific advantages of the vast array of available antihypertensive agents.

In addition to blood pressure control, pharmacologic lowering of lipoprotein levels has been shown to prevent atherosclerotic progression and should be used in the primary prevention of stroke. Agents of the hydroxymethyl glutaryl-CoA (HMG-CoA) reductase group are favored for this indication. Provastatin is being compared with dietary intervention for the prevention of heart attack and stroke in the ALLHAT.

Antiplatelet Agents and Anticoagulation

Aspirin irreversibly inhibits platelet cyclooxygenase, thereby preventing formation of thrombroxane A_2, a proaggregatory vasoconstrictor. In addition, aspirin decreases synthesis of protacyclin (PGI$_2$) in vascular endothelium. This anti-thrombotic effect occurs optimally at doses between 80 and 325 mg per day (Tohgi, Tamura, Kimura, Kimura, & Suzuki, 1988). Ticlopidine is a new anti-platelet agent (antiaggregate) somewhat more effective than aspirin. Combination treatment using ticlopidine with aspirin may be of value in preventing stroke in patients suffering from TIA or recurrent strokes (Hass et al., 1989). Warfarin for full anticoagulation is preserved for the patient at risk for embolic stroke secondary to valvular heart disease, atrial fibrillation, congestive heart failure, and mural thrombus (Yatsu, Hart, Mohr, & Grotta, 1988). Achieving an international normalization ratio of 1.5–2.5 is the goal and is associated with minimal bleeding risk (The Stroke Prevention in Atrial Fibrillation Investigators, 1990).

Carotid Endarterectomy

Results from seven clinical trials have demonstrated the value of carotid endar-terectomy for patients at risk for stroke or death. Trials evaluating asymptomatic patients have not shown definite benefit, whereas clear-cut efficacy has been elucidated for those trials in which symptomatic individuals displayed carotid artery stenosis greater than 70% of luminal diameter. The North American Symptomatic Carotid Endarterectomy Trial and the European Carotid Surgery Trial were both beneficial in reducing stroke risk in patients with TIA or nondisabling stroke (European Carotid Surgery Trialists' Collaborative Group, 1991; North American Symptomatic Carotid Surgery Trial Collaborators, 1991). Patients with high-grade stenosis (>70%), less than 80 years of age, and with acceptable operative risk should be selected before the development of serious cerebrovas-cular dementia.

Management of Behavioral Manifestations

Depression is common in MID and managed effectively with tricyclic antide-pressants such as nortriptyline. Selective serotonin uptake inhibitors (e.g., ser-traline HCI) may be preferable to tricyclics in patients with significant hyperten-sion. Haloperidol and major tranquilizers are useful in controlling psychosis or impulsive behavior. Pseudobulbar palsy may respond to conventional doses of levodopa or amantadine hydrochloride or to low-dose tricyclics. Seizures are managed with phenytoin or carbamazepine. The use of occupational, physical, and speech therapy may optimize rehabilitation and functional ability.

    Cessation of cigarette smoking reportedly improves intellectual performance (Meyer, Judd, Tarvaklna, Roger, & Mortel, 1980). Moderate use of alcohol should be enforced, as stroke risk increases with heavy alcohol use (Criqui, Langer, & Reed, 1989). Most of the risk factors for CVD—smoking, hyperten-sion, elevated serum cholesterol, diabetes, obesity, physical inactivity, stress, and drug misuse—are directly controllable through the behaviors of individuals, their families, the organizations they belong to, and the communities in which they live. Social policies and environmental factors can also play an important role in controlling these risk factors (Green & Kreuter, 1991).

Compliance as a Major Behavioral Factor in the Care of Chronic Health Conditions

Failure to follow advice and recommendations from one's health care provider is a major cause of premature death and disability throughout the world. This is true for all health ailments and is particularly applicable to asymptomatic disorders such as high blood pressure. Inadequate adherence to treatment of high blood pressure is ubiquitous; it affects all types of patient populations, health care settings, and types of health care providers.

Many factors contribute to noncompliance. Inadequate adherence is more frequent in individuals who are less educated, unemployed, and more isolated. This pertains particularly to men and younger individuals of both genders. Practice characteristics associated with lower adherence include lack of or inadequate health insurance, poor access to care, and lack of a specific primary health care provider. Cost of medications may also be a factor, as some individuals may reduce the prescribed dosage in order to save money. Disease characteristics associated with lower adherence to care include other comorbidities such as diabetes or heart diseases, other diseases requiring lifelong treatment, need for multiple behavioral or lifestyle changes, and lack of symptoms. Because all these conditions are associated with the management and control of high blood pressure, the potential for noncompliance is great. Although these factors have been found to increase the likelihood of inadequate adherence, it is also important to remember that adherence problems are prevalent in all patient groups. Studies to date have been unable to accurately identify the sociodemographic profile of an individual most likely to be faced with problems of nonadherence.

It is estimated that approximately 50% of individuals are not able to maintain a yearlong follow-up program to manage their high blood pressure. The management program often includes daily lifestyle changes, such as exercise or diet restrictions, that are extremely difficult to internalize, given the long-term habits individuals have grown accustomed to. Taking daily antihypertensive medication as directed by health care providers has been a major challenge for approximately 40% of individuals diagnosed with high blood pressure. Long-term behavior change is much more difficult to accomplish than one-time or short-term behavior change.

Strategies Found to Enhance Adherence to Treatment

A series of studies and clinical trials have provided evidence as to the effectiveness of doctor–patient communication activities and their role in patient education. The doctor is an extremely influential individual whose advice is generally well respected. Studies have found that physicians who advise their patients to stop smoking more than double the spontaneous cessation rates of about 3% per annum (Li et al., 1984).

Related studies on hypertension have also demonstrated the key role of the physician in eliciting, recognizing, and addressing problems of inadequate adherence to treatment. Even patients who intend to fully adhere to their treatment regimens often have problems remembering to take medication. Physicians can take an active role in making it easier for the patient to remember to take medication. One way to accomplish this is to prescribe medication in a dosage that requires only one dose every 24 hours as opposed to several doses a day. Research has demonstrated that individuals taking more than two different prescriptions more than one time a day are significantly more likely to forget to take their medications (Kelman, 1958). Physicians can also help patients "link" the medication-taking behavior with another activity that is performed on a daily basis, such as eating breakfast or brushing one's teeth. These cueing behaviors have been successfully implemented in many practice settings.

Assessing Adherence to Treatment

Most health care providers are looking for a simple way to assess adherence among their patients with hypertension. Some physicians have used pill counts to assess this behavior; however, this has not been found to be a reliable approach as many patients often combine several different medications into one container. Urine tests or blood tests are other approaches, but they are invasive and cost intensive. A more simple approach has been to ask patients directly about their medication-taking behaviors. However, most patients will try to please their physicians and provide the response they wish to hear. A more successful technique involves asking a series of diagnostic questions posed in the negative direction, such as "Do you sometimes have problems remembering to take your medication?" The health care provider may even generalize the questions by adding, "Many patients have difficulty in following the medical recommendations of their physicians; do you sometimes forget to take your medication?" When the question is phrased this way, patients may be more inclined to answer truthfully. Another diagnostic question is "When you travel away from home overnight, do you sometimes forget to bring along your medication?" Another item that often results in considerable response variability is "Have you sometimes not completed the entire amount of an antibiotic prescription?" These items have been used in numerous settings and field surveys, and approximately 60% of respondents answer no to each of the questions, indicating very high adherence among these individuals. When these highly compliant patients are compared with the group of individuals who respond yes to any item, significantly higher proportions of blood pressure control are found among individuals who demonstrated higher levels of adherence (Morisky, Green, & Levine, 1986).

A comprehensive approach to improving adherence must address both cognitive and environmental factors. Cognitive factors such as knowledge and positive attitudes and beliefs (belief in the benefits of treatment, vulnerability, seriousness) are often described as necessary but not sufficient for the behavior change to occur. Sociostructural factors such as a positive reinforcing environment (family member or significant other support, peer reinforcement, strong communication ties between provider and patient) have been identified as an additional boost that both initiates and maintains the behavior. To maintain behavior change over the long term, the individual must move from simple compliance, that is, performing the behavior under observation, to internalization, in which the behavior is performed because of increased self-esteem and self-efficacy (Morisky, 1986; Hockenbery, 1991). These factors as well as a series of approaches (such as tailored patient exit interviews or short counseling sessions, social influence modeling, simplification of the treatment regimen, telephone follow-up, family member involvement, etc.) have also been found to positively influence adherence behavior (Morisky, 1986).

THE COMMUNITY HYPERTENSION INTERVENTION PROGRAM

Compliance with medical regimens, particularly for African Americans, is low. Poor doctor–patient communication, cost of antihypertensive medication, side effects of drugs, and lack of continuity of care from a primary physician may all serve as barriers to effective therapeutic compliance. In response to this, the Community Hypertension Intervention Project (CHIP), a 4-year program, was designed to address barriers to therapy adherence in the African American population. The overall objective of CHIP is to augment hypertensive care to patients attending the hypertension clinic at the Martin Luther King, Jr./Charles R. Drew Medical Center, whose clientele is predominantly African American. Attainment of this objective will be accomplished by developing educational strategies to improve compliance with clinic appointment-keeping and medication-taking behaviors. The program began in September 1993 and will run until August 1997.

Method

A total of 1,200 patients were randomly assigned to one of four groups at the start of the intervention. This four-group randomized experimental design is being used to test the effects of three educational strategies: E⇃↾, individualized patient education counseling; E⇌, patient tracking; and E⇌, home visits and focus-group discussions. Results will also be compared with the control group, C⇃↾, which will receive standard medical care (Figure 1). All four groups are being prospectively followed for 24 months.

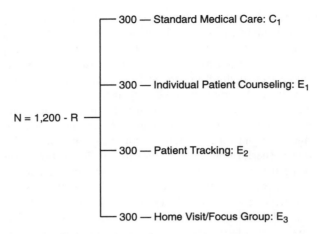

Figure 1 Randomization procedures for the allocation of hypertensive patients to educational intervention study groups.

A needs assessment conducted before implementation on a random sample
of hypertensive patients attending the same clinic as the study group revealed
that the hypertension clinic is almost equally divided according to sex, with
women accounting for 53% of the population. The sample also indicated that
approximately 60% of the enrolled hypertensive individuals were African American. Table 3 presents the Joint National Committee blood pressure classifications
of the sampled clinic population, according to JCND recommendations. As noted
in this table, 40% of the population had blood pressures in the moderate to very
severe range. In terms of the proportion of patients who had their blood pressure

**Table 3   Blood Pressure Control Status of Martin Luther King, Jr./
Charles R. Drew Medical Center Patients Attending the
Hypertension Clinic**

Blood pressure classification	Patients (%, $N = 214$)
Blood pressure classification[a]	
Optimal (<120/80)	2
Normal (120–129/80–84)	3
High normal (130–139/85–89)	13
Hypertension	
Stage 1: Mild (140–159/90–99)	42
Stage 2: Moderate (160–179/100–109)	25
Stage 3: Severe (180–209/110–119)	12
Stage 4: Very severe (>210/120)	3

[a]In accordance with the recommendations of the Fifth Report of the Joint National Committee on Detection,
Evaluation, and Treatment of High Blood Presssure (1993). When the systolic and diastolic pressures fall into different
categories, the higher category is selected to classify the individual's blood pressure.

under adequate control, only 35% had a systolic pressure less than 140 mm Hg and a diastolic pressure less than 90 mm Hg. Forty-two percent of the African American patients did not have their blood pressure under control.

Outcome variables consist of appointment-keeping behavior, compliance with the medical regimen, and blood pressure control.

Role of the Community Health Worker

All educational interventions are provided through trained community health workers (CHWs). The CHWs are individuals trained in blood pressure concepts, measurement issues, factors that influence blood pressure control, and factors that impede progress toward individual patient goals. The workers are familiar with the community, being either current or previous members themselves. This advantageous attribute garners them greater credibility with the community. It also enables them to personally identify the lack of health-related resources in the community, such as exercise facilities, smoking- and alcohol-cessation programs, affordable child care, and counseling services. As part of the targeted group, CHWs are also better able to recognize regional beliefs and cultural apprehension about mainstream care as barriers to appropriate health care. CHWs are also cognizant of prevalent treatment blockades such as violence within the community, transportation inadequacies, access to health care, health care costs, the legal status of some patients, and home or family stress and pressures. Having a comprehensive understanding of these barriers is essential to bring about improved adherence to the health care providers' recommendations among this group.

Job Description

The CHW provides services directed at enhancing the likelihood that hypertensive patients will remain in continued care and control adverse cerebrovascular and cardiovascular risk factors, as well as enhance their quality of life. Services are thus geared toward identifying specific patient needs for information and support, addressing specific patient concerns, encouraging patients to become active participants in their care, simplifying and tailoring patient regimens, and reinforcing patient progress at each clinic visit. Improving patients' understanding of specific therapies and treatment goals, correcting patients' misconceptions of hypertension, adjusting the therapeutic interventions to patients' lifestyles, and emphasizing family and social support are challenges that have been undertaken.

As educators, the primary goal of the CHW is to improve adherence to therapy, compliance to treatment, and control of hypertension. This goal will be achieved by skillfully implementing behavior modification modalities such as self-monitoring, in which the CHW attempts to increase patients' awareness by encouraging them to ask questions and teaching them to monitor their treatment by keeping blood pressure logs; goal setting, in which the CHW encourages patients to set realistic goals along with providing patients with positive reinforcement; corrective feedback, in which the CHW encourages patients to adhere to treatment; self-perception, in which the CHW looks at patients' past adherence behavior in order to tailor behavior-modifying strategies to patients' belief(s); and social support, in which the CHW identifies family members who are willing to work with patients to increase their compliance with medical regimens.

TRAINING OF CHWs

The CHWs completed more than 90 hours of intense comprehensive training in the following components.

Blood Pressure Measurement and Monitoring

AHA guidelines were used to train CHWs in the accurate measurement of blood pressure. In addition, CHWs were instructed in the principles of controlling high blood pressure, learning the standards for measurement, detection, referral, and patient education. Pre- and postexams were administered, in addition to quarterly reassessment by standardized blood pressure measurement video tests.

Strategies to Improve Adherence to Therapy and Blood Pressure Control

The CHWs were trained to educate patients about hypertensive conditions and treatment. Instruction was also given on how to individualize and tailor medication regimens, provide reinforcement and encouragement for compliance behavior, and promote social support, especially with family members. CHWs also collaborated with other health care professionals to comprehensively work to improve patient adherence to medical regimens.

Role of Diet and Exercise

A registered dietician provided information on the importance of controlling blood pressure through a proper diet coupled with exercise. Handouts on low-sodium diets, the daily food pyramid food groups, and an exercise program were provided.

Effects of Smoking

An eye-opening and informative workshop was presented on how cigarette smoking affects the lungs and the heart. The benefits of quitting included decreased blood pressure, a lowered risk of heart attack, decreased incidence of lung cancer, and a savings of more than $500 per year in cigarette purchases.

Counseling Techniques

This consisted of interpersonal skills development, including how to establish a good rapport with patients and being sensitive to specific needs. In addition, interview techniques such as probing and how to follow up on questions were other techniques used during role-playing exercises.

Ongoing Training

Training continues as CHWs are engaged in biweekly didactic forums. These CHIP meetings focus on target organ damage, cardiovascular functioning, medication and its side effects, and special considerations among geriatric patients.

Role Playing

The CHWs were trained to recognize patient motivation and compliance behaviors and in how to identify principles of education designed to encourage patients to adhere to treatment. At the conclusion of the 4-week training period, all CHWs completed a postexamination to evaluate individual comprehension of the material presented.

Evaluation

The CHW will monitor hypertensive patients through exit interviews, computerized patient tracking, and home visits and health information exchange interventions. In exit interviews, the patients are approached by the CHW immediately following their clinic visit in order to assess the patients' understanding of their illness and provide them with accurate concepts of high blood pressure. On consulting with the practitioner, he or she explains the recommended treatment and addresses any patient concerns and questions to clarify any misunderstanding. The CHW also makes follow-up reminder calls to patients assigned to the tracking intervention in order to ensure that appointments are kept and to inquire about missed appointments. Home visits are also provided to patients assigned to the home visit and focus-group sessions to counsel patients and family members on the importance of compliance. These visits serve as opportunities to teach cueing techniques and to provide the family with educational material and referrals. Health information exchanges are conducted, encouraging patients and family members to share their ideas and experiences as they relate to health and high blood pressure. The purpose of the exchange is to increase patient and family involvement in patients' therapy in order to increase patients' compliance in the areas of appointment keeping and blood pressure control.

CONCLUSION

The African American population endures high death rates from stroke, attributable primarily to the high prevalence of hypertension. It is only through the efforts of strong community-based educational programs, such as CHIP, that progress can be made to address the multifactorial problems and concerns identified in this high-risk population. The results of this study and future research will undoubtedly provide invaluable information regarding the design, implementation, and evaluation of hypertension management clinics and their success in preventing premature cerebrovascular accidents.

REFERENCES

American Heart Association. (1994). *Primer in preventive cardiology*. Dallas, TX: American Heart Association.

Barnett, H. J. M., Mohr, J. P., Stein, B. M., & Yatsu, F. M. (Eds.). (1992). *Stroke-pathophysiology, diagnosis and management*. New York: Churchill-Livingstone.

Becker, L. B., Han, B. H., Meyer, P. M., Wright, F. A., Rhodes, K. V., Smith, D. W., Barrett, J., & the CPR Chicago Project. (1993) Racial differences in the incidence of cardiac arrest and subsequent survival: The CPR Chicago Project. *New England Journal of Medicine, 329*, 600–606.

Benson, D. F., Cummings, J. C., & Tsai, S. Y. (1982) Angular gyrus syndrome simulating Alzheimer disease. *Archives of Neurology, 39*, 616–620.

Brant-Zawadzki, M., Fein, G., Van Dyke, C., Kiernan, R., Davenport, L., & de Groot, J. (1988). MR imaging of the aging brain: Patchy white matter lesions and dementia. *American Journal of Neurologic Research, 6*, 675–682.

Casper, M., Wing, S., Strogatz, D., David, C. E., & Tyroler, H. A. (1992). Antihypertensive treatment and U.S. trends in stroke mortality. *American Journal of Public Health, 82*, 1600–1606.

Cooley, S. G. (1990). *Ethnicity and the dementias in the U.S. Department of Veterans Affairs*. Washington, DC: Veterans Affairs Central Office.

Criqui, M. H., Langer, R. D., & Reed, D. M. (1989). Dietary alcohol, calcium, and potassium. Independent and combined effects on blood pressure. *Circulation, 80*, 609–614.

European Carotid Surgery Trialists' Collaborative Group. (1991). MRC European Carotid Surgery Trial: Interim results for symptomatic patients with severe (70-99%) or with mild (0-29%) carotid stenosis. *Lancet, 337*,1235.

Flegel, K. M., Shipley, M. J., & Rose, G. (1987). Risk of stroke in nonrheuatic atrial fibrillation. *Lancet, 1*, 526–529.

Francis, C. K. (1991). Hypertension, cardiac disease and compliance in minority patients. *American Journal of Medicine, 91*, 29S–37S.

Green, L. W., & Kreuter, M. (1991). *Health promotion planning: An educational and environmental approach* (2nd ed.). Mountain View, CA: Maywood Press.

Hachinski, B. C., Lassen, N. A., & Marshall, J. (1974). Multiinfarct dementia: A cause of mental deterioration in the elderly. *Lancet, 2*, 207–210.

Hass, W. K., Easton, J. D., Adams, H. P., Pryse-Phillips, W., Molony, B. A., Anderson, S., & Kamm, B. (1989). A randomized trial comparing ticlopidine HCL with aspirin for the prevention of stoke in the high-risk patient. *The New England Journal of Medicine*, *322*, 863–868.

Hershey, L. A., Modic, M. T., Greenough, G., & Jaffe, D. F. (1987). Magnetic resonance imaging in vascular dementia. *Neurology*, *37*, 29–36.

Hockenbery, B. (1991). Multiple drug therapy in the treatment of essential hypertension. *Nursing Clinics of North America*, *26*, 417–436.

Hypertension Detection and Follow-up Program Cooperative Group. (1982). Five year findings of the Hypertension Detection and Follow-up Program III: Reduction in stroke incidence among persons with high blood pressure. *Journal of the American Medical Association*, *247*, 633.

Joint National Committee on Detection, Evaluation and Treatment of High Blood Pressure (5th report, Report No. 93-1088). (1993). Bethesda, MD: National Institutes of Health.

Kelman, H. C. (1958) Compliance, identification, and internalization: Three processes of attitude change. *Journal of Conflict Resolution*, *2*, 51–60.

Li, V. C., Coates, T. J., Spielberg, L., Ewart, C. K., Dorfman, S., & Huster, W. J. (1984). Smoking cessation with young women in public family planning clinics: The impact of physician messages and waiting room media. *Preventive Medicine*, *13*, 477–489.

Marsden, D. C., & Harrison, M. J. G. (1981). Outcome of investigation of patients with presenile dementia. *RN Medical Journal*, *2*, 249–252.

McGinnis, J. M., & Foege, W. H. (1993). Actual causes of death in the United States. *Journal of the American Medical Association*, *270*, 2207–2212.

Meyer, J. S., Judd, B. W., Tarvaklna, T., Roger, R. L., & Mortel, K. F. (1980). Improved cognition after control of risk factors for multi-infarct dementia. *Journal of the American Medical Association*, *256*, 2203–2207.

Morisky, D. E. (1986). Nonadherence to medical recommendations for hypertensive patients: Problems and potential solutions. *Journal of Compliance in Health Care*, *1*, 5–20.

Morisky, D. E., Green, L. W., & Levine, D. M. (1986). Concurrent and predictive validity of a self-reported measure of medication adherence and long-term predictive validity of blood pressure control. *Medical Care*, *24*, 67–74.

National Heart, Lung, and Blood Institute. (1994). [The Antihypertensive and Lipid-Lowering Treatment to Prevent Heart Attack Trial (ALLHAT)]. Unpublished raw data.

National Heart, Lung, and Blood Institute. (1990). *Morbidity and mortality chartbook on cardiovascular, lung, and blood disease*. Bethesda, MD: Human Services, Public Health Service, National Institutes of Health.

North American Symptomatic Carotid Surgery Trial Collaborators. (1991). Beneficial effect of carotid endarerectomy in symptomatic patients with high-grade carotid stenosis. *The New England Journal of Medicine*, *325*, 445.

Sacco, R. L., Boden-Albala, B., & Lipset, C. H. (1995). Stroke prevention: Importance of risk factors. *Internal Medicine*, *16*, 13–27.

Sacco, R. L., Wolf, P. A., Kannel, W., & McNamara, P. M. (1982). Survival and recurrence following stroke, the Framingham study. *Stroke*, *13*, 290–295.

Smith, J. S., & Kiloh, L. G. (1981). The investigation of dementia: Results in 200 consecutive admissions. *Lancet, 1*, 824–827.

Stamler, R., & Pullman, T. N. (Eds.). (1967). *The epidemiology of hypertension*. New York: Grune & Stratton.

Steckler, A., & Goodman, R. (1989). How to institutionalize health promotion programs. *American Journal of Health Promotion, 3*, 44–56.

The Stroke Prevention in Atrial Fibrillation Investigators. (1990) *The New England Journal of Medicine, 322*, 863–868.

Systolic Hypertension in the Elderly Program Cooperative Research Group. (1991). Prevention of stroke by antihypertensive drug treatment in older persons with isolated systolic hypertension: Final result of the Systolic Hypertension in the Elderly Program (SHEP). *Journal of the American Medical Association, 265*, 3255.

Thom, T. J., Epstein, F. H., Feldman, J. J., Leaverton, P. E., & Wolz, M. (1992). *Total mortality and mortality from heart disease, cancer, and stroke from 1950-1987 in 27 countries* (National Institutes of Health Pub. No. 92: 3088). Bethesda, MD: National Institutes of Health.

Thornhill-Joynes, M., Ward, H. J., Norris, K., & Barbour, B. J. (1995). Prevalence of drug abuse in Black end stage renal disease patients. *Journal of the American Society of Nephrology, 5*(3), 342.

Tohgi, H., Tamura, K., Kimura, B., Kimura, M., & Suzuki, H. (1988). Individual variation in platelet aggregability and sensitivity to thromboxane B⇌ concentration after low-dose aspirin. *Stroke, 19*, 700–703.

Tomlinson, B. E., Blessed, G., & Roth, M. (1970). Observations on the brains of demented old people. *Journal of Neurological Science, 11*, 205–242.

U.S. Department of Health and Human Services. (1985). *Report of the Secretary's Task Force on Black and Minority Health*. Washington, DC: Author.

Wu, S., Schenkenberg, T., Wing, S. D., & Osborn, A. G. (1981). Cognitive correlates of diffuse cerebral atrophy determined by computer tomography. *Neurology, 31*, 1180–1184.

Yatsu, F. M., Hart, R. G., & Mohr, J. P., & Grotta, J. C. (1988). Anticoagulation of embolic strokes of cardiac origin: An update. *Neurology, 38*, 314.

Yeo, G., Gallagher-Thompson, D., & Leiberman, M. (1994, September). *Variations in type of dementia by ethnic category*. Abstract presented at the Ethnicity and the Dementias Conference, Stanford University.

Chapter 18

Dealing with Ethnic Diversity in Nursing Homes

Irene Daniels Lewis
Shirley Kirchen

The ethnic diversity among both the staff working in nursing homes and the resident population is increasing dramatically. Many older residents now in nursing homes grew up in this society when racial separatism was an accepted way of life. The number of older individuals who speak English as a second language, especially those who have recently immigrated to the United States as "followers of children," has also increased as a result of changes in the immigration laws. Those with diverse speech patterns include not only Hispanics, Asians, and Native Americans, but also African Americans who are fluent in "Black language."

STAFF DIVERSITY

Paraprofessionals

Before certification of nursing aides was required by the nursing home reform legislation in the 1980s, the racial and ethnic makeup of aides in nursing homes tended to be more homogeneous than it is currently. Depending on the location of the facility, aides were predominately either European American or African American. In the southern and eastern states, aides were largely African American, whereas in the northern and western states aides were more likely to be European American, although many aides from the Philippines and other Asian countries began to be hired on the West Coast in the late 1970s and early 1980s. After certification was required, the racial and ethnic makeup became more diverse. New recruits were from Hispanic and Asian groups, and a few aides were Native Americans.

Workers in the dietary, laundry, and housekeeping departments of nursing homes frequently consisted of individuals with a similar cultural diversity. Many non-English-speaking paraprofessional staff in these facilities were shielded from conversing in English. Often they worked in pairs, and when both were non-English speaking, they conversed in their own languages.

Licensed Staff

Historically, licensed vocational/practical nurses have been used as charge nurses in nursing homes. Initially, their racial and ethnic makeup was largely European American. After Medicare was implemented in 1966, the nursing home industry grew by leaps and bounds, and more African American licensed vocational or practical nurses were hired in the late 1960s and early 1970s.

Traditionally, registered nurses have been of European American descent. They were in charge of the paraprofessional nurses, and frequently they supervised individuals in other departments (i.e., laundry, housekeeping). Partly as a result of the proliferation of nursing homes after Medicare and Medicaid, registered nurses seeking employment in nursing homes lagged far behind the supply. Thus, foreign-born and foreign-trained registered nurses were recruited. Many came from the Philippine Islands, and most were bilingual.

RESIDENT DIVERSITY

Although the percentage of demented ethnic elders in nursing homes remains small, the advent of Medicare and Medicaid and changing demographics have led to a slow increase in placing demented ethnic elders in nursing homes. Elder Americans of color are the fastest growing segment of the frail elderly population. Although in 1990 elders from the four ethnic minority categories (African American, Hispanic, Asian/Pacific Islander, and American Indian/Alaska Native) were about half as likely to use nursing homes as non-Hispanic White elders, demographic projections have predicted a rise in cultural diversity in all nursing homes (Yeo, 1993). Many monolingual non-English-speaking and bilingual demented ethnic elders are followers of children; that is, they relocated from their county of origin to the United States as older adults to live with family members. Today, the placement of frail ethnic elders in nursing homes is increasing because there are few nonworking women to serve as caregivers. Economic resources and career aspirations and opportunities for minority women have altered the long-standing availability of minority women in extended families to care for frail elder relatives. Affirmative Action laws have opened positions that were previously closed to women of color, and they are walking through those doors, leaving many frail ethnic elders to care for themselves in urban high-rise or rundown apartments or older single family residencies in the cities or in rural communities.

Medicaid has made it more possible for families to place their demented ethnic elders into nursing homes. Having federal and state insurance that will cover the cost of custodial care has removed one of the barriers to long-term care for this group. More and more, consumers of color are discovering the entitlement programs available for elders and their families and are taking advantage of them. Informed, culturally diverse professional nursing home employees are one contributing factor to an increased awareness of resources.

The aforementioned changes in nursing home staff and residents have had and are having a profound impact on the care of demented ethnic residents. Currently, in many parts of the country nursing homes are staffed primarily by minority paraprofessionals, for example, African Americans, Hispanic Americans, and Asian Americans; English is the second language for many of these staff members.

SELECTED BIASES, BELIEFS, AND VALUES HELD BY STAFF

Today's cohort of demented ethnic elders and some of nursing home staff share a common racial prejudicial history in the United States that cannot be denied. This shared history provides the cultural context within which members interact with others. Such biases, beliefs, and values undoubtedly exert some influence on staff's and residents' behaviors. For example, many demented ethnic elders in nursing homes cannot deny their past experiences of living in separate residential neighborhoods and attending separate school and churches while growing up and later living in separate worlds as adults. In some cases, asking residents from different racial and ethnic groups to share the same room may invite conflict. Having immigrant staff direct the actions and dictate responses from demented ethnic elders with short-term memory loss may often result in aggressive behavior because the elders may be "living" during an era when they were at odds with persons from the immigrant staff's racial or ethnic group. For example, hostile reactions have been reported toward Asian staff in nursing homes by demented veterans with combat experience in Asia during World War II, when people who looked like the staff members were the enemy. It only takes the sound of an old familiar foreign accent and the visual imagery to trigger a hostile action.

LIMITATIONS AFFECTING DEMENTED ELDERS

Ethnic diversity is a fact of life in society at large. Generally, people can control or choose their level of interaction with different ethnic groups. However, for residents in the nursing home environment, the society is quite limited. They

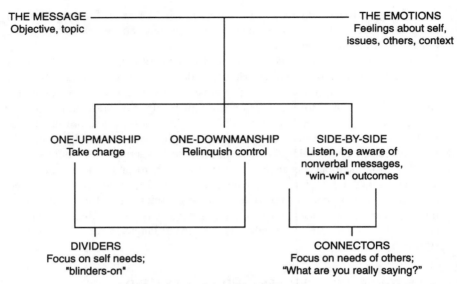

Figure 1 Understanding the concept of power as people communicate. Adapted from *Confronting Diversity Issues on Campus* (p. 38), by B. P. Bowser, G. S. Auletta, and T. Jones, 1993, Newbury Park, CA: Sage.

must interact with the daily and ever-present ethnic diversity of the staff in the nursing home setting. Underlying feelings of prejudice or fears about different ethnic groups may be brought to the surface because of frequent interactions with this ethnically diverse staff. The demented resident is typically lacking the usual controls and inhibitions that operate in normal social interactions. Demented elders may react in an exaggerated manner. The particular concern of the following discussion is the key manifestations of ethnic differences between residents with dementia and their caregivers, the problems that may arise for both residents and staff, and potential ways of dealing with the problems. It is expected that recognition and understanding of ethnic and cultural diversities may prevent negative staff–resident outcomes in the care of demented residents in nursing homes.

COMMUNICATION PATTERNS

Obviously, interactions and dialogue among a culturally diverse multilevel staff and demented ethnic elders in a nursing home will by definition be complex. Although the intent in this chapter is not to engage in an in-depth discussion or analysis of varied communication patterns that may or may not exist between different parties, three patterns should be recognized (see Figure 1). The first pattern is one in which parties talk as equals, the side-by-side pattern. Situations in which culturally diverse, multilevel staff and demented ethnic elders converse as equals fall into this pattern. Each one is concerned for the other. It is a collaborative endeavor. Next is the pattern in which one of the parties talks from a position of power, the on-top pattern. One person (staff or resident) assumes a position of control or superior status. In this approach, the person in control blames the victim: a win–lose situation. Last is the pattern in which one party talks from a lesser position, the on-the-bottom dialogue between two individuals. This is the least effective communication exchange. Here, an individual takes a subservient position and withholds ideas or withdraws support. Neither gets the better of the other. Indeed, it's a lose–lose outcome.

Staff and residents convey messages and feelings about issues as they converse, verbally or nonverbally. Just as culturally diverse staff and demented ethnic elders communicate by one of the above patterns, so do persons of different racial and ethnic groups in everyday events, as discussed in Chapter 13.

Verbal Communication

It is assumed that English will be the common language among the majority of residents and staff. (There may be cases in which a language other than English is the common language of the majority of a given nursing home community, but this is not the ethnically diverse environment being discussed here.) It is common that in an ethnically diverse group, English is not the primary language of a large number, perhaps even the majority, of the community, including both staff and residents. The range of ability to communicate in English may be very broad. Some residents, whether because of their demented state or otherwise, may have little or no ability to communicate in English. Demented elders are frequently reported to lose their ability to speak in their second language late in the progression of their illness. Today in the 1990s, all staff members must have the minimum acceptable level of English proficiency to qualify for their positions. Given the situation, for example, in which an Asian staff member for whom English is a second language is providing care for a native Spanish-speaking resident, what are some of the issues that may arise? When English is a second language for both resident and staff, a particular English word may not bear a common meaning. Connotations from idiomatic expressions present further misunderstandings. For example, when a staff member preparing a resident for bed says, "Let's go to bed now," a resident may react by saying, "I didn't know that I was married to you." An idiomatic expression that seems so commonplace can trigger different reactions in demented residents. The above reaction seems fairly harmless and humorous. However, in some cases, a resident's reaction may be aggressive or sexually inappropriate.

Aside from the problem of explicit word meanings, different accents can make it very difficult for two parties to recognize which words are being used. Tone of voice can also be taken to display attitudes and feelings that are not really present or intended. For example, some Asians may speak in a high-pitched voice that a demented resident may find disturbing and anxiety-provoking. The speed and volume at which a staff member speaks can also contribute to residents' reactions. Although misinterpretation based on pitch or volume can happen between two persons speaking the same language, speed and volume have an exaggerated effect when the native languages differ.

It is well recognized that it is more reassuring and comforting to residents when caregivers talk residents through procedures or activities that they are engaged in. Eating, bathing, preparation for bed, and physical and occupational therapy are typical activities that go much better when accompanied by reassuring conversation or one-way verbal commentary from staff. When a caregiver has a language barrier in communicating with residents, verbal reassurance that should accompany these activities can become problematic.

Aside from direct communications with residents in nursing homes, when staff of different language backgrounds communicate with each other about a resident's care (potentially that of a resident of a third language background), they need to be aware that the explanation of a resident's needs may be crossing translation lines of three different native languages.

Another common problem with diverse language background is the normal linguistic environment that may prevail in nursing homes. That is, if staff speak with each other in a language other than English in the presence of residents, residents may begin to wonder to what country they have been shipped or what the staff members might be saying about them. Generally, demented residents have difficulty keeping oriented in the expected English language environment. Hearing other languages may add to the feelings of confusion, disorientation, abandonment, or suspicion.

Nonverbal Communication

One basic reaction to ethnic differences is the simple reaction to outward physical appearance. Demented residents are subject to uncensored feelings and behaviors that may derive from past experiences and prejudices. Staff should be prepared to recognize these reactions as part of a resident's disinhibition related to dementia and to avoid their own defensive or unreasonable reactions to these apparently abusive attacks.

Different ethnic groups can have different responses and feelings related to physical care. The necessary touching that takes place during bathing, toileting, and dressing are common triggers of aggressive or violent reactions from demented residents (Miller, 1994). Caregivers' ethnic differences can exaggerate an already volatile situation when a caregiver is unaware of or is insensitive to a resident's potential reactions to physical care.

The combination of varied verbal and nonverbal situations, plus feelings about ethnic differences, may evoke aggressive behaviors from demented residents. Staff must anticipate, understand, and accept the likely basis of each resident's potential reactions. Physically aggressive behavior seems to be a defensive response to perceived threat rather than an expression of anger. Perhaps a resident's general state of cognitive or perceptual failure is the reason for not recognizing a caregiver's approach as one of help rather than harm (Ryder, Bossenmaier, & McLachlan, 1991). In some cases, staff may simply be the object of racial or ethnic resentment or hatred. There is nothing staff can do to correct this situation. However, if staff members are to be able to continue to provide quality care, they must avoid taking an act of aggression personally and reacting as if it were meant as a personal affront. Sometimes use of humor in such situations can be a useful disarming approach. Sometimes enlisting the support of other staff members for a particularly hurtful situation involving racial slurs can help a person cope.

IN-SERVICE TRAINING FOR MORE EFFECTIVE CARE

Training is a frontline strategy for instilling desired behavioral patterns in staff. Awareness, sensitivity, and developing competence with regard to potential responses and feelings about ethnic differences are essential first steps in establishing appropriate and professional staff behavior. Experiential group workshops that include role playing can help staff experience a different perspective of demented ethnic elders and enable staff to cope more effectively.

Specific verbal problems in communication—for example, the ability to use English vocabulary effectively according to the needs of different residents—can be helped by improving simple language skills. Likewise, being made aware of the problems, slowing down one's speech, and pronouncing words more clearly can improve communication tremendously. Problems of speed, tone, accent, and volume may require focused work on the part of particular staff. Group exercises in English usage can be part of any regular in-service education program. Education about cultural diversity is appropriate. The regulatory body, the Joint Commission of Accreditation of Healthcare Organizations (1993), now requires culture be included in resident assessment in long-term care, so it should be part of any regular staff in-service training.

CLINICAL IMPLICATIONS

The issue of a general linguistic environment populated by multiple foreign languages can be addressed by adopting an English-only rule. Under Title VII of the 1964 Civil Rights Act, an employer may have a rule requiring that all employees speak only English at certain times. When an employer can show that a rule is justified by business, the individual's rights are not violated. In nursing homes, it may not be necessary to forbid the use of other languages completely, but a rule requiring the use of only English when staff are in the presence of residents may be best for the mental well-being of demented ethnic elders and other residents. Naturally, there are times when it may be more appropriate to address individual residents in their own native languages. Of course, such a rule may be controversial if a large percentage of any staff speaks one language other than English. However, staff are there for residents, not the reverse.

Second, taking a comprehensive in-take assessment of a resident's history and personal characteristics may enable staff to be more aware of potential reactions or behavioral issues related to cultural diversity. For example, a resident who served in Spain during World War II found himself looking for his gun in the middle of a night in a nursing home staffed largely by Spanish-speaking care providers. The resident was so disoriented that the language took him back to past traumatic war experiences. Awareness of the resident's background would have alerted staff that this resident might react aggressively and violently at night, triggered by hearing Spanish spoken. Assessment of an individual's reactions and past experiences should be ongoing and should be communicated among staff and documented in a interdisciplinary care plan. This is particularly true for demented ethnic elders whose memory of the past may be more intact than their present memory.

Third, do not overlook a valuable resource, the family and friends of culturally diverse ethnic elder residents (Barnes & Raskind, 1980). In a multicultural setting, these resources can be invaluable in privacy care matters like bathing, changing clothing, and toileting. For example, a Spanish-speaking resident was constantly combative when being bathed by a non-Spanish-speaking staff. Rather than resort to physical or chemical restraints to bathe this resident, staff asked his wife to be present during bathing. They scheduled his bath to accommodate the wife's availability. The wife came and conversed with him in Spanish during his bath, providing a calming, reassuring environment.

Finally, in a multicultural setting, it is important to carefully assign staff to specific residents. The point here is not that any resident of a particular ethnic background should always or only receive care from a staff of the same culture. For instance, it might on the surface seem that a Cantonese-speaking resident would be most comfortable with a Chinese staff member. However, there may be personality or other differences between particular residents and staff such that these two would not work well together, regardless of their apparent common cultural background. There may be differences in dialect; in their economic, political, and social backgrounds; or in their adjustment to non-Chinese culture that are much more important than their common Chinese heritage. Important issues are to (a) make an ongoing assessment of the needs and sensitivities of each resident and (b) plan appropriate care relationships with staff that take ethnic issues into account and avoid automatic assumptions that assignments should be based purely on ethnicity.

RESEARCH IMPLICATIONS

American culture continues to be enriched by its ethnic diversity. At times, diversity can be a focus of social and political controversy, and at other times it can be a source of national pride. Either way, it is a growing fact of life that the elder care setting must constantly consider. Conditions like dementia are becoming much more common among nursing home populations, and dementia honors no color boundaries. Unfortunately, research and information on issues peculiar to demented residents of different ethnicities and culturally diverse staff are quite limited. Therefore, study is needed for areas such as the following: What, if any, specific ethnic differences give rise to physically aggressive behavior in demented residents? Is there evidence that an English-only language environment makes a difference in residents' cognitive well-being or comfort? What programs are more effective in improving language skills of ethnically diverse care providers? Finally, what in-service educational programs are most effective in cross-cultural awareness and cultural competency outcomes? Such types of research can provide the information and expertise needed to improve the quality of life for both nursing home staff and residents.

REFERENCES

Barnes, R., & Raskind, M. (1980). Strategies for diagnosing and treating agitation in the aging. *Geriatrics, 35,* 111–119.

Bowser, B. P., Auletta, G. S., & Jones, T. (1993). *Confronting diversity issues on campus.* Newbury Park, CA: Sage.

Joint Commission on Accreditation of Healthcare Organizations. (1993). *1994 Accreditation manual for long term care.* Oakbrook Terrace, IL: Author.

Miller, R. (1994). Managing disruptive responses to bathing by elderly residents. *Journal of Gerontological Nursing, 20,* 35–39.

Ryder, M. B., Bossenmaier, M., & McLachlan, C. (1991). Aggressive behavior in cognitively impaired nursing home residents. *Research and Nursing Health, 14,* 87–95.

Yeo, G. (1993). Ethnicity and nursing homes. In C. Barressi & D. Stull, *Ethnic elderly and long term care.* New York: Springer.

Chapter 19

Ethnic Diversity Among Veterans with Dementia

Susan G. Cooley

The U.S. Department of Veterans Affairs (VA) administers the largest health care network in the United States. In 1994, the yearly operating budget for VA health care was approximately $15.8 billion, with the VA responsible for 172 medical centers; more than 350 outpatient, community, and outreach clinics; 128 nursing home care units; and 37 domiciliaries (VA, 1994a). Annually, there are approximately 1 million inpatients treated, 24 million outpatient medical visits, and 30,000 VA nursing home care unit admissions (VA, 1994a). Eligibility for VA health care services is based on a number of specific criteria (VA, 1994b). Veteran race or ethnic status is not a factor in eligibility determinations.

One of the most dramatic trends confronting the VA over the past 20 years has been the aging of the veteran population. In 1994, the median age of veterans was 56.7 years (VA, 1994a). In addition, approximately 32% of the veteran population (more than 8.4 million veterans) were age 65 or older in 1994 (VA, 1994a), compared with approximately 13% of the total U.S. population. By the year 2010, an estimated 8.5 million veterans will be 65 years or older, representing 42% of the entire veteran population at that time (Sorensen & Feild, 1994). More than one half of those older veterans will be 75 years old or older. In 1994, the fastest growing segments of the veteran population were the 85- to 89-year-old, 75- to 79-year-old, and 80- to 84-year-old age groups, with increases of 15%, 14%, and 12%, respectively, over the previous year (VA, 1994a).

As the number of elderly veterans has increased, care for cognitively impaired veterans with Alzheimer's disease and related dementias has become a significant concern for the VA. The number of veterans with severe dementia is expected to increase from an estimated 400,000 in 1990 to 600,000 in the year 2000 (VA, 1989). In addition to those with severe dementia, equal or higher numbers of veterans may have mild to moderate dementia. As the number of veterans with dementia rises, it is anticipated that the number of these veterans seeking VA care will also rise. Since the early 1980s, the VA has been involved in a variety of dementia initiatives and activities, including data collection for VA dementia program planning and development; provision of clinical programs and services for dementia patients at individual VA medical centers; dissemination of educational materials and information to VA medical centers, state veterans homes, and other interested health care providers; and research on a wide range of dementia topics.

The current cohort of elderly veterans includes relatively few non-Whites; however, younger veteran cohorts contain substantially more individuals from other racial and ethnic backgrounds. Thus, the issue of racial and ethnic diversity among elderly veterans in the future, including those with dementia, will assume increasing importance in coming years.

To help the reader understand the changing demographics of the veteran population, this chapter provides information on ethnicity of the total U.S. veteran population, ethnicity of the older veteran population, and ethnicity of veterans with dementia. The tables are derived from information provided by the VA's National Center for Veteran Analysis and Statistics, based on purchased tapes of the 1990 U.S. Census of Population for veteran population data and on the VA's own administrative data files, the patient treatment file (VA, 1983b, 1988b, 1993b) and annual patient census (VA, 1983a, 1988a, 1993a) for specified years. The patient treatment file provides information on patients discharged from VA medical centers during the fiscal year. The annual patient census gives information on inpatient bed occupants on September 30, the last day of the fiscal year. Additional information about racial and ethnic characteristics of the veteran population and the use of VA medical care by minority veterans has been reported elsewhere (Schwartz & Klein, 1994; Stockford, 1994).

ETHNICITY OF TOTAL VETERAN POPULATION

Table 1 shows the ethnic composition of the total veteran population, as estimated by the VA National Center for Veteran Analysis and Statistics, using 1990 U.S. Census data. As the table indicates, more than 88% of veterans at that time were White. The next largest group were Black veterans, at almost 9%. Other races and Hispanic origin accounted for much smaller percentages of the veteran population.

Table 1 Veteran Population by Race and Hispanic Origin (1990 U.S. Census)

Race or ethnicity	No. of veterans	% of total
White	24,107,579	88.7
Black	2,330,229	8.6
Asian[a]	246,242	0.9
Indian[b]	189,788	0.7
Other	309,824	1.1
Total	27,183,662	100.0
Hispanic origin[c]	925,349	3.4

Note. Data from Department of Veterans Affairs National Center for Veteran Analysis and Statistics, Washington, DC.
[a]Includes Asian and Pacific Islander.   [b]Includes American Indian, Eskimo, and Aleut.   [c]Hispanics can be members of any race.

ETHNICITY OF OLDER VETERAN POPULATION

Table 2 shows the ethnic composition of the older veteran population in comparison to the younger veteran population. These data also come from the VA National Center for Veteran Analysis and Statistics, using 1990 U.S. Census data. Of the current 65-years-and-older age group, almost 93% are White. Among younger age groups of veterans, however, there is an increasing amount of racial and ethnic diversity. For example, although the majority of the under-45-years age group are White (83%), the percentages of other racial and ethnic groups are two or more times what they are for the 65-years-and-older group. The 45-to-64-years age group shows an intermediate level of increase of racial and ethnic diversity. Thus, future cohorts of elderly veterans, including those

Table 2 Veteran Population by Race and Hispanic Origin: Percentage of Total for Three Age Groups (1990 U.S. Census)

Race or ethnicity	Age group		
	65+	45–64	<45
White	92.6	90.3	83.0
Black	5.9	7.3	12.7
Asian[a]	0.6	0.9	1.1
Indian[b]	0.4	0.6	1.0
Other race	0.4	0.8	2.2
Hispanic origin[c]	1.8	3.0	5.4

Note. Data taken from Department of Veterans Affairs National Center for Veteran Analysis and Statistics, Washington, DC. Total veteran population (1990 Census) was 27,183,662.
[a]Includes Asian and Pacific Islander.   [b]Includes American Indian, Eskimo, and Aleut.   [c]Hispanics can be members of any race.

Table 3   Veterans with Dementia: Patient Discharges, by Race or Ethnic Origin (Fiscal Year 1993)

Race or ethnicity	No. discharges	%
White	25,953	77.9
Black	5,713	17.2
Hispanic White	1,031	3.1
Hispanic Black	67	0.2
Asian	109	0.3
American Indian	87	0.3
Unknown	323	1.0
Total	33,283	100.0

Note. Data from U.S. Department of Veterans Affairs (1993b).

with dementias, can be expected to be much more diverse than is currently the case.

ETHNICITY OF VETERANS WITH DEMENTIA

The remaining tables provide information about the ethnic composition of veterans with dementia. As seen in Table 3, for those veterans with a primary or secondary diagnosis of Alzheimer's disease or a related disorder who were discharged from a VA hospital or nursing home care unit in fiscal year 1993, the majority of discharges were among Whites (almost 78% of discharges). However, compared with the numbers mentioned previously for older veterans in general, among these veterans with dementia there was somewhat greater ethnic diversity in the direction of Blacks (17% of discharges) and Hispanic Whites (3% of discharges).

Table 4 shows the ethnic distribution of these dementia patient discharges across the four VA geographic regions. Discharges of Black patients were dis-

Table 4   Veterans with Dementia: Patient Discharges, by Race or Ethnic Origin and VA Region (Fiscal Year 1993)

Race or ethnicity	VA region				
	Eastern	Central	Southern	Western	Total
White	7,190	6,721	7,104	4,938	25,953
Black	1,633	1,385	2,169	526	5,713
Hispanic White	97	37	575	322	1,031
Hispanic Black	40	2	20	5	67
Asian	11	4	8	86	109
American Indian	11	29	23	24	87
Unknown	34	108	101	80	323
Total	9,016	8,286	10,000	5,981	33,283

Note. Data from U.S. Department of Veterans Affairs (1993b).

Table 5 Veterans with Dementia: Patient Discharges, by Race or Ethnic Origin and Year

Race or ethnicity	Year		
	1983	**1988**	**1993**
White			
n	10,887	27,220	25,953
%	83.1	81.0	77.9
Black			
n	1,859	5,063	5,713
%	14.2	15.1	17.2
Hispanic White			
n	231	879	1,031
%	1.8	2.6	3.1
Hispanic Black			
n	3	34	67
%	0.0	0.1	0.2
Asian			
n	24	99	109
%	0.2	0.3	0.3
American Indian			
n	26	74	87
%	0.2	0.2	0.3
Unknown			
n	63	230	323
%	0.5	0.7	1.0
Total			
n	13,083	33,599	33,283
%	100.0	100.0	100.0

Note. Data taken from U.S. Department of Veterans Affairs (1983b, 1988b, 1993b).

tributed fairly evenly across the eastern, central, and southern regions, with somewhat fewer in the western region. Discharges of Hispanic White patients were found mostly in the southern and eastern regions; discharges of Hispanic Black patients were primarily in the eastern and southern regions. Discharges of Asian patients were primarily in the western region, and discharges of American Indian patients were primarily in the central, southern, and western regions.

Table 5 shows that ethnic diversity among veterans with dementia who were discharged from VA hospital or nursing home care units has increased somewhat over the past decade. For example, the percentage of discharges among White veterans with dementia declined from 83% in 1983 to just under 78% in 1993. The percentage of discharges among Black veterans with dementia increased from 14% to 17%, and the percentage of discharges among Hispanic White veterans with dementia increased from less than 2% to just over 3%. The other groups increased to lesser extents. Data from 1988 show an intermediate level of increased racial and ethnic diversity.

Table 6 Veterans with Dementia: Patients During 1-Day Census, by Race or Ethnic Origin (Fiscal Year 1993)

Race or ethnicity	No. of patients	%
White	3,772	83.8
Black	626	13.9
Hispanic White	67	1.5
Hispanic Black	5	0.1
Asian	10	0.2
American Indian	4	0.1
Unknown	14	0.3
Total	4,498	100.0

Note. Data from U.S. Department of Veterans Affairs (1993a).

Table 6 shows that for those veterans with a primary or secondary diagnosis of Alzheimer's disease or a related disorder who were present in VA hospital or nursing home care units during the fiscal year 1993 1-day census, the majority were White (almost 84%). However, there was some ethnic diversity, primarily Blacks (almost 14%) and, to a lesser extent, Hispanic Whites (1.5%).

Table 7 shows the ethnic distribution of these 1-day census dementia patients across the four VA geographic regions. Black patients were distributed fairly evenly across the eastern, central, and southern regions, with fewer in the western region. Hispanic White patients were found mostly in the southern and western regions; there were one or two Hispanic Black patients in all regions except the central region, which had none. Asian patients were found primarily in the western region, and American Indian patients were found only in the central region.

Finally, Table 8 shows that ethnic diversity among veterans with dementia who were present in VA hospital and nursing home care units during the annual 1-day census has increased somewhat over the past decade. For example, the

Table 7 Veterans with Dementia: Patients During 1-Day Census, by Race or Ethnic Origin and VA Region (Fiscal Year 1993)

Race or ethnicity	VA region				
	Eastern	Central	Southern	Western	Total
White	1,434	935	1,032	371	3,772
Black	206	121	256	43	626
Hispanic White	11	6	24	26	67
Hispanic Black	2	0	2	1	5
Asian	1	0	0	9	10
American Indian	0	4	0	0	4
Unknown	1	5	7	1	14
Total	1,655	1,071	1,321	451	4,498

Note. Data from U.S. Department of Veterans Affairs (1993a).

Table 8   Veterans with Dementia: Patients During 1-Day Census, by Race or Ethnic Origin and Year

Race or ethnicity	Year		
	1983	1988	1993
White			
n	2,114	7,728	3,772
%	91.4	87.6	83.8
Black			
n	146	926	626
%	6.3	10.5	13.9
Hispanic White			
n	19	123	67
%	0.8	1.4	1.5
Hispanic Black			
n	8	8	5
%	0.3	0.1	0.1
Asian			
n	5	18	10
%	0.2	0.2	0.2
American Indian			
n	0	7	4
%	0.0	0.1	0.1
Unknown			
n	21	9	14
%	0.9	0.1	0.3
Total			
n	2,313	8,819	4,498
%	100.0	100.0	100.0

Note. Data from U.S. Department of Veterans Affairs (1983a, 1988a, 1993a).

percentage of White veterans with dementia declined from more than 91% in 1983 to almost 84% in 1993; the percentage of Black veterans increased from a little more than 6% to almost 14%; and the percentage of Hispanic White veterans increased from under 1% to 1.5%. The other groups show lesser changes. Data from 1988 show an intermediate level of increased racial and ethnic diversity.

CONCLUSION

In conclusion, these data suggest that the issue of racial and ethnic diversity among veterans will become increasingly important over time. The data for the past decade show there has already been some increase in ethnic diversity among veterans with dementia served in VA hospitals and nursing homes, and one should expect future cohorts of elderly veterans with dementias, as well as veterans in general, to be much more racially and ethnically diverse than is currently the case. Potential implications of this demographic trend should be considered in future VA dementia program planning.

REFERENCES

Schwartz, S. H., & Klein, R. E. (1994). *Characteristics of the veteran population by sex, race, and Hispanic origin: Data from the 1990 census* (VA Pub. No. SR-008-94-1). Washington, DC: U.S. Department of Veterans Affairs.

Sorensen, K. A., & Feild, T. C. (1994). *Projections of the U.S. veterans population: 1990 to 2010* (VA Pub. No. SB 008-94-3). Washington, DC: U.S. Department of Veterans Affairs.

Stockford, D. (1994). *Usage of VA medical care by minority veterans* (VA Pub. No. SR-008-95-1). Washington, DC: U.S. Department of Veterans Affairs.

U.S. Department of Veterans Affairs. (1983a). *Annual patient census, September 30, 1983* (Administrative data file). Washington, DC: Author.

U.S. Department of Veterans Affairs. (1983b). *Patient treatment file* (Administrative data file). Washington, DC: Author.

U.S. Department of Veterans Affairs. (1988a). *Annual patient census, September 30, 1988* (Administrative data file). Washington, DC: Author.

U.S. Department of Veterans Affairs. (1988b). *Patient treatment file* (Administrative data file). Washington, DC: Author.

U.S. Department of Veterans Affairs. (1989). *Dementia guidelines for diagnosis and treatment* (VA Pub. No. IB 18-3). Washington, DC: Author.

U.S. Department of Veterans Affairs. (1993a). *Annual patient census, September 30, 1993* (Administrative data file). Washington, DC: Author.

U.S. Department of Veterans Affairs. (1993b). *Patient treatment file* (Administrative data file). Washington, DC: Author.

U.S. Department of Veterans Affairs. (1994a). *Annual report of the Secretary of Veterans Affairs: Fiscal year 1994*. Washington, DC: Author.

U.S. Department of Veterans Affairs. (1994b). *Federal benefits for veterans and dependents*. Washington, DC: Author.

Part 5

Implications for the Future

Although the future is always difficult to predict, especially as it is influenced by the political tides, planning for more culturally competent services in dementia care requires some attempt to analyze needs into the 21st century. Local, state, and national perspectives are provided in this last chapter.

Chapter 20

Implications for Future Policy and Research

Suzanne Hanser
Dorothy Howe
Kathleen Kelly

This chapter reviews federal and state policy recommendations designed to meet the needs of ethnic minority older persons with dementia and their families. In addition, it describes the role of local advocacy efforts in transforming recommendations into legislation.

With an influx of older immigrants into the United States, and with the aging of those who immigrated a number of years ago, practitioners are seeing persons with very different needs than those of the clients they have served in the past. The elderly population has been growing faster among ethnic populations than among Whites. In some parts of the country, ethnic minorities will soon be the majority population among those 65 years and older (American Society on Aging, 1992). In the absence of federal or state mandates to reach out to ethnic minority populations with services for people with dementia, service providers have nevertheless seen a need in the ethnic minority community in their service area and have made a serious commitment to serve that population. Many outstanding programs have resulted from these local initiatives.

FEDERAL POLICY

For the most part, federal regulations and statutes are silent regarding meeting the needs of all persons with dementia, much less of those who are members of ethnic minority groups. Programs that primarily service the health and long-term care needs of older persons—Medicare and Medicaid—provide only very limited assistance for persons with dementia.

However, the Older Americans Act, which provides funding to Area Agencies on Aging for certain in-home services, requires that state plans be targeted to those persons with the greatest social and economic need. Low-income minority individuals and persons with dementia and their caregivers should receive special attention in these outreach efforts. Inadequate data collection, however, has hampered efforts to find out if that goal is being achieved.

The joint federal–state Medicaid program for persons with low incomes is the primary payer for long-term care services. Medicaid pays for half the nursing home costs and for some home- and community-based care, services that persons with dementia need. Rather than meeting the needs of ethnic minorities, Medicaid has been accused of bias against members of minority groups. Federal and most state laws allow nursing home providers to give preference in admission to people who pay privately, who are more likely to be higher income and White. One federal court has held that this is tantamount to racial discrimination (*Linton and Carney v. Tennessee Commissioner of Health and Environment*, 1990).

As the primary federal health care program for older persons, Medicare includes coverage for hospital and physician services. Although it provides limited skilled care at home and in community-based and institutional settings, Medicare does not cover the personal care and supervision needed by persons with dementia over the long term. Medicare also does not cover the respite care that family caregivers need.

As is true for persons of any age with a disability, older persons with dementia need physician and hospital care as well as long-term care. However, there is little integration between acute and long-term care services. The physician is often the first point of contact for diagnosis when impaired memory and other symptoms become apparent. Physicians' knowledge of services in the community and organizations that can provide information, however, is limited (American Association of Retired Persons [AARP], 1991).

Physicians direct patient care in the hospitals and outpatient settings, with Medicare as the primary payer. Family members and nursing staff are the principal caregivers in the long-term care system, either at home or in an institutional setting (AARP, 1994a). It is difficult to ensure quality of care and control costs in such a fragmented arrangement.

The lack of integrated financing for acute and long-term care services also contributes to the fragmentation of care between service settings. Medicare pays for acute hospital services and encourages patients to be discharged quickly from hospitals to another setting such as a nursing home for rehabilitation, therapy, or both if patients are not able to return home and manage independently. An admission to a nursing home means very expensive care that is not adequately reimbursed by Medicaid. This provides an incentive for nursing homes to discharge residents back to hospitals where Medicare will again pay (AARP, 1994a). Another change in acute and long-term care services involves patients discharged from hospitals to nursing homes for subacute care where they receive rehabilitation, therapy, or both. This trend is largely being driven by Medicare reimbursement and managed care contracts.

Despite the lack of federal leadership in addressing the needs of minority elders with dementia, two federal programs stand out as targeting ethnic minority persons with Alzheimer's disease. The Alzheimer's Disease Research Centers authorized by the National Institute on Aging provide a focal point for research on Alzheimer's disease. Currently located in 20 academic institutions, the centers provide outreach to persons who would not ordinarily come to centers with diagnostic and supportive services.

Another noteworthy program is a demonstration project administered by the Health Resources and Services Administration of the U.S. Public Health Service, which has a mandate for outreach to rural and culturally diverse populations. This $5 million program provides matching grants to states and focuses on hard-to-reach populations. The programs are located in 13 states, the District of Columbia, and Puerto Rico and are designed to provide assessment for services and to identify unmet needs in very specific targeted populations. Those programs are often aimed at ethnic minority groups.

MANAGED CARE

A trend that has implications for the older population in both the acute care and long-term care systems is managed care. In early 1995, nearly 10% of Medicare recipients were in managed care plans. Managed care is organized in a variety of models, the most common being health maintenance organizations (HMOs) and preferred provider organizations. Managed care is designed to control costs while maintaining high quality care and efficiency. It includes the following elements:

- agreements with selected providers (e.g., doctors, hospitals, and skilled nursing facilities) to furnish comprehensive health care services to members
- features designed to ensure quality care and cost containment
- financial incentives for consumers to use providers affiliated with the selected plan
- financial incentives for plans and providers to provide only medically necessary services (AARP, 1994b).

Many managed care plans are aggressively marketing to the Medicare population across the country. Some HMOs promise more health care coverage than Medicare beneficiaries can receive from the traditional Medicare program alone without paying an additional premium. They also offer eye exams, discounts for prescription drugs, and small copayments for physician care and outpatient surgery. However, coverage of the kinds of services persons with dementia need, such as home care and skilled nursing facility care, is limited or nonexistent.

Although some health care experts and researchers praise managed care as a way to control Medicare costs, others fear that holding down costs means limiting medical care and access to specialists. Advocates for elderly and disabled persons fear that managed care plans might screen out persons who currently have dementia as being too high risk. However, even if such plans enroll healthy older persons, particularly those in their 60s and 70s, some of those persons will eventually develop dementia. That raises concerns about whether persons who later develop dementia will qualify for the services they need.

Managed care in the long-term care system is quite different. The Program of All-inclusive Care for the Elderly (PACE) and Social Health Maintenance Organizations (SHMOs) are models.

PACE is a national Medicare and Medicaid demonstration program replicating in 10 other communities what worked so effectively in the On Lok Senior Health services program in San Francisco. PACE provides a comprehensive care package of primary, preventive, acute, and long-term care services to very frail elderly persons, all of whom are certified nursing home eligible. About 44% of those in the program have dementia (Van Steenberg, Ansak, & Chin-Hansen, 1993). Although the On Lok program serves a 90% ethnic minority population, mostly Chinese, the PACE sites have served other ethnic minority populations and Caucasians. A multidisciplinary team assesses participants and provides all the services needed from PACE providers for a capitated rate from Medicare and Medicaid. Preserving cultural identity is a hallmark, respecting cultural preferences while helping the participants maintain their lifestyles.

SHMOs are federal demonstration programs in three sites designed to serve Medicare beneficiaries, some of whom are relatively healthy and others who are severely impaired. SHMOs pool funding from Medicare, Medicaid, and private funding sources. Covered services include all Medicare benefits, home- and community-based long-term care services, prescription drugs, and case management for those who are at risk of becoming or are nursing home eligible (AARP, 1994a).

MEETING NEEDS OF CONSUMERS

The needs of consumers often get lost as policymakers and service providers develop service packages. Disabled persons and family members know what the disabled person needs to function at the highest level possible, filling in the gaps that family members cannot provide by themselves or with the help of formal services. However, they are often not consulted about their preferences. This is particularly true among members of ethnic minority groups. Each ethnic group would prefer that care provided by the formal system be delivered in a culturally sensitive way with respect to their unique language and culture. Too often policymakers and service providers use the rationalization that members of ethnic minority groups ''take care of their own'' as a reason for not developing policies and programs when, in fact, many needs remain unmet.

POLICY RECOMMENDATIONS

In 1995, the U.S. Congress debated the future of the programs that provide the backbone of acute and long-term care services to persons with dementia and their family caregivers—Medicare, Medicaid, and the Older Americans Act. A number of policy changes could make a difference in the lives of this population:

- Use a standardized assessment to screen and diagnose persons with dementia in a culturally relevant way before they enter the long-term care system.
- Develop and use care management to coordinate and manage care.
- Provide assistance to family caregivers through information about services, emotional support and counseling, and expanded services.
- Enact a comprehensive public long-term care program based on social insurance principles.
- Provide for a full continuum of long-term care services, including rehabilitative services, home- and community-based care, housing options with supportive services, and institutional care.
- Develop a client-centered system of integration between acute and long-term care.

QUESTIONS TO BE ADDRESSED
IN FUTURE RESEARCH

One area for research is to identify the prevalence and needs of ethnic minority persons with dementia. What are the differences over time in ethnic and racial populations? More longitudinal research is needed on all minority elders, with particular attention to those with dementia. What is the incidence of dementia in different population groups? What are the causes of dementia, and how do they differ among the groups? Does the onset of dementia occur at an earlier age among ethnic minority groups?

The role of family caregivers in providing care is important to recognize. Who are the family caregivers in these groups? Comparable data are needed to explore differences between ethnic minority groups, as each group has very unique characteristics and issues.

What are the most important cultural elements in meeting the needs of ethnic minority persons with dementia? Is translating materials into different languages enough to serve the targeted population effectively? Are there enough trained nurses and social workers who speak the languages of ethnic minorities and know their cultural preferences?

Another area of study is evaluation of programs developed to serve minority elders with dementia. What are successful interventions? What are the components of programs that can be transferred to other population groups? What aspects are unique to a distinct group? What strategies work to involve families successfully? What are the important linkages between formal and informal care?

STATE PROGRAMS AND RECOMMENDATIONS

As the number of ethnic dementia patients and their caregivers grows, various states have taken action to ensure that publicly funded programs are modified to meet special needs. In the bellwether states of California, New York, Texas, Florida, and Illinois, where the demographics of the elder population have shifted dramatically to reflect a more multicultural universe, some efforts have been made to accommodate these clients.

In California, the key programs serving Alzheimer's patients and caregivers with diagnostic services (Alzheimer's Diagnostic and Treatment Centers), day care (Alzheimer's Day Care Resource Centers), and caregiver assistance (Caregiver Resource Centers) have recognized the needs of ethnic patients and caregivers in their strategic planning processes. All of these programs are committed to serve a more diverse population and have made program modifications by conducting special outreach programs, training staff in cultural competency, hiring bilingual and bicultural staff, and forming partnerships with existing community service organizations to extend service capabilities.

Other states have undertaken similar activities. In Florida, the Memory Disorder Clinics have translated diagnostic evaluations for ease of use with Spanish-speaking clients, and the model day care programs have conducted community outreach programs and public awareness conferences. Illinois has stimulated the provision of home care and day care services to ethnic communities by allowing the bids for services to focus on a target population (e.g., Asian and Korean) rather than on a broader geographic service area. Illinois has also printed home care manuals in Spanish, Arabic, Chinese, Korean, and Polish. These manuals contain general information on home care but have a brief chapter on caring for patients with Alzheimer's disease.

Other states, such as New York, are driven by general targeting initiatives for low-income persons and minorities within their service eligibility guidelines. For some specific Alzheimer's legislation aimed at the creation of respite services and Caregiver Resource Centers, the mandate was to serve those with the greatest social disadvantage. There is great variability across the state in the implementation of these programs with regard to ethnic caregivers.

STATE POLICY IMPLICATIONS AND RECOMMENDATIONS

Increase Resources to State-Funded Programs Serving Alzheimer's Patients and Their Families

Generally, state-funded programs for targeting Alzheimer's patients and caregivers are relatively small, with limited geographic range. Resources need to be increased to expand Alzheimer's-specific services and capabilities within existing services throughout the country.

Increase Funding to Improve Access to Health and Social Service Programs for Minority Caregivers and Adults with Alzheimer's Disease

Small, targeted efforts have been made in some communities across the country to improve the access to health and social service programs for minority Alzheimer's patients and their caregivers. However, much more needs to be done in the areas of improved language capabilities, culturally sensitive program modifications, transportation, and financing of specialized services for Alzheimer's patients and families.

Increase Funding for Applied Service and Social Policy Research for Minority Elders

Although the research literature is increasing in the area of minority elderly persons, more needs to be done in the areas of applied service and social policy research on caregivers. More research needs to be conducted on subgroups in the Asian–Pacific Islander (e.g., Japanese, Chinese, Filipino, Korean, etc.) and Hispanic (e.g., Mexican, Central American, Puerto Rican, etc.) communities regarding family caregiving for Alzheimer's patients.

Provide Technical Assistance to Community-Based Minority Aging Service Providers in Order to Improve the Quality of Alzheimer's Services

Often, community-based minority service providers are unfamiliar with Alzheimer's disease and its impact on the family. Technical assistance and training to those providers of aging and general information services need to be available in order to build an infrastructure for support in minority communities.

Disseminate Best Practices and Facilitate Communication Between Programs Specializing in Services to Minority Elders

Increased funding could be provided to support clearinghouse efforts to disseminate guidelines for practice and service provision to minority elders and to facilitate communication between service providers by means of conferences, electronic bulletin boards and newsletters.

TURNING RECOMMENDATIONS INTO ACTION

The reader of this volume may agree with these policy recommendations. It will, however, take an organized advocacy plan to convert these sorts of directives into national, state, and local legislation. Although it is often difficult to see how one individual, agency, or center can have an impact on a vast system such as government, there are many ways to make changes.

Vote

Voting is basic to the democratic process, yet voter apathy exists in all too many elections. Because voting is something that every adult citizen can do to influence legislation, helping constituents register to vote and get to the polls is an important and fundamental strategy. Voter registration forms and sample ballots are available in many languages, and nonpartisan groups such as the League of Women Voters help new voters to participate in the election process. The voting records of public officials are available to support an informed vote.

Although becoming educated about candidates and specific propositions at election time is important, keeping abreast of bills that are coming before state and federal legislatures all year round will help determine the timing for a grassroots effort at influencing governmental decision making.

Be the Voice of Others

Providing a voice for those who cannot speak for themselves must be the responsibility of anyone who is concerned about ethnicity and the dementias. The challenges for ethnic minority groups are many. They are more likely to be affected by chronic dementias caused by potentially treatable conditions. They are less likely to receive community-based services once they become demented. Furthermore, they are more likely to have extremely burdened and overwhelmed caregivers.

In addition, they face multiple barriers to care, including language and communication difficulties, differences in cultural values and beliefs, socioeconomic factors, isolation, lack of knowledge among service providers, limited access to diagnostic and medical evaluations, and a lesser likelihood of receiving treatment for reversible conditions and for caregivers in medical, mental health, or social service supports. These barriers ultimately place the responsibility on those who serve these constituents to provide the voice, representation, and leadership.

Identifying specific needs of constituents is another significant part of the process of advocacy. The 1995 Mini-Conferences of the White House Conference on Aging provided one avenue for focusing attention on issues of concern to older adults and articulating policy directions for federal legislation. These conferences were planned by older adults across the nation to develop recommendations for consideration at the White House Conference on Aging. The Public Policy Forum of the Alzheimer's Association, the AARP's active advocacy conferences, and other similar functions by community not-for-profit agencies teach constituents how to participate in government and translate individual problems into solution-oriented recommendations.

Analyzing the potential impact of present and pending legislation also enables service providers and individuals to raise relevant policy concerns. When more than one person encounters a barrier to service delivery, this may be a clue that a broader social issue is lurking. This should be a stimulus for investigation and action.

Communicate

The next step in an advocacy plan for public policy is to communicate these issues to those who can affect legislation. When the solution to a personal problem is a change in regulation or law, it is important to bring this to the attention of an official. Letters, telephone calls, and visits to public officials are all appropriate ways to initiate contact.

Communications based on personal experiences that describe the impact of the problem on family and community make a strong case for needed change. Personal stories carry considerable weight, especially when they relate to the effects of a specific bill in the legislature. Public officials count on constituents to voice their support or disapproval of bills directly. Clear statements of the issue at hand; the constituent's position, pro or con; the personal history to back up this position; and follow-up after an initial contact comprise some key elements of the process. Interested legislators may ask for testimony to be provided on behalf of a certain bill; others may offer to introduce or sponsor legislation. These aspects of the democratic process require participation from citizens so that their views are represented. Getting involved often helps caregivers take control of an uncontrollable disease and give back to others who share their challenges.

Communicating with other agencies that share similar concerns helps build even more powerful coalitions of constituents. Collaborating not only spreads the workload out among more individuals and provides strength in numbers, it also offers multiple perspectives. Most legislation has some impact on interests other than those targeted. A compilation of views from a variety of agencies builds a more comprehensive case for or against a piece of legislation.

Communicating with the media about these concerns often yields coverage that brings visibility and meaning to an issue as well as increased public awareness of the problem. Whether it is through print, audio, or visual media, a message may receive wide recognition when it is brought to the attention of others through the press.

Advocate

Gathering statistics and background information, gathering allies, and developing coalitions are all useful strategies. Irrespective of the technique, the focus should be on promoting a solution to the problem rather than on global complaints. Advocacy means identifying an unmet need in the community, drawing attention to it through the press or other avenues, and taking action to legislate change. From listening to the problems of ethnic minorities experiencing dementia to identifying a legislator to sponsor a bill, advocacy may be one of the most important tasks health providers can undertake. For without advocacy, decisions regarding support of research, services, reimbursement, quality of care, and other areas relevant to the future of ethnic minorities with dementia will be based on views of those who have other priorities for governmental spending and regulation.

CONCLUSION

Taking constituents' concerns seriously, taking action, and taking the responsibility to advocate must be part of a concerted effort to meet the needs of every person from an ethnic minority who has dementia. By meeting these needs, service providers can help people with dementia to live healthier, more satisfying lives, and society as a whole will benefit.

REFERENCES

American Association of Retired Persons. (1991). *Local information on long-term care: consumers' and providers' points of view.* Washington, DC: Author.

American Association of Retired Persons. (1994a, August). *Integrating acute and long-term care: Advancing the Health Care Reform Agenda Conference Proceedings.* Washington, DC: Author.

American Association of Retired Persons. (1994b). *Managed care: An AARP guide.* Washington, DC: Author.

American Society on Aging. (1992). *Serving elders of color: Challenges to providers and the aging network.* San Francisco: Author.

Linton and Carney v. Tennessee Commissioner of Health and Environment, WL 180245 M.D. Tenn (1990).

Van Steenberg, C., Ansak, M., & Chin-Hansen, J. (1993). On Lok's model: Managed long-term care. In C. M. Barresi & D. E. Stull (Eds.), *Ethnic elderly and long-term care* (pp. 178–190). New York: Springer.

Index